Amanda Smith

"Funny and sad. A passionate, personal tale of survival and triumph. A brilliant piece of work – a revolution on the inside."

Dan McCulloch
producer of BBC 1's Victoria.

Copyright ©Amanda Smith
2004 – 2013

Cover design
Amy Pettingill
www.amypettingill.co.uk

Layout & formatting
K J Bennett
www.kjbennett.co.uk

Contents

Foreword	7
Dedication	9
Introduction	11
PART 1 - THE MIDDLE	15
Chapter 1: Pride and Prejudice	17
Chapter 2: Cruel Intentions	31
Chapter 3: The Belles of St Trinian's	40
Chapter 4: Love Story	50
Chapter 5: The Grass is Greener	61
Chapter 6: Four Funerals and a Wedding	73
PART 2 - THE END	97
Chapter 7: Lost in Translation	99
Chapter 8: Girl Interrupted	130
Chapter 9: Meet the Fockers	157
Chapter 10: Gas Light	175
Chapter 11: The Great Escape	188
Chapter 12: Dirty Dancing	221
Chapter 13: Return of Dracula's Bride	231
Chapter 14: Second Chance	250
Chapter 15: The Borrowers	276
Chapter 16: Without a Paddle	291
Chapter 17: The Sixth Sense	300
PART 3 – THE BEGINNING	307
Chapter 18: Predator	309
Chapter 19: Natural Born Killers	322
Chapter 20: Keeping Mum	333
Chapter 21: As Good As It Gets	350
P.S.	353

Foreword

Several years ago now, I met Amanda Smith. She was withdrawing from a living nightmare, a toxic relationship, a kind of lethal 'drug' on legs. Amanda alternated between confusion, fear and hopelessness.

Her recovery from alcoholism was an incredible feat, however she had started to awaken to the realisation of another addiction, the addiction to a "trauma bond" relationship. Amanda revealed to me the inner terror she was experiencing, and yet she had started to see beyond these toxic bonds, and the controlling and abusive behaviour. Toxic ... No More is a testimony to her escape from these bonds.

When I looked through the first draft, I was in awe of her willingness to go to any lengths to free herself from the prison of her own mind. She had miraculously survived, and then she began to write about her journey.

Now, reading the almost unbearable and emotionally bleak story of Amanda's childhood, I wondered how she'd managed to survive at all. In the chapters about her adult life, she gives an achingly candid, painful, and eloquent account of her inner world. It made for harrowing reading, and at times her words became blurred by tears in my eyes.

Writing in vibrant prose Amanda brings a raw and streetwise power to each chapter. Toxic...No More is moving, mesmerizing, and profoundly life-changing. It is a hugely important work that I believe will empower individuals to break free from the tyranny of addiction and trauma bond relationships, a dynamic which includes the Stockholm Syndrome.

Although I have been working on my own mission to bring healing to those who struggle with these issues, I know Amanda's book will reach a far wider national and international audience. She brings amazing clarity, and challenges the myth that addicted people never get better, by showing that fundamental change is possible.

Whether you've been touched by addiction, addictive relationships and trauma bonds or not, I think this brilliantly written and desperately needed book is precisely what those seeking understanding have been waiting for. I was moved and deeply affected by the sad, touching and inspiring beauty of Amanda's life. It is a story of survival from childhood trauma, addiction to alcohol, and addiction to trauma bonds. It's an unforgettable story of recovery and hope, of surprising triumphs, written in the language of insight and personal growth.

What is outstanding about this book is that Amanda is so generous and unashamed. She dares to use it as an instrument of truth about addiction to a toxic personality type. The abuse was relentless and yet she stayed and couldn't leave. Whatever happens, we must be extremely thankful to Amanda for her undoubted love, courage, faith in God, and resilience, and grateful for her message that if committed to change, it's possible to be free.

Hilary Betts MSc
Addiction and trauma therapist - Harley Street
Former manager Addiction Treatment Programme, Priory Clinic, North London
Member of the Federation of Drug and Alcohol Professionals
www.hilarybetts.co.uk

For the children

Introduction

I could be anybody.

Many stories deserve to be told, silenced voices set free. Mine may be no more or less fascinating. Rather, my hope is firstly that you're entertained – it was sometimes humour that skipped alongside then dragged me through set-backs and I *never* believe that message should be told at the expense of story – an honest story. However, since the genius that is screenwriter Paul Abbott (Shameless, State of Play, Clocking Off) tells me I'm good at writing the small details, that I make things accessible, I wanted to use that to set out my own life as a framework to show specifics of why and how people get into, stay in and get out of toxic situations and relationships. And that it's addictive, compulsive. And that it starts in childhood.

Some of the action reads heavy, necessarily so, yet Fay Weldon (author The Life and Loves of a She Devil) says the book is also "very lively and fun and highly readable". I want to share my learning, spread a message of hope so that if even a moment of grief is prevented or a bit of understanding understood – then I shall be very grateful.

Toxic...No More had an unusual journey. Taken on initially by a mainstream publisher, it battled to survive against powerful odds where many don't. It sits in front of you now, the stronger for its struggles. I wonder if some things are meant to be.

I wasn't always this sensible though and as you read on you'll see I'm lucky to be alive. Problem is with being life-long discounted by my controllers, it snatched away my ability to read subtext. From the simple

"Don't be stupid, you CAN'T be cold" or worse – it punches out a person's own reality and when continued or intensified it denies their very sense of self and their ability to self-protect. Reality becomes unreal, lies become truth. I was taught to accept what I was told at face value, rather than be attuned to my own gut feelings, whose job is to alert us, me, to danger signs. Bad behaviour, boundary breaches, abuse, become normalised in childhood and unknowingly get passed on through generations if not intercepted. Addicted to toxic relationships and behaviours, my necessary denial protected me from truths – and from change – because I *just didn't notice*. They say if you throw a frog in a pot of boiling water it'll jump out – but put it in while the water's cold then boil it up gradually – it'll stay. Big business knows this. *Abusers* know this. Consequently I couldn't keep myself safe. I put myself in danger, never seeing the truth.

Other times danger was masked under the guise of 'having a laugh' like the time I went to New York. Reeling from grief and addictive withdrawal from my first husband after we split, my safety was once again on the line...

The next night I'm back at the Waldorf. It's okay because Mr Salesman has gone home. The prostitute with the fur coat's back. She's quite attractive in a black-dyed-hair-God-knows-how-many-bodies-have-laid-on-top-and-underneath-her type of way. It's like those almost but not quite invisible lines on her face are a tally. A shagging tally. I've had a few to drink and someone asks me if I want to go to a club. Awww, it's nice to be asked so I agree I'll go. Next thing I know, a gang of about eight penguin-suited blokes (can't tell if they're Mafia – they're not telling and they're not wearing hats) and the prostitute and me are getting into a white limousine.

We go to a club called Tattoos. The entrance is cordoned off like it should be a crime scene but it's not. It's just the entrance. The men pay for the limousine and for me and the prostitute to get into the club which is really sweet of them. And it turns out the doormen only let the blokes in because they're with me and the prostitute. So that's lucky.

Almost immediately I'm on my own, which is how I like it. It's dark in here, with small coloured lights, red ones and blue ones, dotted about on the bars. The dance floor is big.

I get a drink then get on and dance — squished up as there are so many people. It's different from a club back home. Here it's a bit more 'everyman' and there's a weird psycho in the corner dancing on his own. Dancing on his own. What a freak! I look away from him, pathetic creature.

It seems like quite soon I spot and am spotted by a gorgeous man who slides over and starts dancing with me. He's Italian-American and the gorgeousest bloke I've ever met close up. He buys me a drink and we dance and chat. I talk to him about my search for the Mafia.

"Come here," he grabs my arm.

"What?" God, he's gorgeous. He pulls me over to the wall. I think we're less conspicuous here. I bet he wants a snog. God, he's gorgeous. And a quick worker — not a problem. God, he's gorgeous.

I stand with my back to the wall looking up at him. I'm smiling as English rosy as I possibly can. He stands over me with his arm against the wall above my head. I am so ready for this. I hold my stomach in.

"I wanna show you su'mnt." Here it comes.

He bends down. No — not here surely! Even I would draw the line at cunnilingus on the dance floor. I'm just about to suggest we kiss first when he pulls up the hem of his trousers. On his ankle there's a holster. And in the holster there's a gun. This is so exciting.

We leave the club and sink down into his black sports car – a Corvette thing – which is parked a block away at an underground car park. He drives us back to my (cheap shit) hotel and somehow I get the key to fit the door of my room. It's not so easy, what with the walls moving away from me, then up-close to me. Away. Close. Away. Close.

This man is stunning, late twenties – early thirties.

"Can I see it?"

"Pardon me?"

"Your gun – can I see it?"

"Sure." He takes it out of its holster and empties the bullets onto the bed. I hold the gun in my hand, stroke it, giggling.

I think he likes me as much as I like him. He tells me his uncle, who lives over by Westchester Racecourse, works for the Mafia. Job done.

Oooh no, hang on, I won't be a sec. I rush to the bathroom and vomit good and hard, emptying a fair bit into the toilet. Oh, please God, no, never again. While I'm in there I hear a firm click as the door meets the frame, determined. Shit shit shit!

The next day I can't reach Mr Italian-American on the number he gave me. Oh well, I must have written it down wrong. I feel like I've more or less achieved my goal to find the Mafia. It's a laugh all this, isn't it?

PART 1 - THE MIDDLE

Chapter 1: Pride and Prejudice

"Fucking black bastard!" He's a laugh, my dad. He's not normally bothered about all the 'fucking kids running all over the house'. But this new one! And I know he likes the brand-new Vauxhall Cresta Mum buys him with the fostering money. It's his first – brand-new motor, that is. Be a joy then, not having old greasy, blackened, dead, exhausts, gearboxes, spark plugs, solenoids and other body-parts all over the garden and front room and hall and kitchen.

He keeps the doors wide open come all weathers too, like the place is begging attention from the wider world, convinced there must *be* one out there. As if they're trying to shout with useless, smothered voices – *Can you SEE the shit going on in here?*

It's freezing in the winter, let me tell you. My twenty-three-stone, six-foot-four dad, whose friends call him 'Tiny' rather than Martin, doesn't feel the cold. He wears this big black coat with leather patches on the elbows and chest. The gas company gave it him when he drove their tankers. They looked for him all over the country once when the tanker – as in OIL tanker – had a leak in it. Him, chain-smoking his usual forty fags a day. Eventually the police hunted him down, rescued him and he lived happy ever after. Ha.

Once, Mum says, wearing her 'sexy' smile, she had 'Cresta' imprinted on her backside for ages, from the car's bonnet. It's not me she tells – rather I overhear her tell a friend. Mum likes talking. She even sees a psychiatrist for years. She tells him things about Dad. Things like he doesn't want sex much, only once a year but when it does arrive it's an all-nighter. In the end the psychiatrist tells her it's Dad should be making appointments to see him, not her. So she gives up going.

Mum likes a chat round the bakers too. Sometimes they knock money off the cakes, bung an extra one in the bag. My twenty-stone mum likes cakes. Specially Eccles cakes packed with juicy currants. And she gets these small round ones with a nest of sugary, coconutty straw glued to the cake with icing. Flippin' gorgeous… puff pastry too. Though I cannot be disloyal – I always was more of a biscuit person. Gingernuts and chocolate bourbons. And what about fig rolls? Smoothing your fingers along the ridges on their backs. Sometimes there are bags of broken biscuits. Yum. We never care if they're a bit stale. Funny, Mum prefers the bigger more whole bits while us kids and the dog get the rest. You're right – the dog, *then* us kids get the rest.

While Dad's away a lot on the lorries Mum does private fostering. But when he's home he's not so keen if the kids get in the way of the telly. What can you do – it's money, eh? And he's a laugh, Dad. He is. Really. Specially when someone's round for a cup of tea. Someone like Keith the Milkman or Roger the Lodger.

"Give her one if you want, the ol' woman," he says, nodding towards Mum.

They're both a laugh, specially Keith on his eighty fags a day, him with one lung. The hospital got rid of the wrong one, can you believe? Then the other one got better – silver lining and all that.

"Cheeky bastard, I'll have 'im for breakfast." she grins, bathing in the attention.

They're all in stitches.

When Roger's our lodger it means I share Mum's bedroom as he's in the box-room, obviously, with Dad having the other big room due to his snoring. He gives Mum 'the clap' too, Roger the Lodger, before he goes off to prison for fraud. But Mum won't tell me about Roger's rodgering for a few years yet.

It'll be during one of our late-night talks in my kitchen in 'the big house' in the early eighties. I like these talks though I'll be tired because it's often two in the morning and I'm pregnant again. But she's sort of neutral, doesn't snap and almost speaks with respect like I'm a stranger in the post office. Almost. So long as I keep listening. And listening. And asking her things about being pregnant and having small children. And about new-born babies who, she says, are revolting ugly things. *Can't stand 'em – they're like baby rats*. But not about breast-feeding. No, stop! That makes her feel physically sick. But I find out it's good for the baby so I have to go in the other room to do it.

She'll talk as if hypnotised, eyes like they've got milky cataracts that old dogs get. I think her new eyes will flit away from her coffee cup as she then floats to the kitchen ceiling, out through the window (no squeezing), leaving me as she flies along the high street and whooshes off. Is she the ghost of Christmas Past or of Christmas Yet to Come? Back, back, back to those better times. *Were* they better? She did have all of her teeth, and all her children were still alive. But I'm getting ahead of myself...

Dad's always got something exciting to sell. Like

watches, lighters, cameras. Specially when he drives a lorry for Dixons and goes to Glasgow every week. Tells us about this stand-up comedian he sees, Billy Connolly, who swears on stage.

He's a good bloke, Dad, a real grafter. Always getting something for someone. Takes orders for things. I'm not sure what sort of discount he gets but he's fairly popular.

"Wanna buy a watch?" Puts him in a good mood, selling things. He's nice when he's in a good mood though he's not always. When dad sits in the front room, legs out in front of him, I tell you what – you don't want to walk in between him and the telly. God's honest, you don't. Not even if he's relaxed, sitting in his baggy cotton underwear, his bollocks dangerously near saying hello while he has a scratch and gets himself organised. Specially not when he's 'doing' his ears. Gets a pen, digs it in his ear and waggles it, sharing the squelching noises with his audience.

Mum prompts from backstage. "WHEN ARE YOU GONNA GET YOUR EARS SYRINGED, YOU DEAF OL' BASTARD?"

"What?"

"Nothing."

He loves his telly, my dad. And it *is* his! He likes the cowboy films, war films, the football – can't miss the Spurs matches even though they're a 'Yids' team – and some funnies like Till Death Us Do Part. He's Alf Garnett's mate, *loves* him.

Mum, she's a musicals person – likes Seven Brides for Seven Brothers and anything with Maurice Chevalier in. And on Sunday nights it's dead exciting because the London Palladium's on. Me and the foster kids are allowed to watch it. We sit lined up, still and quiet on the settee, spilling onto the floor. There's Jordon, he's Greek, quiet and a couple of years younger than me. Maria, a year younger than him. Shirley, Neesy and their brother Jimmy then me and my own brothers, Tony and Adrian and Patrick, then Charles. Charles, yep, the *new* one. Patrick isn't really a brother but he lives with us. He doesn't get on with his two younger sisters. Or his little two year old cousin, Mabel. His mum, Sheena said he's always aggravating them and last time she caught him at it she threw him out. Since he came to us Sheena's handed Mum the family allowance she gets for him. Patrick's dad's a butcher and sometimes sends round; the odd joint of beef or a nice hock, strings of sausages, a few pounds of mince or misshaped bacon pieces. Once even some fillet steak! And *always* bones for the dog. Patrick's a year above Tony at school, they're best friends and he's tall too like Tony and Adrian. Mum loves him, good as gold, even makes her a cup of tea sometimes. *Such a nice bloke.*

You seen it though, the London Palladium show? Don't you love 'Beat the Clock'? There was this bloke once, stood in a phone box (looks like) and it's completely full of balloons. He's got one minute to burst all the balloons and he nearly does it. Nearly. And what about that quiz show Take Your Pick? *Now* you're talking. Do you shout out 'Open the box' or 'Take the money'? I always call out "Open the box!" We all do in our house. "OPEN THE BOX." The words get pinged at the telly and hit it on the first shot. Determined, they arch straight through the air from our settee island. Opening the Box is so much more exciting than Taking the Money. The mystery. Living on the edge. The unknown.

Deano, the huge boxer dog from Battersea Dogs'

home, commands respect in the house and protects Mum. Say if my older brother Tony goes to hit her then Deano will go for him. Sometimes even bites him. Mum thinks highly of Deano – so does Dad – and the dog gets fed a lot from their dinner plates. She tells us we have to share too and when we've finished we all have to give him the plates to lick clean before they're washed up.

Charles is different from the other foster kids. He's two years old. And black. He's scared of the dog too which goes against the grain for Mum and Dad. Though he's not Charles anymore, he's turned into something else. Some*one* else. Moving into our magical home he's no longer known as Charles. He's been renamed Boo Boo by Mum and Dad. Boo for short. I never know why or even dream of asking – that's *not* what you do in our house. And like the other foster kids he has to call my mum 'Mummy'.

The only one who refuses is Shirley. Her own mum, Hilda, goes to prison for making girls be prostitutes. Hilda's occasional visits to her kids are something else. She brings with her a whole tinful of sweets including lollipops, Black-Jacks, Rhubarb and Custards. We can only guess what other delights are contained within as Mum takes possession and doesn't share such privileged information. Instead she ekes them out as currency, used sparingly in exchange for; jobs, being good enough, having manners and asking properly for that which she covets for herself.

Shirley doesn't play the game, won't call Mum 'Mummy'.

"No, I've got me own mum!"

I shiver. Not for anything would I be in her shoes. But she doesn't care and says so. I don't think Shirley likes it here. She takes the younger ones up to the end of the garden, takes their pants down and pushes them over so they're sitting in the stinging nettles. She leaves me alone though she towers above me, her eight grand years to my five. Instead she tells me how much she hates Mum.

"Oh," I say, not really understanding, but…

Shirley doesn't stay during term time. Not like her sister Denise, renamed Neesy Boots. Mum thinks Neesy's 'ok'. She's got asthma, like Mum. But their little brother Jimmy won't get potty trained. *He's the only one I couldn't get clean.* So he goes to live with neighbours across the road. They've got four kids of their own, lino instead of carpets and butter on *every* door handle, so don't mind where he shits. But it's a bit hush-hush. When Hilda comes to visit no-one's allowed to tell her he hasn't been living with us, that he's been staying instead in shit-heaven. It's a *secret*. Mum gathers all the kids in front of her. Her eyes wide, enthusiastic.

"Jimmy's been staying here – *hasn't* he!" She nods, measured – slowly up, slowly down – while she utters this, saying it over and over till all the kids nod along with her saying their yeses. *Her* yeses.

Anyway, Charles takes a while getting used to the dog and you know what dogs are like – they can sense fear in the meat around them. Dad nearly pisses himself when Boo Boo climbs onto the settee, trying to get away as barking King Dog towers over him, its shadow completely covering the boy.

"Go on you black bastard!" It really tickles Dad.

Boo Boo, formerly known as Charles tries climbing the wall but it's no good. His hands scratch then pad flat against the flowery wallpaper, like someone trying to get out of a coffin they've found themselves buried alive in. They're keen enough to help, his hands, but ultimately powerless to save him. Charles screams and screams, his tears mixed with snot which joins his nose and mouth like his head is a piece of knitting unravelling. Eventually the dog gets distracted with biscuits, a pat on the back and some stroking of his silky ears.

"Fucking wogs. Wass for dinner, Joan? JOAN! Out the way Deano – mind the telly!" A firm shove with his foot. "Good boy."

There are many photographs of our family – of the kids anyway. Dad likes taking photographs. He's always got the latest camera. You should see us… at the seaside or in the garden running in and out of the sprinkler in our swimming costumes, admiring, when Mum points it out, the small artificial, perfectly formed rainbow. There are pictures of us kids on the steps outside the pub with a bottle of perfumy, red, fizzy Tizer *with a straw* and a packet of crisps with the blue salt bag. Oh, the excitement of seeking out the little blue pouch of salt, the paper twisted at the bottom. Look at that… a picture of Fireworks Night, me and the foster kids in the back garden each holding a sparkler. The only ones smiling though are me and Neesy. Everyone else looks glum. Even though the picture isn't in black-and-white the other kids look… grey.

"Come on Mand, smile!" Both of them say this, though mostly Mum while Dad fiddles with the camera. So I smile harder, as hard as I can, knowing it's important to do what they say, safer. I don't know where my big brothers are this time; Tony, seven years older at twelve, and Adrian, who's fifteen. I call Adrian 'Aijee' because I could never pronounce his name and it stuck. They're both real, not adopted like me. At thirteen even Patrick is real – to his own mum and dad at least. But as I say they're out of the picture. Aijee left home at fifteen because he doesn't do as he's told. Dad even had to break several smacking sticks on him. I miss Aijee loads. He used to give me more cornflakes when Tony wouldn't let me have many. Or he'd give Patrick a flick-ear when he caught him doing the same to me. Tony's still here, Patrick too. Tony and Mum, they're alike, she tells him. He's clever, not like Aijee, who, the school said 'will never be able to learn'. I dunno if the years spent in hospital with severe eczema made any difference. And Patrick, well, him and Tony – two peas in a pod when it comes to liking the same things including girlfriends.

Tony and Mum though have stand-up fights. Sometimes they pin each other up against the wall. It's all so loud then, the shouts and the thumping sounds, huge bodies competing for the winning position. Patrick tells me he thinks it's funny they do that. Hiding is difficult. I'm not really allowed out the room so just sort of sit further back in the settee like I haven't noticed. Tony's over six foot tall, like Aijee and Dad and Patrick too. They're all big except me, who's slim and short. Sometimes I hear Mum talking about the runt in a litter of dogs and how some people have the runt put down.

It's not only camera photography that Dad likes. He watches films too. Super 8's. Sometimes he brings home cartoons for us. He hangs this big white cloth on the wall in the front room. It's unbearably exciting. Me and the foster kids patiently wait and watch the screen, the rest of the room still and dark. Suddenly black numbers flash up in front of us. Real quick they go backwards from ten to zero like a space ship is about to take off in the front room. The cartoons appear *in colour* and as they unfold their stories they bring their illusory lives into the room, blending their world with ours. There are no sounds from the film, just the flick, flick, flicking of the projector as the tape goes round.

Sometimes Mum brings out an extra treat, a cup of milk and the sweetness of broken biscuits. They're a bit soft. Who cares!

It's good of Dad to do this and Mum makes sure we thank him. Often though, or always, he takes the screen, projector and a big cardboard box of films up to his bedroom for a private viewing. I don't think they're more cartoons. If they are that's not fair, when us kids could be seeing them too downstairs. Wait, though. Not yet but later, when I'm ten, I find out a bit more when I go to the toilet and can't resist a peak through the keyhole of his firmly closed bedroom door. All I can see is the film playing away on the wall opposite. Awww – wish I had lovely long blonde hair like her.

Mum took me to the hairdressers and got all mine cut off. There was a lot of it, nearly three feet so she took possession, got them to give it back. She said she might sell it. It's in a brown paper bag in the kitchen drawer ready to be made into a hairpiece. Be alright if I go bald or need to get down from my tower. Ha. Perhaps I'll spin it into gold and fuck off with a handsome prince. It's dead short now, my hair, just sort of hangs there. I look like one of the Beatles. Or like a big potato with cocktail sticks coming out of it, the cheese and pineapple long gone. So now my ears stick out even more.

"Jug handles," Mum and Tony call me. "With a wog nose!"

It's all a laugh. They crease up 'laughing policeman' style.

Trouble is I really do look like a boy. Some girl over the park, someone I don't know, asks me, "You a boy or a girl?" Just like that. I tell her I'm a girl. After that I go home – it can get nippy once the sun's gone in. Back on the landing, spying into Dad's bedroom, the flick, flick, flicking of the projector seeps through the keyhole. Awww – yuck! Repulsed, scared and guilty I bolt quietly into the toilet. I give a little cough to show I really am in the toilet now so don't anyone go accusing me of anything! One thing I know – it's definitely NOT a cartoon.

The house is in a Close, the houses surrounding a 'green' in the middle. In the summer all the kids from around the adjacent roads gather on the green to play games like British Bulldog, Sticky Toffee and Knock Down Ginger.

A few other families have a car like we do, but not many. When the Tonibell van comes everyone runs shouting into their houses for money. Mum lets us have an ice-lolly but if Dad's about he pays for ice creams – for the dog too. Sometimes even a '99 with a flake in.

Anne Drewitt and her brother Mike live in one of the corner houses. An old woman lived in it before them. One day she went in and found her son hanging from the stairwell. Blue, he'd turned blue. She ran to the neighbours saying, "There's something wrong with my son." Just a bit.

The family in the other corner, the Jensons, well, it's said their mum put her head in the gas oven. Killed herself. But no one, not the dad or the boy and the two girls, ever speaks of it. The boy has a bit of trouble with the ol' Bill but I think the dad was always that strict and miserable even before she did it. But why would anyone try and kill themselves? My advice is never live in a corner house.

Mind, our Close could be a big wrestling ring like they have on Saturday afternoon telly. They could wrestle over who's had the best death, who scores highest on the 'Oh, no, what a tragedy' scale. There could be a referee like the ones that keep Mick McManus and Cat Weazel in their places. He'd be stood, 'counting out' in the middle of the green – away from the dog shit round the edges.

"IN-ARRR the blue corner… a lad, early twenties, body hanging over the stairwell. Maybe he could never speak to his mother. His aged mother-ARR! He's certainly strung up about things." (Here the crowd roars/laughs). "AND-ARRR in the red corner… Mrs Jenson bending over the cooker-ARRR…leaving three dependent children."

He stops while the families attempt to give refreshments to the bodies, which strangely don't respond. The referee points at the boy, now cut down, in a heap, one leg bent underneath the body.

"ONE-ARRR…" (no response)… "TWO-ARRR… THREE-ARRR…" Still no response so the bell goes and the referee announces that Mrs Jenson's leaving three kids makes her the winner in the game of death. Maybe death was the only say she had over her life.

"Fucking idiots," says Dad about them all. He thinks everyone else inside the Close or outside our family is a fucking idiot. He should know because when he was in India during the war they wanted him to stay behind and become an interpreter, so quickly had he picked up the language. Mum relays the story often.

"How can you be so *stupid* when you're so clever?"

"All fucking idiots. Give it a rest, will ya – yip yip yip!" He goes back to chewing the side of his mouth that way he does. The way that says don't even *think* of walking in between him and the telly. Don't even think about it.

Years later when a new boyfriend and Tony's new girlfriend and Patrick's old girlfriend are round for the evening, Mum and Dad will start up. Mum'll be yip yip yip, while Dad sits there apparently unaware of her existence. It's coming, I know something's coming. I can feel it in the air, bubbling up from the floor getting louder and louder. It seems only I can hear it – while everyone else carries on watching telly. So I sit still and smile at my new beloved. Wriggling, I squeeze back into the seat. Trying to disappear is always worth a go… until he blows.

"SHUT YOUR FUCKING RABBIT. You've got more mouth than a CAMEL'S GOT CUNT!"

I'll feel sorry for Mum then, Tony with his serious face on. This time though, Mum doesn't cry. She stays quiet, says later she didn't mind because he showed himself up. As she always says, don't you see (hear) some sights when you ain't got a gun? Except she doesn't say ain't. Wouldn't dream of it.

"Who wants a cup of tea?" Patrick grins, slowly gets up, darts a look at his woman.

Mum also tells me about how she's had rock-solid Cintique chairs broken on her by Dad.

"Probably deserved it," she says wistfully, like it was a long-ago romantic trip on a gondola, being serenaded by Cary Grant under the Venice moonlight.

Sometimes she tells the funny story about the time

when Dad was with a prostitute (also in India). When he tells Ms Working Girl his name, Martin Trent, she says she knew a Trent once, Captain Trent. Only turns out it was his own flippin' father. What a laugh. Great minds think alike eh?

He's strong-minded too, Dad. When we do The War at school I ask him about Hitler, about the Jews he'd had killed.

"He didn't kill enough of 'em," he tells me. I know by now because Mum's told me, that my birth father is Jewish.

"I wouldn't walk across the other side of the green to save one of them," my dad tells me.

"Oh."

Chapter 2: Cruel Intentions

How the fuck did this happen? One day I belong with a gaggle of young foster children, the next day I get back from school and they've all gone. What? Speak to me someone! No warning. Nothing. Gone. Gone home. Back, left, departed, returned as in to *their own homes*.

"I've had enough," Mum says, sitting in 'her' chair.

There's a plate of cheese on toast and tomatoes on 'her' coffee table right at her elbow. There's not one spare inch free on the table. The dogs sit in front of her, heads tilted like a doggy charity poster, dribbling onto the carpet, waiting for treats.

There are two boxer dogs now, Joker and Jess. Deano had to go *because of HIM* because he kept biting Tony. *Only* Tony. Aijee and Patrick always got on well with Deano. Look, there's her special sharp knife! *Where's my special sharp knife? Where's that stick?* She needs the knife to carefully prize the skin from the tomatoes, brow sweating, and to remove each pip one by one before cutting the toast into minute squares. She divides up the equal-size squares, spreads them around the plate. Each one gets crowned with an equal-size piece of tomato. The eating itself is painfully slow while she savours each mouthful, or fraction of a mouthful. She's like a Holocaust Jew with a raw potato, though no-one came out of Auschwitz her size. Or did they? Perhaps it truly is in the genes, eh? Not her responsibility at all.

I'm not allowed to stay in my room. She wants me where she can see me. *Children should be seen and not heard.* So I sit next to her, as many cushions away as possible on the far end of the fake leather settee, trying to concentrate on the telly, trying to block out the sounds of her eating. The whole process lasts hours and the dogs will stay till it's over. Till the fat lady sings, then picks her teeth in front of 'her' special mirror.

The plate of food stands next to little groups of sweets. *Don't touch!* (bellowing) *They're MINE.* They're piled up in neat rows, graded by colour. Next to those are several bottles of pills, rubber bands round each bottle, one of which contains her diet pills. Ha. Filon. Bright orange smooth shiny pills like siblings of the only Smarties she'll eat. Don't even think of bringing a tube of Smarties to our house, expecting you'll eat all of them. She'll make you take out all the orange ones and give them to her. *They're the only ones I can eat.* Don't think you'll get away with it just because you're a visitor. Dad's a mini-cab driver now. The other drivers buy the Filon from Mum so they can stay awake at night, work longer hours. I overhear this rather than get it from the horse's mouth – that's the mare who is my mother.

Later she opens a bar of Caramac, breaks it up, leaves the pieces lying in their golden foil inner cover. She says nothing, instead maximises the use of food currency. My mother lets it sit there for an age. She knows I know it's there. We all do. Me and the dogs, Joker and Jess. ("Does that mean Jess is my sister?" I ask her one barmy summer evening. "Yes," she says. Blimey, and I thought I only had brothers.) Everyone pretends they don't know it's there, this little piece of chocolate heaven that is driving us all nuts. Eventually she says I can have a piece after I've done the washing and wiping up. The dogs get some without having to do a chore. I guess that's the down side of being the eldest sister. Their task is only to sit and wait. And wait. And wait. Fucksake – it's only food. Yet it becomes this really big important thing – ammunition, weapon, tool, style of management and drug of choice.

Enough. What about the other children, the foster kids? Where the flip are they? There literally are no signs they were ever here. No toys, drawings, puzzles. Not that there was anything of theirs on display when they were here. Mind, the house isn't big enough for *so many bloody kids* as well as things that would show an identity, interest, habit or opinion. I suppose the house has to stay minimalist as clutter makes it look shit real quick.

Did I imagine them? All of them? Shirley, Neesy, Jimmy, Boo Boo, Jordon, Maria and Vickie Drippin' (why?) and others before them. Perhaps I made up not one invisible friend but seven. That's it, isn't it? All the time it was just me and Mum and Dad and the dogs. Did I make up my two brothers too, the ones I said are real? And Patrick? How real are they, though? Am I the first under-ten to get Alzheimer's? Or am I living a different version, a cheaply made council-housey version of that film The Three Faces of Eve?

Maybe all along the foster kids have simply each been a different part of myself? Was Neesy really just a cuter, nicer, more lovable part of myself? Certainly I will go on to become asthmatic. And Jimmy – was he the very small, very frightened part within me somewhere, shitting myself at every opportunity? Was Shirley the big tough brave part of me that would like to stand up for myself, have courage and stand up to the Big People? The Really Big People like Mum, Tony, Patrick or the many others who are more important than me. Tony with his Chinese burns on my wrist and Patrick, laughing, with his thumps on my back and sticking his foot out, tripping me up. Can you imagine?

Take this washing upstairs, Mand. It's easier for you. You haven't got all this weight to carry around. While you're up there, change the beds. Just imagine if...

"No."

"DON'T SAY NO TO ME."

"NO."

At this point her lips curl up and away from her teeth like a Rottweiler. She sharply sucks air in between her teeth, while she reaches round for the smacking stick, a three-foot cane most folk use to prop up tomato plants. I'll stand up on the settee and peer down, hands on hips, one foot proudly forward, Supergirl cape flapping behind me (from the draught of 'her' special fan because she feels the heat so easily).

"I WILL say no. HEAR ME as I say NO now to you. And to all others who like you come from the DARKNESS to destroy THOSE FROM THE LIGHT. If you EVER shout at me or raise your hand to me again, you will be sent through the wardrobe back to Narnia, upon which time you will, on bended knees, have to clean up the shit left behind by the Ice Queen's horses. You will use a dinner knife, the same one you make me use to clear up the sick and dog-shit off the carpet, from your animals." *Who's Mummy's lovely dog then? Yeah, Mummy's favourite boy, Mummy's favourite girl.* "If you refuse you will be turned into stone. ALSO... also you will first be made to eat like a normal person, like it's part of life rather than life itself."

The house is so empty. Tony's left now too, obviously, because he doesn't do as he's told either. He stays longer than Aijee – doesn't leave until he's sixteen. Perhaps because he's like Mum (and HRH Her Dad, she says), so they get on better, have more in common. Patrick left the same month Tony did though he'd promised to visit.

HRH Her Dad is known as Pip to us kids. Dad's Dad is called Pop. He's alright, Pip. I'm not sure what got him to HRH status. Never see him smile much and not at all any more, of course, seeing that he's dead. But he was a small, unassuming man. He used to wear a hat, did Pip. Or a flat cap, like Prince Philip but without the money and the fwar fwar accent. Yet her dad *he never wanted me to marry your father* was an HRH. Mum's always slagged off Nan or Lillian, a big woman, who perhaps *did* assume things. Mum says things like, 'You can't trust women.' 'They're catty.' 'At least you know where you are with a man.' The only time I can see she stood up for her own mother was during the war when HRH Her Dad made Nan have margarine while he kept the butter rations. Mum reported him though I'm not sure who to. The butter police? Mum tells me when she was little she was HRH Her Dad's mate, helping him out in his workshop attached to the back of their two-up, two-down in North London. And he was a radio ham, doing his City and Guilds after he retired. But as soon as they were out in the workshop, Nan *that stupid woman* would call them in for dinner or anything else she could think of, such as a chore for 'John' – HRH Her Dad's earth name. Nan was twelve years older than Pip. They lived in the same street and she used to push him in his pram when he was a baby. Maybe he was ever after grateful so he married her.

Whereas when Pop's wife, Maud, got cancer, it was only then that he bought her a fur coat. Yet Rose, his secretary at his firm where he ran a fleet of lorries, got a fur coat long before this, long before Maud got ill. So if you're married it's best to get that cancer early if you don't want to wait for your treats. Then Pop only goes and marries Rose the year after Maud dies. S'true! This was all before I was born which is why Maud never progressed to Granny, Nana, Grand-mater blah blah.

Flip knows what has happened to the foster kids. Suffice to say it's not long before life in 'the house' settles. With Patrick, Tony and Aijee gone, and they rarely visit, even Patrick, it turns into a place that almost echoes and the only real sounds are those coming from the ever-present telly. Or the occasional dog barkings. Dad's away a lot once he starts on the lorries for Dixons – away all week and only home at weekends. Mum says she doesn't miss him.

Every day after school it's just me and her. She's clever though, knows a lot. If I say I'm cold, she says "Don't be stupid, you CAN'T be cold." Then somehow what I thought I thought and felt I don't think and feel any more. It all disappears, me with it. Clever.

And when I get an itch I need to scratch she makes me stop just with a little bellowing…"Don't scratch MY arm!" Clever again, because the scratch goes away once I know I'm not to scratch it and it's not my arm or my body anyway.

She's good at getting me to stop saying no too, though I sometimes try.

"DON'T SAY NO TO *ME*! Where's that stick?" Call me picky but I really don't like the stick. So my head does an unspoken deal with it and for the most part it stops me saying no.

When she makes her decisions about what I'll wear it's always browns, dark blues, blacks and greys. And always trousers. *Won't show the dirt.* Is that it, though? Her antidepressants find a comfortable home on the coffee table next to the diet pills. And me, the dogs, the tablets, the house – all her other possessions and her past settle around her in endless days that become threaded together like the dullest, dullest paper-chain left on the ceiling. Once lively and colourful, no one knows or cares that it's still there, its fibres a useless container of memories.

Occasional words break the silence but...

"What do you want for your birthday?" I ask.

"A *good* daughter," she snaps, with that face on, the face that shows just how bad I really am.

There's no one to talk to at home or at my new grammar school either – at first anyway. With everyone moving on to other schools I'm to start again with a load of fresh faces. It's posh though, at the grammar school. Somehow I passed my eleven-plus though my handwriting is so shit they move me to the front of the class, thinking I can't see the board properly.

At school there are loads of Jewish girls with loads of money. They have all the gear – full school uniform and I mean *full*, including all PE equipment. No visits to lost-property for them on a freebie hocky-boot search! And the biggest range of stationery ever. Always the latest brightest felt-tips – even cerise pink! And no blunt pencils for them either, with their own sharpeners. Mind, for us it's an excuse to go 'up the front' to the teacher's desk and whiz 'em round in her electric sharpener.

I always have this fear the pencil will get sucked in too far and I'll lose the end of my finger. Always the fear thing.

The school is huge and set within twenty-seven acres of woodland. We have our own drinks machine. You can get this watery hot chocolate if you have the money. If. Mum chose the school because of the grounds. She likes gardening and nature and things *au naturel*. People, though…

By the second year my marks are diabolically crap but I get through the long, long days by having a laugh. So do my new friends. School work can be dead boring but entertaining myself and those around me comes easier. I seem to be able to come up with ideas for a crack. It's easier than working and I can't concentrate on all that, my head's too jumbled. But it's after the 'set- my- desk- on- fire- and- tell- the- headmistress- I- did- it- because- I- was- cold' crack, that the school decide to send me to a child psychiatrist. Does he want me to entertain him?

The appointment arrives. Great – a day off school. Me and Mum both go. I don't know where we are but the complex where this bloke's office is, is surrounded by trees. Soothing, for others – not for the likes of me, obviously. Inside there are two of them but only one speaks. Perhaps the other bloke's here to fetch the tea. *See*! He's only going to get a drink for everyone! And there's only a dolls' house! If they think I'm going to play with *that* they can shove it up their arse.

When they speak to me, ask me questions, all I can say is I don't know. They tell me it's important to be honest. So I am. I honestly don't know why I do the things I do at school. No, nothing's wrong.

Hello, what's this? I think me Mum's been sprinkled with magic dust since we walked in here. She's being so nice – lovely, in fact – someone I'd love to have as a mother. I didn't know she could be like this. Well, I suppose she's a bit like it around strangers or men, specially men but never with me. And here she is answering this bloke's questions in the calmest, gentlest, loving way. A half-smile here. A grin there. A tiddy little shared joke with everyone in the room *including* me. She's the loveliest, loveliest person anyone ever met in the whole world. Even in films.

And the visit goes *so* well we don't have to go back, though they say we're welcome to any time. As we leave and walk towards the car, Mum spots them watching us through their window.

"Come on, let's show 'em," she says, smiling and hooking her arm in mine, in a jolly jape way like we've just stepped off a boat in Swallows and Amazons. I join in and off we swagger, giggling, to the car.

As we pull out of the drive Mum speaks up.

"You can clear your fucking room up an' all when we get back."

The familiar darkness pulls me back into its cosy depths.

Chapter 3: The Belles of St Trinian's

Diary. I keep a diary and if someone like Mum were to read it there's a code for days when I've had a bunk-up with a boy. At school we've all got different codes except Leanne, who's never even had it away like the rest of us. (She will hold out till she's seventeen, can you believe?) My way is to colour in the number of the date with biro. Easy when the numbers have a hole in like say: 4, 6, 8, 9, 10, etc. Harder though when the numbers are 1, 2, 3, 5, 7. I just do my best. That's all you can do, isn't it? That's what Mum says when we have a test or exam at school. *Just do your best.* Ha.

"Do I look any different?" I ask Sandra after telling her my cherry got popped last night. I reckon I look odd, unusual, and I swear people can tell something's happened, something's matured me.

She cackles, that special quiet rasping sound she uses when something bad happens to someone. We all do it – crack up at each other's bad stuff. It's a wonder we keep any friends. Will we stay in touch, years to come?

"You won't tell anyone?"

"Course not!"

A strange calm floats from the sky and pitter patters over me, surrounds me, soothing. I feel grown up. A flit of self-respect visits me briefly. Acceptance? Apart from Leanne I'm the last to go. I'm fourteen. I carry a good figure and my tits are becoming decent. This I know because I stand in front of my dressing-table mirror, both hands held flat against my bare breasts and lean forward, looking up at the glass to see how my cleavage is doing. And I'm getting there, I really am.

"It true then Mand? You had it away with Simon F?" says Dawn minutes later as Beth and Leanne join in the giggling. We're walking out the school gates at home time. I've kept myself to myself *all* day. How though, I do not know. It's all I could think about every stretchy length-wise and width-wise minute. I'd wanted to spill to Leanne sat next to me but held back the too-special information.

Sandra quickly turns away and the molecules of self-respect zoom off to seek another, more deserving, where they'll be welcome, appreciated, can build themselves a home. Instead something else slithers back inside my gut, head, legs, seeps into my skin, and takes up its place again, flowing round my body. Heavier and darker than before. Sandra's slight grin vanishes like a nervous twitch.

Simon's asked me back round to Nathan's next weekend, where we did it the first time. God, I really do love this bloke. I'm ecstatic he wants to meet again... but he hasn't phoned and I'm pining something rotten. SIMON F SIMON F SIMON F. I write his name on my diary, desk, pencil case and school books – with the others.

And because of this precious new love I try wiping the memory of his testicles trailing between his legs. Hard balls in a soft bag, which slapped against my arse as they swung back and forth. The Earth didn't move at all, not one tremor, a perfect zero on the Richter scale. Cynics might suggest there's a lot of fuss about nothing. Pigeon-like, it didn't take long for this really tall bloke to do his thing on top of me, way up there somewhere, my face shadowed by his chest. Simon's blonde with a sharp-cut nose that's focused on where he's going. Afterwards I noticed spots of blood on the sheet. Nathan's eau-de-Persil sheet.

Oh, I'm right to love him – we're going out now right? I remember what I'd said before it happened, too grateful to say no.

"But I'm not even going out with you."

"Will you go out with me?"

"Yes." But he doesn't turn up at Nathan's the next time and I never hear from him again. Just hear *about* him when he tells friends everyone's been up me. It hurts he couldn't tell it was my first time. When he doesn't turn up I have sex with Nathan instead, who seems as surprised as me when his friend doesn't arrive. He asks me and I like the attention. It makes me visible, nearly.

I almost forget Simon and fall head over heels in love with Nathan. I really am in love this time. Completely, deeply, wholeheartedly, and he gets the diary, desk, pencil case, school book treatment. Sadly I won't hear from Nathan again either but I don't know that yet. In his bedroom I play 'Yesterday' by the Beatles over and over, a love substitute. A musical hug. Nathan bounces downstairs for a laugh, coffee and cigarettes with my friends, who are ready to crease up at this boy-god's jokes. I place the Durex wrapper in my purse, a 'love' keepsake that'll stay there for months.

It's not that Nathan can't love or that romance is dead – we obviously just aren't suited, right? He falls madly in love with beautiful Leanne, who makes him work hard for moments of her time while I get scrubbed from his memory like a failed spelling test. Over the next few weeks, to ease his suffering while he waits for her, he has sex with Dawn and Ellen too.

I'm heartbroken. Again. It's this wretched heartache (and it *is* physical) that forces me to have words when I find out about Ellen. It's a perfectly harmless day and I've taken a bunch of mum's dieting tablets. As Ellen walks towards the front of the class I bravely jump her from behind. There's some hair tugging and some on the ground action but not much else. We're both small and she's better than me at both applying make-up to her face, and herself to her school work rather than to being a good scrapper. So, not much happens.

And me, what am I good at? Sometimes I'll start on someone and come off worse. The buzz of it is good – gets me noticed for a bit. Face it – I'm shit at fighting, standing up for myself. Do I secretly think I'm always wrong?

"He's not yours," Ellen says, wise beyond our years.

"Fucking bitch!" I grab another clump of hair for good luck.

By lunchtime all is forgotten. By then we're 'group-ignoring' someone else, someone who's a total slut, slapper, whore, slag and bitch.

I should pay more attention to what's around me – someone's only gone and stuck down the lid of my desk with black gunk and I can't get it open. Fucksake. Beth and Leanne are pissing themselves so much you can taste it. Strangely, they know 'nothing' though Beth later confesses it's some sort of car glue.

Then one of the Jewish girls shares her sweets, only it turns out they ain't, aren't, sweets. They're stones –

pebbles that she put in a sweets bag. Fucking teeth nearly went for a burton! Bitch scumbag. What a day. It's not easy being a teenager!

It's good at school in winter, though. The snow covers all the green bits and you could be anywhere: Switzerland, Canada, the Arctic, or Dead. There are many trees in the woods, so many. Once some men came to shoot the grey squirrels. They've been breeding a lot and they're worried about them taking over from the orangey squirrels. As if that'd ever happen! (What has a hazelnut in every bite? Squirrel shit!) We had to stay out of the woods while that went on which was a shame because I like to be right in the thick of it. In the woods, stood in my bottle-green skirt and black jumper I can become a blur and almost, almost, almost disappear.

It's autumn now. Ron the gardener rakes up all the leaves into piles and later when we're out the way he'll bonfire them. They're oblivious, innocently being blown around, not realising they're for snuffing out. I wish I could make them green again, give them back their lives to start all over, do things properly. I wonder if they'd have stood a better chance if they'd come from different trees. Maybe they wouldn't have ended up in a heap on the floor.

At break we have the usual cigarette behind the green hut.

"EURRR Leanne," says Dawn, "You've bum-sucked it!"

Leanne sniggers the same way she does when she's been busted for farting. It's infectious and some of us laugh. She passes round the fag with its now soggy end, the short stubby Number Ten which we make do for five of us. Ellen doesn't smoke but always comes with.

Let me tell you though, this short stubby bum-sucked cigarette is a joy compared to what happens next.

We're about to discover what Caroline's brought into school, making it her own bring-and-share day. There's loads of fuss, everyone's crowding round, so we call her over, curious. It's in a jar. She's got this thing **in a jar**. It's only a fucking turd! A full length of mid-brown once-steaming shit. Did she think of us all at school while she gave birth to it? (Why is shit tapered at the end? So your arse doesn't go off with a bang!) There's something wrong with that girl. She needs a right whack if anyone ever did. Nah – she's taller than me!

After that we discover this perfect pile of crispy autumn leaves. Huge! It's a kaleidoscope of rusts, reds and creams, some struggling to stay green. I dive into the pile, burrowing underneath. There are so many leaves in this cavern I can't be seen from outside. Bliss. I could stay till Spring if the ground wasn't so damp.

Sandra, Ellen, Beth and Leanne follow me in but Dawn doesn't make it under before a teacher turns up. Oh no! Mrs Stevens, the chemistry teacher. Scarier than scary. Her daughter Kim is in our year. Imagine having a chemistry teacher for a mother! How depressing. Dawn, meanwhile, makes herself useful and, noticing Leanne's head sticking out, she covers it with her foot.

"Is there someone underneath those leaves?" Mrs Stevens snaps in an atom- splitting way.

"No," says Dawn in that same innocent 'common sensey' voice she used to tell me she shagged Nathan – the voice that gets you, me, feeling sorry and makes you feel bad all over again.

We're busted completely when one by one we piss ourselves giggling. Mrs Stevens demands we get out and grow up.

When I get home Mum proudly shows me some clothes she's picked up from a charity shop. A coat. As in mac. She's chuffed to fuck, tickled to shit – just because it's reversible. It's something an old woman might wear and I'm not talking forties, but fifties or sixties! It's cream coloured on one side and greeny-turquoise on the other, with pert white buttons that spin around laughing at their own private joke. They know like I do that I'll have to wear this coat no matter what. There'll be no choice and it won't matter whether I cry, or how much, nor what I say. I do try but Mum's version is the only one that counts. The coat may be reversible but her decision isn't. This while my mates are wearing black crombies and stack heels like the skinheads we admire.

Then she produces these shoes, pleased as punch with her bargain. They're repulsive – flat, or almost, with a slim, slim wedge heel, and holes punched in the fronts in the shape of a flower. And they're olive green she tells me – she's good at her colours – but she dyes them brown as we're not allowed green shoes at school. Again they're something an old person would wear, a *very, very* old person. They wouldn't look right unless they had massive, fat, swollen ankles hanging over their sides, with wiry varicose veins fanning outwards and upwards, pointlessly searching for the good old days when their hosts danced away the nights to the sounds of the big bands.

I'm nearly fifteen. Crying doesn't help, but I can't stop the huge wailings that fight their way from my mouth like lemmings over a cliff, as I lay thrown across my bed. The lump in my throat won't go away as the air in the room hangs heavy as wallpaper paste. It's all so grey, grey, grey. What can I do? What will my friends say when I turn up at school dressed like this? They'll give me shit, take the piss, obviously, as anyone would. Like I would.

Next day Mum gives me a lift to school. She checks I'm wearing the coat and shoes.

"Hmm... nice, Mand." She makes her point.

Before we've gone past the next road she pulls up at the post-box.

"Post this!" She orders, hands me a letter.

I slowly look back and forward to case the place, check the coast is clear, without her seeing.

Oh no! Hell has decided to bring me a hand-delivered invitation. That's only Jack Nyman walking up on the other side of the road on his way to school! Oh. Please. God. No. In around thirty-eight seconds he'll pass the car. Inside the car is horrible fat Mum who can't stand him so pretends she hasn't seen him when she has. And next to horrible fat, dresses-like-a-man Mum, there's a horrible coat and horrible shoes. And inside the horrible coat and horrible shoes is me. Stupid, pathetic, ugly, waste of space, should-never-have-been-born me. Let me die now. I can't do this. Truly I can't.

Jack Nyman is so dishy he should be in films. He moved into the close a few years back. Loaded, the Nymans are. Absolutely rolling in it. His dad runs a newsagent's *and* they've got a chalet at Leysdown on the Kent coast. His mum Doreen is short and round with jet black dyed hair, caked on make-up and earrings. Big earrings. Huge.

Jack's always well turned out with the latest loafers *with* metal Blakeys he's put on the bottom so you can hear him click-clacking up the road, announcing that a wonder of the world is approaching. You might though, smell the Brut aftershave before you hear the shoes thing. Never short of cigarettes or chewing gum, he wears brand-new stay-pressed trousers, Ben Sherman and Fred Perry shirts, tonic suits with silk hanky – the whole bit. Even a sheepskin! *And* he wears it to school *and* he's got it on now!

I take the letter like it's toxic, count to five, sort of in s-l-o-w m-o-t-i-o-n, hoping she won't notice. My head stays down so that Jack won't see me.

"Go on then. What you playing at? What the…?"

She looks at me, then at Jack just as he's almost level with the car.

"That's it! Out! NOW."

He sees me.

"Alright?" I greet him like it's a normal day but I wish again that I truly could die. He nods back, barely acknowledges me, flicks his dog-end away then clip-clops on with his future, a smirk enhancing his already beautiful face.

Wouldn't it be great if you could just eat something, say a sherbet fountain, and disappear? At school I draw coffins with my name and 'RIP' on the front. There's usually a cross on the top. I'm not alone in this. School can be a laugh and a couple of the teachers are alright too, but…

When I get to school the first time with the 'coat and shoes,' I make a joke of them. Luckily, as I'd hoped, everyone laughs along with me. Hey, look at me being a little old woman. Ha ha. Just call me Gertrude. Ha ha.

Most days I catch the bus. As soon as I reach the bus stop I roll up the coat and stuff it in my basket. We've all got these wicker baskets now instead of bags. Some of the girls even have covers that stretch over the top to keep the rain off. Sensible Dawn does anyway. Her mum makes cakes, the works! After I put on the once-white gym shoes, nicked from lost property, I stuff the coat and shoes down deep into the basket. It's cold when it snows, what with no coat over my short-sleeved jumper but what else can I do?

Mrs Lewis, our form mistress, who teaches needlework, keeps me behind after school one day and starts having a go at me for not doing homework blah blah. At least that's how it starts but God only knows how it gets round to the coat and shoes. Somewhere in the middle of all that she starts to get really nice and – I don't know where it comes from – I start to cry. She only offers to alter the coat for me! How nice is that? *Specially* for a teacher. But I have to say no, obviously. Mum would kill me, a) for telling someone, b) because she likes the coat as it is, and c) there's a part of her that gets a kind of pleasure out of making me wear said coat (and shoes). So why spoil all that fun she's having? And, as I say… she'd kill me.

Chapter 4: Love Story

"You slag!" He grabs my ponytail and pulls me along behind him.

All this attention! I know then it's real love.

At school I gouge New Bloke's name into my desk. On my arms too. At fifteen we're all doing it. With compasses we scratch the names of our beloveds until globules of blood pop out, shiny and honest. The plan is to pick the scabs so the scars will prove our undying love. Doesn't always work. Sometimes they rebel and just heal.

By the fifth year a new class gets created for the six of us. It should have been four but Ellen and Dawn were given the option to stay with us, their friends. I suppose it's the first sin bin. I never think we do very much wrong, more that the school is so twinset and pearlsy they can't cope.

We need a pig's heart to dissect in biology. So me and the then 'Pears Soap' beautiful and innocent Leanne go to the butcher's at lunchtime to get a heart. When we ask for a pig's eye as well, the butcher gives it us, no questions asked and we rush off giggling to Leanne's house, her back garden backing onto the school. Leanne's brave as we, she, puts it in a Marmite sandwich. The eye seems surprised at this.

Back in class we put the sandwich in Beth's desk. The bell goes. A wasp buzzes inside the window, conscious of its heavy workload. Beth reads the forged 'note' we've written on the blackboard from 'Venetia,' telling her about the donated sandwich inside the desk.

Miss Stanway looms in, in her blonde loomy way to read the register. She's irritated as usual to dip her toes outside the sanity of a French lesson.

"I wonder what's in the sandwich," says Beth lifting one of the edges. She's always so curious.

It's a ... big... long... scream. All shivery.

"For goodness' sake, Elizabeth. Stand still – it's only a wasp!" Snaps Miss Stanway in her thundery, Thatchery voice.

I won't touch Marmite for two years now. Beth recovers more quickly. Others can, it seems.

New Bloke is different from most I've been out with. He's seventeen to my fifteen and so sensible – so grown up – *so* mature.

We meet at a party. I'm stood near the top of the stairs with my new friend Sally, who I've just met tonight. Tony and Patrick were going out and I begged if I could come along. ("Go on, take her," says Mum – result!) They were going out in a foursome with their women, who (this time) are sisters. There's a third sister my age – Sally. Nice gel and she's as short as me!

Anyway the two couples go off somewhere else so I tag along with Sally to a party. There are no other decent blokes except this one I notice near the bottom of the stairs. He looks alright, not as in 'Phoarr! Bit of alright!' but as in 'Ok, the best here' – not that there's much else here.

"Push me into him," I say to Sally.

"What for, Mandy?" she says, coming in a head

behind the rest.

"Just push me into him as we go past."

So that's how it happens. It's love at first flight – of stairs. As we make our descent, me in front, I muffle a laugh at my skilfully devised plan. Just as I reach this bloke, Sally shoves me into him and I nearly fall down the stairs. He remains standing, barely raising a considered eyebrow.

When New Bloke speaks he keeps his glass up, covers his mouth. He always does that. Almost as if the words trip from his lips without permission to go public. Like they're on their maiden flight. As if he tests them according to the response he gets.

"TESTING – TESTING – TESTING. Stand back. Newly used words approaching, first airing with YOU!" Maybe he's alright *and* all right.

He's drinking Pernod and lemonade. I'm not too fussed about a drink as long as I have my fags.

"So what O levels are you doing?"

Blimey, who could care less about school exams, I think, as a giggle jumps defiantly out through my mouth and lands on his face. Oops. But what sort of bloke *is* this? Obviously very grown up. Tall, almost six foot. Slightly porky. We talk for a short while.

"I'm a loner," he says.

"Oh." I haven't heard of this before. I smile and nod. Anyway, it doesn't concern me does it?

New Bloke's an electronic wire-man working at the local telephone exchange. After a bit more stimulating talk which goes over my head, he guides me upstairs and into a small bedroom. I'm awe-struck and happy to be guided anywhere by this bloke. That he takes the lead makes him all the more grown up in my book.

He goes towards the bed and shoves off the big

bundle of partygoer coats, abandoned there like puppies in a gutter. Then he lays me on the bed.

You know what? He's not so bad at all! My heart's in my throat though there's barely room, what with his tongue being in there too. He sucks and tugs and pulls and slobbers all over my neck, face and mouth. I feel privileged to have this attention from one so clearly superior.

The doorbell goes and I can hear the voices of Tony and Patrick and some female giggles.

"Oh shit, it must be eleven o'clock." The last thing I want is them seeing me walk, flushed and dishevelled down the stairs with a bloke. But that's exactly what happens. Patrick gives me a knowing look as I descend the stairs followed by New Bloke. I hold the banister and come down tentatively like Bambi on the ice.

After I say hello me and New Bloke go into the front room where we dance to Still Waters Run Deep by the Four Tops.

We dance, not too close me and him, though he does reach across to blow gently in my ear. It both turns me on and repulses me at the same time.

Tony, Patrick and their women stay for a couple of drinks. Hazel's the same age as Tony but Paula is seven years older than Patrick and has a four-year-old daughter. Patrick is twenty three. He likes older women. And younger women. And women the same age.

He fancied my friend Susan Jacobs from school. Mind, she was four years older than me. She was in the fifth year when I was in the first. He liked Susan because she's got big tits. Or so he tells Mum.

Just before I have to go, New Bloke gives me the record we've been dancing to. He doesn't tell me it wasn't his to give. And his phone number. This is so romantic, I'm thinking. Tony tells me to cover up the love-bites on my neck.

Me, Sally, the boys and their women go back to Paula's flat, a high-rise. It's dead exciting staying at someone else's place. I feel so free it's fantastic. But I can't shift New Bloke from my head. In the end I think about him so much I struggle to remember his face.

The next day I try to phone him. A lot. But strangely he's out every time. And once, his eldest brother Trevor answers.

"He's out with his girlfriend."

I'm distraught, like you are when you've known someone less than twenty-four hours. But meeting him was meaningful... so I make Sally take me round his house to investigate.

He's just going on a driving lesson with his dad. He gets out of the car and says "Sorry, eight miles – it's too far." I walk off crying.

"You can keep the record," he calls out. As he drives off I know his love is lost to me forever.

So how many times does that record get played over the next few days? Well, definitely once or twice.

The next day I try his number again.
"Yep?"
"Hello, can I please speak to—"
"He's gone out."
"Do you know what time he'll be back?"
Click, prrr prrr.
I dial again.
"Hello, could I—"
"I told you, he ain't here."
"Is that you?"
He laughs. I slam the phone down but dial again.

"What now?" Still laughing.

"You've got a fucking cheek. I want an explanation."

"Look, what am I supposed to do? You live too far away. Why would I want to go out with a giggly little schoolgirl? You're no good to me."

I'm thinking…here's my lesson for today: finish my homework then ring someone else. But will I do either?

Click, prrr prrr.

"Look," it's my turn now, "you owe me an apology. *You* gave me your number, *you* asked me to ring you – then *you* did a runner on me!"

"Told you – I'm a loner."

But after a few days he takes my calls.

Every day at school I dig out more shallow graves in my desk. 'Mand loves New Bloke OK?' 'Mand + New Bloke 4 eva + eva OK?' 'Mand + New Bloke rule OK?' 'TRUE 4 EVA SO IF U DON'T AGREE FUCK OFF OK?'

Every evening after school I play Still Waters Run Deep on the big grey square record player Dad got me for passing my eleven plus, getting me into grammar school. I leave the arm off so it plays over and over. And over and over. And over and over. In my mind I try to hang on to the events of the party though I can barely remember what New Bloke looks like any more.

You know what it's like when you stare at a washing machine – all the colours mix together and you can't tell if it's your over-knee socks, your old red jumper or Father Christmas bubbling around? That's what my head's doing. It's got Him-Him-Him stuck on permanent spin-dry.

And every evening after my dinner I sneak upstairs to call him from the other extension. We talk for ages.

Specially we talk about bunk-ups. New Bloke says it makes him want to pole-vault all the way over to my house (as in using his prick to do it with – yeah I have to get him to explain it!)

Then one night after about a fortnight, IT happens. He calls me! *He* calls *me*. I'm really grateful as we arrange I'll catch the three buses over to him. I'm so excited though I've no idea where we'll go or what we'll do. It doesn't occur to me to ask. I don't care anyway.

As Diana Ross sings to me Ain't No Mountain High Enough – I've reached the top of love's mountain. Fifteen years old and I've got myself a date with this gorgeous bloke who's already seventeen. Seven-bloody-teen!

New Bloke's waiting for me at the bus stop and we go into the Wimpy Bar.

"Can't you use your fork?"

How embarrassing. He's so mature!

"I like using my fingers for chips. Makes 'em taste better... " But the last few words tail off in shame.

He takes me to his mate Paul's flat. Paul's parents are out. For a moment I'm worried he expects me to sleep with his friend!

"I'm going up the shops. See-ya." Paul disappears. Phew!

New Bloke tells me to follow him into Paul's room. I do. He takes a rubber Johnny from its packet and we do it on the bed. I feel a bit sore so I'm glad when it's over real quick.

Afterwards me and New Bloke walk back along the stream to the High Street. *He* walks – I float. He buys me ten Number Six and a box of Swannies. Back in the Wimpy Bar he looks at me over his cup of tea and my Coke (which he's paid for).

"Will you go out with me?"

Did I hear right? Lights spring from nowhere. The whole Wimpy Bar is illuminated then disappears as New Bloke's 'Catherine Wheel' face fills the room from the floor to the ceiling, bashing out the walls, blocking up my eyes, my ears and covering my head. Truly I've reached the top of the love mountain.

"Yeah."

"I've gotta go."

"You out tonight with your mates?"

"Nah! You've worn me out – I'm gonna get an early night."

After he leaves I sit in the Wimpy Bar ready to leg it outside when my bus comes.

This bloke suddenly appears. He's wearing black leathers. Dunno why, but he comes and sits at my table.

"You waiting for the bus? I'm Malcolm."

'I'm Malcolm' with his greasy lank hair takes me back home on the back of his motorbike.

"Let's go to the train station first – get our photos taken." I can be a good suggester. We have a laugh at the photos. I don't like the one of him kissing me – he kept his sunglasses on – but at least it's another 'set of four' for my diary.

"Phone me, won't you?" He drops me home but I lose his number.

Brrring brrring.

"Watcha – did your dad tell you I phoned last night?"

"Mand…I've been thinking. I can't go out with you anymore."

"What's wrong?"

"I feel tied down. You're a lead weight on my shoulders."

Click, prrr prrr.

Monty Python's Flying Circus is on the telly but I can't laugh or even watch it through the tears or, behind them, the thoughts juggling around in my head.

"MANDY. UP!" Here we go. She'd be crap as a newspaper, my mum. The Daily Shout. There wouldn't be any news – just old recycled trash that's been said plenty of times, over and over and over.

"GET OUT OF BED, YOU DIRTY LAZY COW. LAYING THERE STINKING. PUT THIS WASHING AWAY, WILL YOU? AND CHANGE THE BEDS. AND TIDY THAT FUCKING BED-ROOM – shouting a good 'un now –"I WON'T TELL YOU AGAIN."

She always orders. I never notice it but my friends do. Not that they're too welcome at the house. Well, Dawn's welcome. Mum likes overweight Dawn. To me the way Mum speaks to me is normal. It's only when I'm round other people's houses that I notice the difference. It's strange the way some mothers speak to their kids – as if they genuinely don't hate them.

Yet Mum and Dad always moan about everyone else as if our family is the normal one! You can have a laugh with Dad, though. And he'll give me a cigarette if I ask for one, whereas with Mum I always have to nick one… Well, I still nick Dad's too, obviously.

Spoiled rotten, I am. Mum's always telling me that I'm spoiled compared to my brothers. She's right in a way. The smacking stick's never once broken on me, whereas it broke regular on Tony and Adrian, specially when Dad used it. She hasn't used it much lately, though it still lives by her chair, her best friend ready to leap to her defence in times of duress.

I light a cigarette then fall back asleep. When it burns my fingers I reckon it's time to get up. Today I'm excited because I'm going to colour my hair auburn. I'd love to be blonde really but would look like a pig, what with my snub nose. And being short. And with my ears, which stick out like jug handles, as Mum, Dad, Tony and Patrick often joke. If only I could look like the blonde woman in Abba. Most probably I'd end up looking like the red-haired one, like a bloke.

I colour my hair in the bath. Temporary, it says. Comes out in six to eight washes, it says. I hope it's true as I've not asked Mum if I can do it.

When it's done I'm not sure what to expect. We don't really have mirrors in the house. Mum doesn't believe in them. Only her special face mirror (for her special face) for when she needs to pick her spots or look at the holes in her fillings. She's very particular about the goings-on in her mouth. Finicky.

She's always moaning at Dad that he eats too quick. He should eat slowly like she does. Digest it properly. *You can't even taste it, you eat so quickly*. All that time cooking and it's gone in a moment. She used to spend all day Saturday baking cakes and biscuits when they were first married. But, she said, it all went in an hour so she stopped. Eating so quick is probably why he weighs twenty-three stone.

"Yeah, but Martin carries it well being as he's six foot four," she'll tell you. "It's easier for him."

She doesn't like being fat, often telling me (snarling) how *lucky* I am not to be overweight, or have my face all covered in eczema like she did as a girl. *You don't know how LUCKY you are!* That's how she got fat: spending so much time in hospital with eczema, being forced to eat white fish that when she came out she ate and ate and ate. Or is she fat because during the war she was allowed to eat only two ounces of butter each week, then went mad when the war ended? Or is she fat because Dad eats so quickly that the only way she gets to have a second helping, she says, is by putting it all on her plate in the first place, otherwise he gobbles it up before she gets a(nother) look in? With all the odds stacked against her it's no wonder she's so big. Plus her mother was big built too. Well, no chance then!

Dad says he's fat because he eats what Mum gives him.

She's in the hall, just hung up the phone as I come down the stairs. I wonder if the girls at school will like the colour. Beth's already gone auburn. Would New Bloke have liked it even though it's not blonde?

Mum stops, glares, lip curled.

"You look like a right slag!"

Chapter 5: The Grass is Greener

Somehow I'm blessed. Simply by phoning New Bloke everyday for two weeks and going over to his and having sex, he forgives me for being the lead weight on his shoulders and we get back together. Bliss. Relief. Deep joy. Because I cannot live without this bloke. You know that by now right?

The heavens must be shining on me to give me another chance. I know he's too good for me – I keep telling them at school. Dawn's had enough. ("For fucksake shut up Mand!")

Occasionally Mum gives me a lift to his which saves me catching the three buses. She loves driving, and swimming too. She could swim a mile when she was six. Maybe driving and swimming make her feel free, weightless. She approves of New Bloke, prefers blokes all round. She even wears men's clothes; tops, jumpers and always trousers. Always dark colours. Only if it's an unbelievably hot day she'll wear a skirt around the house, thundering like a steam train. It will be homemade, a huge piece of cotton with elastic threaded round as a waistband, sweat dripping down her red, red face.

You can't trust women, never got on with them. Fickle. Two-faced. With a bloke what you see is what you get. All that messing around with make-up, how they look, it's all they care about, so they can trap some poor bloke. My mother, wicked cow, used to say "I know my faults," and I'd say "Go on then, name one!" But she never did! Nearly died having me… and then I turned out to be a girl. A GIRL! Didn't bother with a middle name, just switched the boy's name they had ready: John – after '(HRH)' my dad, John Henry Augustus Richards – to Joan. Joan! I was Dad's mate (wistful), his little helper… He was a good old stick, my dad, told me not to marry your father. Not many like him around.

Her spirit goes back then to whatever's on the telly, oblivious of me, wherever I am. *Put the kettle on, NOW!* Oh, *there* I am! Call My Bluff is her favourite programme. She likes words, calls out the answers, gets a lot correct. *See, told you it was that!* Proves to the world once and for all how fucking RIGHT she is. *If a job's worth doing, it's worth doing properly.*

Maybe she's completely right and I'm completely wrong. Is that why she has this unusual brand of motherly love? Motherly hate. Did I not give her the mothering she'd expected from me? Is she wishing those nice men 'Fwank' Muir and Patrick Campbell would jump from the screen, were here instead of me as she throws the dog a biscuit? *Good dog, Mummy's favourite girl!*

So I'm back with New Bloke, who's becoming Utter Hero of my Dreams. Sometimes his dad gives him a lift here, but mostly it's me going there. Three buses? I would go to the ends of the earth for this bloke. He's like a god to me. *A* god? He *is* God.

It's good at his, gets me away from mine. There's a coal fire in the front room though the council are talking central heating. The cheap furniture is clean and tidy. Even the melamine and chipboard kitchen proudly made by his dad. It's cosy... safe, though the cupboards open awkward.

His family are so nice to each other. *No-one* shouts or swears. Will, his father, has depression but he takes his tablets and you'd never know it really. Probably. Dorothy, his mum, hardly speaks – she's such a gentle woman. Well, sometimes she does and sometimes Will tells her not to. Like the time she said my beloved's birth was difficult – and curiously how *she* nearly died!

"Have you seen how big a baby's head is? And the size of the ho—" She puts thumb and forefinger together, forms a circle.

"Ay, ay – told you not to talk about that didn't I?"

She buttons it then, pursing her lips into a cat's bum and carries on clearing the table.

Every day after dinner there's a pudding, can you believe? Dorothy cleans offices. It pays for extras like puddings – cakes too. Depending which day it is you know what's for dinner, week in week out; Sunday morning – fry up, lunchtime – roast (cheap beef you can't chew and you nearly choke, politely trying to get rid of it), teatime – tinned tomatoes and scrambled egg on toast. Monday – leftover beef with chips. Tuesday – bones (stewing lamb), blah blah. Hoovers every day. She divides up her housekeeping and puts it into different envelopes for the bills. Every Wednesday she buses to the market, buys a bunch of flowers and she does bingo round at the church hall twice a week. Bliss. The regularity. The safety of it.

She never knows how much Will earns as a storeman. Nor how much redundancy he got from the Gas Board after a thirty year stretch. Dorothy won't know until years later after he's dead, when the welfare man from the Gas Board explains what those black figures mean on the bank statement.

"That's interest which has built up over the years," he tells her.

"Oh, thank you." At last she clocks how she's struggled when she didn't need to, had to count every penny to stay above the cake line. That's the thing – she didn't bloody *need* to. She utters then the only words I ever hear her say against King Will.

"He was a mean man, your father," she quietly tells my beloved. Then as if Will's ghost drops a pebble onto the window-ledge, threatens to seep through the walls of the front room to insist on her silence, her mouth returns to a cat's bum.

Her son doesn't answer. Does he think he misheard? Although she'll dare to speak out occasionally, the fifty years she's spent with Will have squished the life from her soul. She no longer knows how to be a person.

Dorothy has been anaemic for years. Even the good bits of her blood have been drawn from her, the energy sucked away. Her rightful place is as audience, not speaker. She gets Guinness on prescription for the drops of iron that splodge their way through her system, chug, chug, screaming at the corpuscles to blossom, strut their stuff and bring her back to being a living, breathing, feeling, *speaking* person. But she rarely drinks from the stubby bottles, giving them to her husband or son instead. God helps those who help themselves eh? So she stays a powdery white like a weakened version of Queen Elizabeth I, instinctively knowing and avoiding the danger of being either royal or important in any way.

Tony and Patrick have moved back home for a while. I really miss Adrian, who rarely visits. He brought his girlfriend to stay once but she and mum had a row. Mum asked her to peel the potatoes. She started to but admitted, crying, that she didn't know how. When Mum had a go at her, shouting, potato knife pointing, she left, still crying. Adrian didn't go after her.

Patrick still does that thing where he blows in my ear, breathes, licks it till I shiver, then he laughs. He does it to Mum too. She thinks it's funny. Patrick moans about Adrian's girlfriend who doesn't like it. Patrick gets on *really* well with Mum sometimes. They go for a drink to a well known country-side pub then sit in the car park and watch couples in action. When they come back they tell funny stories about steamed-up windscreens and legs out of car windows. Mum tells about the family whose garden backs on to our neighbours', where this woman had a thing with the teenage boy she was fostering. Mum says she was 'teaching' him.

Mum and Tony decide I'm to study computing when I leave school. Tony's a computer operator. College is near where my beloved lives but the course is weird, with binary this and COBOL that. So I bunk off a lot and visit Dorothy. I can't go home – Mum'd kill me.

Dorothy tells me stories about when she grew up in Forest Hill. She tells me about her first boyfriend, the one before Will. He was a pleasant boy; polite, friendly. And posh. At fifteen she earned money cleaning doorsteps. One day she rang the doorbell of this big smart house on the corner and guess who answered? Yep – Mr Nice Boy. She ran away and never saw him again. Then she met Will on the bus on the way to work at the sewing machine factory.

Choices. I wonder if everyone has that – 'The one that got away' thing. The one we should have stayed with. The nice one. A few months before I met my beloved I went out with James. He was the kindest, most respectful, decent and funnest bloke you could meet. Loving. Rich. Adored me and me him.

He was a year older than me – sixteen, had already decided he would do Business Studies in sixth form at his grammar school. He played water polo. Blimey. We met at a disco when I nicked his drink off him. James lived in a five-bedroom detached house in a leafy village, swimming pool in the back garden. His mum was Scottish and scary with thick black eyebrows. His dad was the director of a building company. A proper one, *not* like a one-man-band bricky. James even had his own bathroom. I loved going in there. It smelled so… clean. I loved to hold his flannel to my face, drink in the smell of his soap. Of him. Life boy.

James wanted to get engaged, wanted us to marry and have four children. He wrote and told me so. From that moment on I wanted four children. One night we went to his older sister's Bistro on Shepherd's Bush Green. She owns it with her boyfriend, Pierre, who's blind. So…if love is blind and he is blind they must be really, really in love.

I had scallops served in real shells – you don't get that at the Wimpy Bar! And guess what? There was only that woman in there who's on That's Life on telly, being all loud and flash with her friends. What's she called? Esther Rantzen, that's it. This is one for the diary!

What went wrong between me and James? We even survived the time his dad came to wake him but couldn't find him. He was still fast asleep in my bed, hadn't woken in time to go back to his own. His mum was funny about it, ignored me. *Scary*. His dad had a go at James, about his disrespectful treatment of 'that poor young girl'. Love it.

So what was it went wrong between us? Not enough, probably. So I got meaner and meaner, blanking him in front of my friends etc. Till in the end he chucked me. But we did two months and two days, my longest before my beloved. And sometimes I wonder...does everyone have someone like this? Someone we let slip through our fingers? Choices. Ha.

My beloved goes on a week's holiday with his mates. How I miss him. Over and over I play Still Waters Run Deep. It makes me feel worse so I carry on. I get hardly any sleep while he's gone and bore everyone rigid talking about him. Cry, too.

I do a bar job in a working men's club where I constantly play Diana Ross singing Touch Me in the Morning. It's difficult pulling pints without bursting into tears. So instead I cry when no one's looking. Or in the toilet. My greatest hope is that my man doesn't meet someone else and chuck me when he gets home. He's gonna get rid of me for someone better, I know he is. Why wouldn't he? He loves blondes. And all his other (prettier than me) girlfriends were blonde. Sometimes I ask him if he thinks I'm pretty.

"To *me* you are," he says. Why doesn't that help? Thing is, I know how ugly I am.

"I'm fat!"

"Well..." He looks down, consoling, "You *have* got a bit of a tummy. But if you just get rid of that... " I'm seven and a half stone. But I know he's right. If only I could look like Farrah Fawcett, the blond Charlie's Angel, who he really likes. Even if I'm the same build as her I'll never be that tall..

On his return I'm excited about seeing him on the

one hand, dreading it on the other. We go round to his local pub. All his mates are there and he tells me to put my hands over my ears, which I do. Then he tells his mates about the girls he 'met' on holiday. I feel stupid sat like that so I pretend I can't hear and look away when he puts both hands out in front of him, meaning 'big knockers.' Or did she have arthritis? Nope – it's the tits thing. It's OK though, because no one notices me anyway. Maybe a couple of his mates do but they look away, awkward. Specially the one who told me before, on our own, that he thinks I've got 'class.' The main thing is my beloved doesn't want to finish it. Relief.

Five months and three days after we first met we're at a pub with a load of my friends. My beloved takes me outside and draws me to him.

"There's something I want to tell you and I'm never gonna say it again after tonight." Oh, no. Could be *anything*. When we first met he told me he was a test-tube baby and carried the 'joke' for a couple of weeks before he let on it was bollocks. Funny one. Or will he have a go at me for being stupid? He does that sometimes, doesn't like it when I get loud with my mates. Says I'm like a giggly little schoolgirl and should be quieter. People he knows are so suave, grown up, cool and mature. So what can it be? Please don't let him chuck me– anything but that! No, no, no, no, no, please no…

"What?" I put my hand around his crotch and squeeze but he grabs my hand, forces it still.

"I love you but I'm never gonna say it again… and… I want us to get engaged."

Fuck me! If he never says it again I won't mind. Once is definitely enough. I have never been so happy in my entire life. The whole sixteen years. Life can only get better from now on. I tell my mates but they're not allowed to say anything to him. Though I'm chuffed I also feel bad, ashamed, like I've done something wrong.

I don't think it's made Dorothy's day but she could at least act as if it has. She doesn't speak to me for a whole month. She doesn't say a lot to her son either, makes him *really* suffer. When she takes him his usual breakfast in bed, she just leaves the tray without saying anything.

I guess she doesn't like it that he's growing up. She misses his boyhood, misses him being hyperactive, never sleeping. Misses him being the school bully, which, he told me, he packed in after another boy beat him up.

The ring, *ooooohhhhhhh eeeeeeeee yipeeeeeeeeeee* is ordered from a catalogue – £26.00 paid by instalments. It was number 13 on the page. An omen? Nah, be alright.

The day the ring comes we go out with Dorothy and Will to the social club at the firm where my beloved now works. It's a proper do with a band so we get dressed up. Just before we leave the house me and Will are in the hallway. He holds out my coat like a real gentleman. And I feel so… looked after. A really nice feeling washes over me, something like soft white feathers in an eiderdown and the crisp, cold cotton of a plumped-up pillow at a guesthouse. "I wasn't going to say anything but I will," he begins.

"Oh." Oh, indeed. What's coming next?

"Didn't like you at first." Here we go. "I thought you were trouble. But now I do and I think you're good for him." As I put my other arm into the coat-sleeve, like a joint of beef into a mincer I can't believe I'm hearing this. Something bad will surely happen next. Really it's a nightmare and I'll end up in a burger. But it's not a nightmare or even a daydream. Simply a lovely thing to hear.

Dorothy enters the hall, pulling her polyester scarf carefully over her newly blue-rinsed hair, then buttons up the bottle-green coat she got from her husband for Christmas. Cat's bum. A twinge of guilt then shame creeps up my spine as I realise that really I'm no good for her son. She knows it. I know it.

When me and my beloved give her the heated food tray she wanted for Christmas she's not pleased either.

"Poke it!" She leaves the room. Five quid from the market and she's turning her nose up! Still not forgiven then. I've heard people, usually older people say that time's a great healer. Is it though?

Trevor, my beloved's brother, said that when he was twenty he came into the kitchen and his mum was at the table, crying.

"I'm having a baby," she stummered.

Now she seems more concerned about *keeping* the baby whose life surprised her. I don't think she can handle him growing up, leaving.

A few years back she'd got used to having her grandchildren, Trevor and Delia's kids, Nigel and Cindy during the holidays. It's what Trevor reckons, anyway. There's a little surprise for Will one day when he gets back from work. My beloved's out and Will guesses Dorothy must be in the front room. But there's a pram in the hall which is a bit odd as all their friends' children have grown up now too. When Will goes into the front room Dorothy is bouncing a baby on her knee.

She turns her head when she hears the gentle summons of the squeaky door.

"I couldn't help it… " Dorothy, tears streaming down her face, eyes wild as redcurrants, looks like she's away with the fairies. Which she is.

It turns out she was round the shops and saw this pram. And in the pram was this baby. Did she hear voices? Fair enough if she did – then anyone might be tempted...

'Please take me home with you. She's no good for me – she's not even watching over me. Look at her, with her short skirt – what's she need me for? She won't care, nice lady. I just need to be loved. Can you? Will you? Yours are growing up and don't care about you but I do. I need you and I need you now! Please. She won't miss me and I'll be better off at yours.'

They kept it all quiet and in the smoothest operation since D-Day, Will went round to the shops where it didn't take too much detective work to discover where the child lived and where the frantic parents waited. So he gave the baby back, the couple grateful for the chance to be better parents and Dorothy and Will carried on much as before. Why wouldn't they?

Once Dorothy has forgiven the engagement and gets back to normal she talks to me about putting things away for our bottom drawer. So I do. The first thing I buy is this shopping list thing. It's a notepad glued to a small turquoise plastic-covered board for the wall. We keep it in the bottom of my beloved's wardrobe. He's got more space than me so he keeps all the things I buy.

Thing is, I really like his parents – love them, truth be told. They're so *normal*. And I want me and him to be exactly like them as we grow old together. Together forever.

On the other hand my beloved is used to a very quiet life and thinks my house is exciting, Mum and Dad shouting and swearing at each other, often having a ruck. Mum likes him a lot, specially when he does her favours like brings her fags over. And once he's driving, goes and gets milk blah blah. She doesn't know he slags her off behind her back.

"He's alright – not so bad, well dusted. *And* the poor bloke has to put up with *her.*" Mum says, lighting up. *But I don't inhale like your father!*

"What d'you think of him, Dad?" He rubs his cheeks back and forward like he's Sherlock Holmes, confounded that there's a dead body in the library but the candle-stick's nowhere to be seen.

"Hmm. I'll reserve my judgement." And he will never give me an update on this.

One day, though, my man is helping Dad dig the garden. My darling boy-man – he's not on the same buzz as Dad so Dad says he's thick. His timing's not great, that's all. They say that timing is everything. Anyway, my beloved and my twenty-three-stone dad are digging in the back garden. It's a hot one and the sweat's pouring off Dad, trickling down his cotton vest, baggy grey trousers.

"Martin."

"What?"

"What would you do if I got Mandy pregnant?" My beloved keeps digging.

Dad slowly, slowly straightens up his achy, achy back.

"You see this shovel?"

"Yeah."

"I'd wrap it **RIGHT ROUND YOUR FUCKING NECK**."

Chapter 6: Four Funerals and a Wedding

The church is booked for next year. That's it. We've been five years together now and we're going for it. When we tell friends about the wedding my fiancé moans accusingly about little things like the hall, church, my mother, flowers, food, and my family – specially my mother – and the amount of money it'll cost. And my mother.

It's impossible at times to hide the heat of my reddening face, like nappy rash with no relieving Sudocrem. The shame. I laugh, quickly tell them it'll be really good being married, and hope they don't notice what a bad person I *really* am.

"Guess who I saw?" my beloved says one day in August. It's those little surprises that keep love strong.

"The Queen?" I say.

"Sally!" He tuts. "Don't be stupid. Remember... the party where we met!"

"She alright?" Should she get an invite to the wedding? That's what's going through my head.

"Asked me who I'm with. Told her that, believe it or not... *you*!" The echo of a smile curls its way to his lips, "*and* we're getting married!"

"How is she?" I don't notice, never do, the way something slides its way inside my gut, like a fish blind to the hook. Instead I feel guilty again, ashamed, and that lumps itself onto the darkness that is already there. The darkness that knows I'm wrong and he's right. The darkness confirms just how wrong I am, how bad I am, but it's really deep down, way, way down, quietly simmering. Mostly I don't notice it's there. It's covered me like an ill-fitting cloak for so long that it's part of the world. My world. Me. Life rolls on and I try still harder to make my fiancé happy.

It doesn't roll on for all of us, though. Later that week we're watching telly when a man's voice announces he is "INTERRUPTING THE PROGRAMME" with "IMPORTANT NEWS."

Elvis Presley is dead. The King is dead! The funny thing about death is that you expect people to go on forever – not only famous folk like Elvis, who's old but not *that* old, but people you know too. Oh no look at that! It's only the dead body of Elvis, in a very grand white open coffin, fronting all the newspapers next morning! Argh!

What, no halo? Have you noticed how dead people turn into saints no matter what their worldly selves were like? Not only that, but those they leave behind become saints too, rather than simply grieving (or not) families who are essentially the same people, good and bad and somewhere in between. The world is rocked by Elvis's death. But never mind us – how is his family coping? I bet they're all shook up.

Elvis's death makes me even more grateful to be this happy now. To be marrying the nicest man in the whole world. I know my man; he's kind, sensitive, generous and funny. He's good with my friends too, plays with their kids. Rough-and-tumbles on the carpet. I'm so proud of him. While he kneels on the carpet he sneaks a sideways look at my friend until he knows he's being watched, then, reassured with an audience he carries on playing the game.

So happy, we're so happy that I feel sorry for others who cannot possibly know this heightened happiness. Poor other people, I say! I wish everyone could have this.

Friends may cringe when my fiancé slags off the wedding but when we're on our own he tells me he loves me so much, wants to get inside my head, cries, tells me if only I'd change we wouldn't argue. So I try harder to make him happy. It's just that I get insecure and jealous. I don't know why.

One day we're driving along and as we pass this gorgeous woman he swivels his head like he's an understudy for The Exorcist.

"Look at the tits on that!" He laughs, says he forgot it was me sat there, thought it was one of his mates. I laugh along with him. He's such a joker. Ha.

But he's right – we *do* argue. We're living together now, got a mortgage on our flat when I was eighteen. There are holes punched in most of the doors from his fists where we've argued.

I blame the doctor. My fiancé went to see him. He said he was worried he wants to hit me when we argue, so the doctor says hit the wall instead. He tries but hitting a brick wall hurts so after that the doors get it. It's all very well showing off our National Health Service to the rest of the world – free hospitals, free care and all that – and we're lucky, I admit, but if you want answers look at the details. Replacement hips? It's fucking doors they want to start giving out.

Patrick gives me 'brotherly' advice.

"Don't argue back, Mand!"

"What? Stand there and take it?"

"He's bigger than you... keep your mouth shut."

Adrian doesn't know about it and Tony laughs when I mention it.

Dinner on the wall. How common is it, I wonder? How many times in all the houses in all the roads last year did someone throw their dinner at the wall? Maybe Esther Rantzen should do a survey for her telly show That's Life. Does it run in families? Is it genetic?

I think my beloved gets bored with smashing his fist into the doors. There's nothing wrong with wanting variety – a sign of intelligence, I reckon. So one evening he throws his dinner at the wall –burgers, baked beans, bread and butter. I clear it up quick before someone sees it, sees the evidence of my badness.

When Trevor and Delia got married they lived in a caravan while they built their house. Sometimes in his job as ceiling fixer Trevor works with itchy fibreglass which worms its way into his clothes, irritating his skin until he gets home to wash it away. Perhaps this day was a fibreglass day, eh?

"This pie's not cooked right," he says, when Delia puts the plate on his lap.

"Should be alright!" What can go wrong with a meat pie?

"'You can't go wrong with a meat pie," the woman at the Co-op had said.

But clearly Delia had. Though normally a good cook, she'd clearly gone very wrong with the pie.

"It's NOT COOKED RIGHT."

WHAM – Boeing 747 pie flies through the air and makes an emergency landing on the wall.

"I'll see what else there is." A puzzled Delia, cloth in hand, quickly and quietly mops up. Trevor needs refuelling so she cooks again.

Delia and her three brothers did time in a children's home but she won't talk about it. Funnily, she doesn't say much to anyone about anything. Small children, she speaks to small children.

It's Trevor who's the centre of things. You can have a laugh with him. He makes sure of it. Whereas it's Delia who's moody and has suffered from bad headaches for years though the doctors never find out why. They wouldn't, would they?

When the dinner-on-the-wall story comes out twenty years later Trevor's still adamant Delia should have cooked it properly.

Then there's Dad. One Saturday before I left home, it's pissing it down with rain. The doors are wide open and Dad's working on his car again. It won't start. Again. Spark plugs, thick with oil, are laid out on the foot-stall in front of him. Next to these is a grimy wire brush, the golden wires curled up, delicate, like an old man's pubes that've seen a lot of action but not for years.

"Be nice if you washed your fucking hands for once," says Mum, bringing in his dinner.

"'Ere we fucking go. Yip, yip, yip. Be nice if you kept your fucking trap shut for once," Dad responds. It looks like a discussion is about to get under way.

"Don't even wash 'em when you've had a shit. Don't even pull the chain properly!"

"Shut your fucking rabbit."

"Fucking animal!"

Woosh. Yup! Dinner on the wall. Dinner, dinner, on the wall, who's the fairest of them all? This time, it's beef casserole with mash, so... lots of gravy.

When people come round they clock the patch on

the wall but say nothing. Sometimes Mum explains. Sometimes she doesn't. The wall is covered with thickly varnished planks of tongue and groove. The dinner stays there for a year, at least the mash and gravy do though the meat never stuck. The pieces fell to the floor where they were instantly cleared by the dogs who licked their lips and were back fast asleep on their settee before you could say... well, anything really.

"I'm not clearing it off – I didn't fucking *do* it." And she's right. This time she's right. After said year he gets a cloth and scouring pad and cleans it off the wall.

Dinners on the wall. Three. They say things come in threes, don't they? Usually?

The day my beloved agreed to live with me last summer I was so chuffed. He'd come to pick me up in his Austin Cambridge (and Bessie was her name). I worked in the West End, a postal clerk at a Canadian airline. He was pleased with me when I got the job in London. I'd been invited to leave college for non-attendance and the man at the careers place had arranged the job interview.

"You won't go dressed like that, will you?" Cheeky fucker, I *love* this T-shirt! Four weeks after leaving college I start the job, dressed smartly.

"Well done," my fiancé said proudly. "I didn't think you'd ever get a job but you have." I glowed then, rewarded.

It was 1976 and the hottest, hottest of summers. There was a drought too. Mum and Dad, like many others, had to queue to get water from a standpipe in the street. The newspapers were full of the heat-wave. At Lords cricket ground, play was stopped for an hour due to a bit of rain. Everyone applauded, grateful at this offering from heaven. The heat was almost unbearable.

When we got back, me and my beloved lay down on the cool, cool, lino of his mum's kitchen floor, at opposite sides of the room. The temperature was way up in the 90's – unheard of.

First though, we were at Green Park, near my work, being kissed occasionally by a virgin breeze. There was an ice-lolly van but we'd no money for extras. My beloved got a football from his car and we kicked it around, played catch for a bit.

I've never told anyone this before. For the briefest of moments as he stood there on the few tufts of green velvet, in the blazing London summer, surrounded by crowds of different, possibly interesting people, i.e., alternatives, just for the tiniest flash of flashes I felt repulsed when I looked at my fiancé. Repulsion and a sinking feeling that there could be something more 'out there'. For moments in that still, still heat I was overwhelmed by a truth that he was not enough. Quickly I buried the thought and feeling, making sure I patted down the sand on top as we headed home.

Our savings were growing. I'd opened a building society account, worked it all out, what, how, when and where, and we flippin' did it. We actually saved up for a holiday on the Norfolk Broads then carried on with this delicious new saving habit. I liked the way it made me feel. Grown up. Though my beloved got annoyed, said we were saving too much. On the drive back from Green Park we talked about getting a flat, living together. In the end, my fiancé agreed to give it a go, try it for six months.

"Alright," hesitant, "I'll give it a go, try it for six months." Am I the luckiest girl in the whole beautiful, pink, rosy world or what?

My beloved became a roadie for Keith. Keith's the singer in a band and Den, our best man-to-be is the drummer. Keith, who's a bit *Look Back in Anger* is too cool to pack his own stuff away so my man does it for a while. He's paid a fiver, which mostly gets spent in the Chinese after the gig. Spare ribs. Mmm.

"You know, Mand, me and you could make sweet music together," Keith says once when my beloved's not looking. I grin, embarrassed and tingly but *nothing* would take me away from my man.

It's New Year's Eve and we're at this gig in a hall. One of the band members, John, has brought his girlfriend. She, whose name escapes me – let's for argument's sake call her Slut – has had her eye on my man all evening. She's much older than her boyfriend – forty if she's a day when he's late twenties. I discover later that, on the quiet, she's kept asking my beloved to dance all evening.

Me and Amy, Den's wife, are in the Ladies, impatient to get back because I know it's nearly midnight but there's a queue and I'm in danger of missing seeing in the New Year with my beloved. Fuck it! I'm right across the other side of the room when the band starts up with 'Auld Lang Syne.' Are you thinking what I'm thinking? There they are – my fiancé and Slut – in a slow-dance clutch *and* they're kissing. It takes me ages to get through the crowds, hack through the thicket of 'happy people out celebrating' to the other side of the room where he and Slut are still lip-locked. When I reach them I dig my nails into her arm but *still* they carry on kissing. Fucking; eyes closed, tongues, round and round, sounds from a blue film my dad might watch in his bedroom. Looks like they're determined to slurp off any loose bits from each other's face, inside and out.

NO! I go mad then, revving up a big scream but it hardly lifts off instead falling to the floor unnoticed as I watch them continue like I didn't exist. I shout at her about how we're meant to be getting married, how she's ruined everything, the slag, slapper, whore. Slowly they come up for air.

"Don't be silly," says Slut, nonplussed, pleasantly tanked up with booze. "It's *you* he loves."

She's not too fussed either when her boyfriend gives her the elbow.

"It's happened before. I've had enough." He packs his stuff away, resigned, drives off alone.

Although my fiancé sleeps solo in his car and Slut cabs it home alone, tonight they've been together in the driving seat. I go home with Den and Amy. The pain of what's happened is physical. The adrenalin won't let me sleep or eat or think of anything else. My betrothed. He means everything to me. More than land and sea. He's the flesh and blood of my world. How could he let this woman do this to us eight months before the wedding? Perhaps we should cancel it? No – hang on, maybe that's a bit rash!

"I couldn't help it," he says when he turns up at Amy and Den's the next day.

"Why didn't you say no to her?"

"Didn't want to offend her." He hangs his head, eyes flick up at me, then down again, a smile hinting. I feel a bit sorry for him. That bloody woman!

We patch it up enough to go shopping with Mum and Dad for our belated Christmas present. A new carpet for the flat. Chocolate brown. Sixty pounds at Allied Carpets and by a stroke of luck they've got a sale on!

"Leave him alone," says Mum. "Let him have his bit of fun. At least he's working."

"I think you're overreacting," says my American friend, Grace, at work. I've known her since I started here at 16yrs, she a wise, grown-up twenty-one. Kris Kristofferson is her hero. She likes men with beards, she says, not long after my beloved grows one. Or was it comment first, beard second?

"This woman obviously had her eye on him all night. What's the poor guy to do?"

It's good she's so wise. Calms me down a bit when I realise he couldn't help it. She's right, Grace and I'm wrong. With a woman like Slut what chance did he stand, eh? I'm glad we've got Grace in our lives rooting for us like that.

She's been through it herself. Got sent away to 'boarding school', she says, as a teenager in Nevada. But before that, she says, she, her mum and brother had to escape one night through a window to get away from her dad. He was violent to her mum and brother but never to her, she says. And she wishes they'd stayed or at least that she'd lived with him instead of her mum. At Court, a Judge asked her to choose when she was four, and she chose her mum, she says, because she knew that was what was expected of her. But always, *always*, Grace regrets not choosing her dad.

The first time we ever got invited to dinner or a 'dinner-party' was to Grace's. I felt so grown up, not sixteen at all. This one time we were all at Julia's, another friend from work. Julia had these inflatable boxing gloves and kept play-fighting with my beloved. She gets on well with him anyway but they *kept* on, getting real close, grabbing each other in a tight grip, faces almost touching. Then she'd straddle him. Over and over. It was OK but I was getting asthma from the cat and as no one really noticed I went to bed and left them to it until about three in the morning, they said. It's good my beloved gets on with people.

During Christmas and New Year my father-in-law-to-be is still not well. Will has been unwell for months but he's getting worse. The doctors reckon it's indigestion. After tests they tell him it's a hiatus hernia. It's real bad so they book him in for an op. Meanwhile they give him medicine, giant indigestion pills as big as sherbert flying-saucers but they don't help. We'll all be glad for him once the operation is over, flippin' dragging on. The rest of the family comes visit the house more than usual.

Even brother Wayne who's ten years older than my beloved. He's a TV cameraman. How exciting is that? Went out with one of the Top of the Pops dancers, Pan's People and the singer Lindsey de Paul, he says. Likes a drink. His wife Stephanie isn't about much. The beautiful ex-model doesn't show her face since they had a bit of a row and, Wayne said, he'd broken a bottle over her head.

Trevor went over after they'd rowed. It's so funny, he says, where Wayne's smashed up the telly and thrown it in the aquarium. The elegant tropical fish have to do a channel swim to avoid the soggy, wiry guts of this encroaching monster. We hardly ever see Wayne. He flits, disappears, says things that don't always make sense – all a bit inside out and upside down. Promises we'll get together, says he'll ring. Yeah, yeah. The family say "That's just Wayne." No one says Wayne tells lies. Certainly not *to* him.

Life's become full on over this hernia thing. When Will and Dorothy go to the doctor's he asks to see

Dorothy on her own. Such a fuss! Is there a new NHS drive on hernia patients?

It's February. My beloved's twenty-first birthday is in April. He's wanted a Black & Decker Workmate for ages but they're over twenty quid. For some reason, like an early spring clean, Will makes sure all his paperwork is in order. He even writes a will and gets me to witness it though he folds it over so I can't see the goodies inside. It's a bit like that game. 'He Says, She Says' where you write what 'He says' on the sheet of paper, fold it, then pass it to the next person to write what 'She says'. At the end it's read out and everyone laughs once all the words and their meaning are revealed. I wonder, will the will that Will wrote get laughs?

After Sunday dinner me and my fiancé finish the washing-up then Will takes him into the dining room, fiddles about with something against the back wall that's been covered in a blanket. As soon as he enters the room the light of my life bursts out crying. He and his dad hug. Will cries too. Stood there, proud as punch, is a Black & Decker Workmate.

"For your twenty-first. I know it's not yet." Hands something over. "Receipt and Guarantee."

"Thanks Dad."

"In case you need to change it." Sensible now, both stood straight. Men of honour.

Will and his son come back to the front room as I notice Dorothy, drinking her tea, wipes a tissue across her eyes.

The next day Will goes into hospital for his op. The trouble is he doesn't wake up after the procedure – not properly. Dorothy says he came round, said he loves her.

"I love you." Just like that, whispered. Trevor and

Wayne say afterwards he never said it. Well, Dorothy says he did.

Me and my fiancé gave up smoking six months before this. But now we're back on it, of course. First thing we did when they said there were complications was shoot up to the hospital in a cab, fags on the go.

Will's lying there, bare-chested, a line of wrinkles separating his chest from his stomach, like a misplaced half-way line at a football match. He's covered in tubes, fresh clean sheets and hospital blankets, the soft waffle-cotton type that make you wish you were a baby again.

No sign of any babies though, or any new life to celebrate. The smell of death mixes with disinfectant. My senses go awry. I can't see anything properly, don't know what to do, say, touch, where to look. My hands are in my pockets, sweating but cold. My beloved's right close to the bed.

Everything's gone white. It seems we've all been transported into the middle of a cloud, soft, gentle, but firm enough to hold us all. This is serious shit.

"Hernia, Mum?" None of this makes sense to my man.

"Cancer," Trevor whispers for Dorothy.

Will lays there on display, forgiven, his depression cleaned out by the machine that parents him like he's a premature newborn. Dorothy, Trevor, Wayne, my fiancé and me fan out like lily petals, powerless to help their centre. The family has always rotated round him. What happens when you don't have a nucleus? Delia's outside with the children, Nigel and Cindy.

As I keep looking, the others disappear. White blankets everything. The walls, the floor – all are simply white and light, the strong Intensive Care strip-lights above Will's bed try to shine strength into him. But fail.

Even the sun's gone in and it was gorgeous out there earlier. The hospital mask Will wears moves gently as the machine helps him breathe. My eyes refocus on my man. His head moves side to side as if that will cancel out the truth, his cheeks now a slalom course for his tears, eyes and nose red. How must this feel for him? I can never know.

They all knew about the cancer. We find out over coffee in the canteen, we consume loads over the next few days. Coffee, fags, regrets.

"Why didn't you say earlier?" My beloved cannot believe his mum never said.

"Didn't want to ruin your Christmas."

My beloved's not happy. He hates being treated like the baby brother. Twenty years he's been around, not twenty months! After a few days of hospital visits a roster is agreed so we go home. It's not our turn, we'll come back later. There is no later. Will dies that night.

You ever seen a dead body? I haven't. They have all this make-up put on Will. That's what they do, says Trevor, so the dead person looks alive. Then they charge you (or Dorothy) thirty quid for the make-up so you can go and look at him. He's in a room at the funeral parlour.

Dorothy, Trevor, me and my fiancé all go together. The others walk straight over to Will, husband and father, whisper a last message. For the first time in Will's life he doesn't say any of the usual Will things; "Did you turn off the gas?" . . . "The lights?"... "The car needs petrol"... "There's no overtime this week"... "I told you not to say that" or "Tomorrow I'll do a bonfire." Dorothy might ask for her rights, finally, now that he can't say no. I look away from the body, stationary on my spot just inside the door. No more time for Will. Emptiness. Nothing. I liked Will. He was nice to me. He had a comfortable way of doing nothing much. After the funeral, my first, I thank God not everything comes in threes.

In April I organise a surprise birthday party for my beloved at the flat. Lots of organising but it seems to work, though I'm so nervous that once the champagne's open I announce I want to 'protose a post'. He misses his dad. A lot.

There's a new estate they're building near Dorothy so we decide to buy a three bedroom house. We sell the flat and move in with Dorothy till the new house is ready.

The wedding's in six months. My beloved wonders if we should delay it. I think not. Everyone says it's what Will would have wanted. So, on we go.

The night before the wedding I stay at Mum and Dad's. Dad wakes me up early.

"Wake up. It's pissing with rain," he laughs as he brings me a coffee.

He's right. It's flippin' pouring down. When my fiancé phones I ask Mum to say I love him and he says it back. I'm sort of in a daze. Can this be happening? At last. Security. Someone to wake up next to every day for the rest of my life. Someone who really loves me and won't ever leave me. Trouble is I've been concentrating on the sunshine, ignoring the clouds and you can never guarantee how it will turn out, can you? Just look at that sky!

When I return from the hairdresser's I put on the dress Aunty Celia, dad's sister, made for me. In the shop I fell in love immediately with this beautiful dress, with a sort of ultra-fine, floaty coat over the top of it. I suppose it's a bit nighty-plus-negligé or plain angel-like. It's white and it's gorgeous – quite magical. But it's not the dress I'm getting married in. I bought the pattern but when I showed Aunty Celia she said it wouldn't suit me – it's meant for tall people and I should choose something else.

I wanted white but Mum said I should have ivory and she gave me lots of reasons why. And she likes a square neck. I suppose it looks alright with a square neck, my wedding dress, but do you want to know a secret? I don't like it. Think I look shit in it. It's kind of Aunty Celia especially with her arthritic fingers which means she sews less and less these days. But it's made of some funny material which feels like a parachute. Am I meant to bail out? Nah – can't wait to be married to my beloved.

Nice, isn't it, the bubbly fluff of a wedding? The trouble is, by the time we leave the church we're not speaking, me and my *new husband*. We've had a falling-out. I dunno... I love him so much but he seems to notice others more than he notices me. I know I'm not that interesting and, don't get me wrong, I'm proud that he gets on with people, and I know everyone likes him and hates me. It's not that at all. But when we're out he stares past me like I'm not there – at home too. It's just he mostly talks *only* to others. Even at our wedding he acts like he's doing it alone, like it's his birthday or something.

I know he doesn't mean it – why would he? He tells me he loves me and sometimes, after an argument, after he says it's over, we're finished and I say sorry again, we then talk for yonks. About how I'll be different, be better next time (at whatever it is), will try harder to make him happy, do whatever he says he wants. I don't mind the effort – you expect to work at a relationship. Let's just stay together, that's all I want. And eventually when he's ready we make up and have sex and it's alright again.

Sometimes he's at the end of his tether with me. He loves me so much, to bits, he says and if only I'd change then life would run smoother. I wouldn't want to live if we weren't together.

At the wedding reception my new brother-in-law Wayne asks the photographer to take pictures of their family and it happens. I'd like one of my family but it doesn't happen. My husband says I'm too sensitive, when I mention it. Although we're not talking we carry on business as usual and don't let it spoil our special day. Everyone has tiffs, I know that. People tell you that all the time – ups and downs.

We're talking by the evening, at the do at his works social club. We're given money so can now afford a night at a hotel. By the time we get there we're probably tired, probably why we don't say a lot, probably the reason we go straight to bed. We get into this huge bed, a quick peck on the lips then my new husband turns over and we sleep away our wedding night.

In the morning, having only the clothes we arrived in we go to breakfast in our wedding attire; my husband in his off-white suit, me in my (polyester parachute) ivory dress with the square neck. The breakfast is included. Have what you want, juice, coffee, fry-up – anything. So I have kippers. A few people look over at us. Nosy fuckers – what's up with you? Never seen anyone eat kippers before?

As soon as we move into the new house our fortunes

change. Without doing anything different we seem better off. Brand-new house and brand-new everything in it – mostly wedding presents.

Dorothy is still upset about Will. It's six months since his death – get a grip woman! All she wants is her son over there all the time. We keep going over for dinner blah blah – it's a right pain in the arse.

I talk about it with a woman from work. Karen lost movement in one of her hands when she tried to slit her wrist when she discovered her husband was dying. She thought she couldn't live without him. Imagine life being that bad you want to kill yourself! He was furious with her and though he died, she lived.

"Six months is nothing. Stop being so selfish!" Blimey, you expect a bit of sympathy from your workmates, don't you?

But… now something niggles. When I see Dorothy I wonder how she survives without her man. I know I couldn't. We visit a bit more too. I watch her, notice how grey she's gone – her skin, and her eyes, always dull, are now watered-down versions of themselves. It's like they're not in the same room – not with her, not seeing for her. How would it be, this death, loss thing? To lose someone you're that close to? I can't stand it if my beloved spends too long on his guitar!

It's Christmas and we're in the new house. Been here ten days! I want us to spend some of the day on our own. My husband doesn't want that so we share ourselves amongst both families. It's the first Christmas without Will for Dorothy, for everyone though it's she who feels it most. Dorothy hasn't become her own person. She's not half of a whole, much less than that. I've got us a free trip to Seattle from work but delay it till New Year to help Dorothy over this year's cruel

Yule.

"You kids are my life," she says and it's not even a guilt thing, simply the truth. Imagine that – the man in your life gone and your kids are your whole world! What sort of world would that be?

As the year dies out and births a new one, Dorothy becomes ill. I *knew* she should have drunk that Guinness. After a spell in hospital she stays with Trevor and Delia because Delia doesn't work and can do the looking-after. Dorothy is laid up in bed. She's got thrombosis and she's to take a bunch of pills. She has these 'turns'.

"I felt as if the life was draining out of me," she says after one had hit. So dramatic. Talk about exaggerating!

Trevor calls and by the time my husband arrives they're taking her out in a body bag. So, not exaggerating, then. After a year-long attempt to call her own shots the life does indeed drain out of Dorothy.

This time I give the body-viewing a miss. So does my husband.

My brother Tony and his wife Hazel have been married a year. Patrick and Ruth have been married two years. He likes a drink. Patrick and Tony sometimes drink at the same pubs but Patrick drinks more.

"I drink because I'm thirsty," says Patrick.

"Why beer, though?" says, well, everybody.

"I could drink water. But I like beer."

If we see them it's in the pub. Pick-a-pub, pick-a-pub – any-pub, any-pub.

"I give it five years." Dad's got relationship counselling skills ahead of his time.

Though Ruth's own dad's a violent drunk and wasn't invited to their wedding, she still can't handle the shouting and swearing in our house. Her upbringing is Catholicism but it's a language she hates. Me too, since I found out my birth mother speaks it fluently and the adoption agency refused to handle the adoption once they knew my birth father was Jewish. Another language I hate. Anyway, as Mum's always told me, being adopted makes no difference to me so there's no point tracing my mother.

Tony and Hazel, Patrick and Ruth are round for coffee when the phone rings. I've taken to not answering it lately because it seems every time I do, someone's died. Mind, its three months now since Dorothy left us.

"Ruth, can you get it? Every time I answer it, someone's just died." They all laugh. I know, it's stupid of me.

"I've told you a thousand million times not to exaggerate!" My husband leads us in another laugh.

Under the laughter I hear Ruth's silence. She sits on the stairs, says the odd word into the phone. Mostly she listens.

"Mandy – it's your dad." She's so serious sometimes, Ruth. No. Something's wrong. With hot-cold hands I take the phone. I can hear dad crying. You're joking, my dad crying? No, fuck off!

"Mand... Adrian's dead."

My nice brother. Aijee who protects me from Tony and Patrick. Heart attack. He's the only one in the family who isn't a fat bastard. Never smoked, tee-total, goes to the gym, wins trophies at table tennis. And two weeks away from the decree absolute for his divorce. Twenty-nine years old.

Ouch. Ouch. **Ouch. Ouch. Ouch**.

Funny, he's so funny. Dry humour. When he started

the divorce they hadn't spoken for a trillion years. So after he gets his solicitor to send his wife of nearly ten years a letter telling her she's being divorced it gets awkward.

They're still living in the same house when things start to disappear. Little things; his favourite LPs (the Carpenters, Glenn Campbell, the Honeycombs), ornaments, kitchenware and money from the joint bank account.

He thinks it strange but it doesn't kill him. Yet when his giant Swiss cheese plant disappears from the corner of the front room Adrian takes action. He goes to the police station.

"I want to report a theft."

"Where from?"

"My house. Front room."

"Right. What's been taken?"

"My Swiss cheese plant."

"Oh deary, deary."

"Yes, it's terrible."

"Do you have any ideas who might have done it Mr Trent?"

"Yes." Looks at expectant policeman. "My wife."

Twenty-nine. How fair is that? And the nicest one in the family. My second time at seeing a dead body. His wife says if we want to view the body we have to pay for the make-up – so we do. She never wants to see him again, with or without make-up. Me and Brenda go to see him together. Brenda's his new girlfriend. Mum likes her – she's plain and overweight.

Brenda glides to my brother and kisses his forehead like she's starring in Sleeping Beauty on Ice. I can't do that, I'm too scared. I love him and from my spot just inside the door I call out to him, "I love you Aijee." But

I can't kiss him. Not here, not now, not like this. He's too full of life to be here like this.

He doesn't respond. Just lies there as if I haven't said anything, as if he doesn't care that he's dead and I can't bear it. My brother – protector from my brother and Patrick. He was the only one who encouraged us when we were buying the flat.

"*Yes, do it. Even better, buy a house!*" All so exciting, starting this new life.

"No, don't buy it. Put your name on the council waiting list," says Trevor, Russian doll-like from within his golden Draylon armchair, in his open-plan lounge with a real log fire, in his four-bedroom detached house. "I was a *lot* older than you – wait till you can afford it."

"Yes, do it," said Adrian, my brother. My brother whose new life after the divorce won't now come to fruition. My funny brother with the 'Afro' perm. My brother who was a mod with a scooter then a skin-head with a gorgeous brown sheepskin. My brother the Spurs supporter, with a wife who's a Chelsea supporter who stood at opposite ends of the football ground when the teams played each other. My brother who's himself at the opposite end of the ground to me. The underneath end. My brother. My dead, dead brother.

At the funeral when I hold Mum's hand she shakes it off. Later I tell her I wish it could have been me instead of Aijee because I've already found the happiness I want and he hasn't. Didn't. She says nothing. I guess she agrees with me.

Next month it's my twenty-first. My beloved's arranged a surprise party. We drive round to different friends but they're all out. When we go home I recognise all the friends cars parked outside, open the door and I see and smell fag smoke. Surprise!

Adrian's girlfriend gives me a slim, gold 'identity' bracelet. On the back, engraved before he died, "All our love, Adrian and Brenda 2.8.79." A few weeks later, we're on holiday in Devon. I lose the bracelet. I can't possibly admit how much it hurts. It is far, far too big for that.

PART 2 - THE END

Chapter 7: Lost in Translation

I'm pregnant with my FOURTH child. The darkness is debilitating. When my husband enters the room I stop speaking.

In company it's all a right laugh. We even have this split-second banter in true stand-up style. And friends laugh along with us. The wine flows and I'm grateful. When the friends leave, the silence sneaks back in under the tightly shut doors. Always silence. Except for the screaming and laughing and bouncing of our surface-happy chaotic kids.

Probably stupid of me but we have friends round and I give my husband a Father's Day card with a crap made-up poem about becoming a dad again. I think it's romantic. He's furious. So unfortunately he has a go at me in front of everyone.

"What d'you mean? What's going on? Telling me like *this*!"

I feel it again. The guilt. The shame. The humiliation.

Trying to fix our marriage is like pinging an elastic band and expecting it not to return to its original shape. But it always does. Strange I don't see the insanity of keeping on trying.

This man is everything to me. He flows through my veins like I'm still fifteen, only now I'm reshaped by his patterns.

I try talking to my friend Theresa.

"How do you know if you're depressed?"

I ask her because I know she's had this type of 'problem'. When she backed out of her marriage two days before her (first) wedding her parents went mad (ha) and got her put into a psychiatric unit. Fuck! Imagine!

"Why – do you think you are then?"

"Dunno. Don't know what it's like."

"You just *know*."

I like being friends with Theresa. She went to school with my husband so I get to talk about him. A lot. Her garden backed onto his garden. (Eventual) husband did a runner and now she lives with her son, Robin. She swears at him a lot, threatens to send him to a children's home a LOT. Robin is a quiet boy and I don't like it when she does that. But her house is beautiful, immaculate. It's a brand-new council house with a downstairs toilet and a garage.

She makes all her own curtains and cushion covers, sews for others too, bumping up her social money. My husband tells me he likes her all the more for backing out of that first wedding.

I try talking to Mum.

"What've *you* got to be depressed about?" Whoosh – the guilt is back. Its heat fills my cheeks. Then it slices into my stomach.

Is she right? It's true we've got boxes full of happy, smiley photos.

"You should put salt in while the vegetables are cooking, Mand," she goes on. "That's why your cooking's got no flavour."

Maybe she seriously is right. So many people don't

have all this. The house is nice. Big, anyway.

I'd always wanted a big family, at least four, since James got away. My husband wanted just two, he says after we've got four – another unpreventable, unfixable trap he places me in, another way it's all my fault. We don't use contraception. Well, the Catholic kind. So changing from 'don't want to get pregnant' to 'do want to get pregnant' is quite simple. And two-way.

But I did pine, cajole and beg him for the others. Actually I pined, cajoled and begged for all four. We put loads of money away and move upwards, as they say.

These houses have four big bedrooms, hundred-foot back garden, eighty foot drives. They were called the 'higher income' council houses when they were built back in 1957, with ugly brown brick and horrid metal window frames. But good to know we're in a house built for Mr and Mrs Doctor and Mr and Mrs Teacher – provided they'd shown proof of income.

I'm twenty-five when we move in. This is our third property. I've been with my man ten years. Good, eh?

My husband used to say he knew he'd end up with a big house so I made sure. Had to pine, cajole and beg though and it cost me a blow-job plus the promise of many more.

I started my small business back then selling leather handbags etc through party-plan. You know, like Tupperware. At first I did the handbag parties with Mum, sharing her car till I got my own. After we went separate I got agents, then managers who got their own agents. It was hard doing sixty-hour weeks and still doing parties myself, always with two still in nappies.

"We can't afford a cleaner," he says.

"How do you even know when I do the bills?

Sometimes we live off the bag money, not touching yours."

"You just get a gut feeling," he tells friends. It's good he's being assertive, listening to his gut feelings.

One busy Christmas period I hire a nanny for three months.

"It's bad for the children," he tells friends who come over. Guilt shoots me in the place an ulcer should go.

"She should never have had kids," says the woman of the couple, a mother of one who, when their baby's a few months old arranges to get sterilised without telling her husband.

I smile and dish up the treacle sponge with custard. I make it in the microwave. It's dead easy.

To me, my small business is a big thing. I know I'm thick as shit, not capable of jack. Woollies-worker thick. Dad always used to joke "You're gonna end up working in Woolworths, you are!" Sorry Woolworths – I did like your stationery – God Rest Your Soul. But it's not easy, specially when my beloved 'forgets' to pass on important messages from customers and manufacturers or when he works late but doesn't tell me so I have to find last-minute baby-sitters. Then he turns up and they have to be paid anyway blah blah. I love the sound of his voice, though, bask in his aura when he talks to friends about how well *our* handbag business is doing.

And I love him. Truly, madly. Definitely madly. Idolise him. Worship him. Kissed my wedding ring 'good night' and 'good morning' every day for the last eight years, my engagement ring for the five years before that.

I always knew I was lucky to be with him. Me and him, we have a heart-to-heart once when we're teenagers, in Mum and Dad's dining room. He tells me the girls he went out with before are prettier than me. Sat on his lap I snuggle into his neck.

"I'm *glad* you're not pretty – I might lose you." He speaks softly and I feel his closeness.

Where did all that warmth go? I loved, love, him masses. Obsessively. More than life itself. First the boy. Then the man.

And now we have the children. All our kids have been invited. A child should know it's wanted, *feel wanted*, not just not bothered about and released into the world floundering like a lost baby whale. Or shoved around from pillar to post. Or given away.

A baby and its birth should be special, a celebration. Not an accident, unwanted, hated, wrong, bad, rejected, sullied, soiled goods, covered with darkness, alone and empty. A baby isn't a piece of shit. A baby is an angel – and needs to know that.

The talking completely disappears except for the 'what's for dinner?' kind. I'm not sure there was ever much of it, truth be told, except in front of others. Most of the relationship has been in my head, safely tucked in there nourished, fed and watered by my fantasies.

The sex reappears sometimes. It's only *ever* fucking, *never* making love and no kissing for years. Prostitution without the payment. Or the equality.

Gutter loneliness. Dog-shit on the pavement. So ugly. I'm so ugly.

It takes me years to realise there's friendly conversation every Saturday evening but it's gone by the Sunday. The attention's lovely and makes me realise why I love this man so much. We always have a box of wine. And sex. Always the sex.

Wine, wine, come and stay, make the pain go away.

Yes, it works its magic. Tomorrow's not here yet. See, things are OK really. I fall asleep happy and with hope – always that hope thing but once the sex is done, he withdraws the chat and the darkness comes back.

So a few months back I look up the phone number for Relate, which used to be called the Marriage Guidance Council. The appointment comes up and I sneak out, telling a fib about going to the library. I reckon it's not a big lie because Relate is in the clinic next to the library. He doesn't like me wasting my time reading so many books but I go anyway.

The counsellor is called Gloria. She's posh but warmish in a posh, scary way. She makes the room smell beautiful.

"It's 'Paris' by Yves St Laurent," she says. She talks about ground rules, like confidentiality blah blah.

She asks me why I'm not happy. No one's asked me that before or talked about my happiness. Ever. I cry. A lot. I tell her he doesn't know I exist. I know many people say that but if you come round for dinner you won't notice it if you don't know. It can be quite a jolly evening yet not one word will pass directly between him and me. Not one. And we can go a whole holiday like that – usually do. Yet he ingratiates himself with other holiday-makers, creates a jolly, charming image of himself in the swimming pool. Ho, ho – look at my beloved, the softy family man.

But you have to know what to look for and I'm not telling anyone. Would you? I'd rather have a laugh, play the game, look at the smiley photos, watch my kids play noisily showing everyone how *happy* they are. We are. Our family.

Gloria tells me people give off messages by how they dress. I look down at my sloppy Oxfam three-quarter-length cardigan – rust-coloured and stretched out of shape, covering a scruffy T-shirt and baggy trousers. I know my long hair has no shape. I lie – it has a shit shape. It's messy and wavy and after I wash my hair it dries itself, making up its own rules, dancing at the ends frizzily.

The disappearance of myself is almost complete. If only I could get a ride on the *Starship Enterprise*. "Beam me up, Scotty". He won't do that for me though because he's not listening. No one's listening. *I'm* not listening.

Neither am I on the *Starship Enterprise*. I'm here, but it doesn't feel like it. The world isn't clear to me. There's no colour in it and I watch it as though through glass. I can't touch or reach it. I can't see the people properly and nobody sees me. Nobody knows me. I don't know me. And I don't want any of us to know me. They'd hate me if they knew me – you would too.

But I can't leave the kids. I've gotta stay and face this shit, this desperately empty, grey continuance, like a human hamster wheel surrounded by darkness, making it even harder to keep going, round and round. I'm no good at anything. I've failed at everything – including disappearing. I can't even do that properly.

"You should think positively – you've had three children and are expecting another," Gloria tells me.

She's being nice… but it amounts to being shagged four times, I tell her.

I like the attention from Gloria. A whole hour of talking. Of being heard. Heaven.

"I'd like to see you and your husband together."

"I can't tell him. He'll go mad."

"It's better if you tell him yourself."

"You're joking, he'll *kill* me."

Will he, though? He's not all bad. For example, he's a terrific decorator. When I was pregnant with my THIRD, our daughter, he decorated our bedroom and it's beautiful. My design, his graft. It's all in the preparation, he tells me, so he spends ages rubbing down walls, burning paint off skirting boards. He did it *so* well that when he threw a hammer at my head when I disagreed with something he'd said it barely even dented the beautifully papered wall. That's how good he is!

"Would you like me to write to him?"

"Yes, please." I like it in here. Safe, soothing, smells of 'Paris'.

We each get a separate letter from Relate offering a joint appointment. We each say nothing.

I'm in early-ish pregnancy, the second trimester. I read about it in 'Parents' magazine. I read everything in 'Parents'. That and loads of books on pregnancy, birth, child-rearing. My Hugh Jolly book has grey corners on its pages where I consume the information like I can't get enough. Which I can't. And I love its still-new smell as I bring it up, open and trusting, to my face. I inhale, closing my eyes. Mmm.

Mum tells me snippets but it's not in the books. None of them say I'll need a smacking stick at the ready. Mind, she went a bit soft when I was pregnant with my FIRST. She even got me a baby journal (brand new) and lots of babies rattles (jumble-sales). I needed her most then, when I was happy with the baby inside but unhappy with my outside, becoming fatter and even less attractive to my husband. He's handsome and I'm proud of him when my friends tell me how charming he is, it's just…

Mum's softness drifts off at some point the next time

I'm pregnant.

We were driving to a handbag party when we argued. We were late and she was driving painfully slow. When I told her that, her arm shot across like a rabid dog as she whacked me across the face with it. I was bleeding inside my mouth and my lip swelled, mirroring my seven-month pregnant belly. I checked the back seat. My gorgeous eldest son, at twelve months old, didn't seem to notice. Mum said sorry and I let her. Saying sorry was a big thing for her. Huge. It was OK again. I hated her then – but not as much as she hates herself.

She and Dad didn't come to the hospital when my SECOND was born. Dad said they would've come if they both hadn't had colds but I later found out they had to have the dog put down the day my son was born.

The first birth was a caesarean. I'm small-built and the baby (7 pounds 4 ounces) was breech – that's the wrong way up if you're single or a teenager. I desperately wanted a natural birth the next time and fought the consultant, who knew better. He threatened I could have my pelvic bones cut to let the baby through and they'd heal themselves afterwards. *What?*

I pined, cajoled and begged and the consultant said he would 'let' me try for a natural birth *if* I was induced but if there was *any* sign of anything then we'll have to operate blah blah.

So labour is induced. It's quick. And it's the most excruciatingly white-light-pain experience in my life. My vision is snatched away by the screaming shunts and blows trying to rip me open. That and the injection of pethedine (*morphine/heroin*) they jab, without asking, into my leg, locking in the pain while taking away the ability to react. I think then – if I can make it to a window I can jump out, end it all, stop the pain.

My husband watches the James Bond film on the hospital telly. I'm moaning. It's hardly bearable. Truly, it's like dark thunder claps from Hell have come to permanently mangle and tear my body apart. Blow it up. Stretch. Rip. Pull. What I mean is **BLOW IT UP. STRETCH. RIP. PULL**.

"Come on Mand, you're making it worse than it really is... " Then during a particularly painful contraction, "So *now* are you glad you're having it naturally?" His laughing mouth and eyes go back to Bond... James Bond.

After he's born, my beautiful snowy haired son (7 pounds 2 ounces), I'm not 'allowed' to hold him till after I've had a cup of tea with sugar in. My husband goes off to get himself fish and chips. The midwife checks for something – has she lost her watch? She only puts her whole hand inside me. I whimper, try to pull away.

"Oh come on now, you've just had a *baby*!" Exactly, you fucking bitch.

I get my hair cut into a short tidy bob, order some clothes from the catalogue; a jade-coloured jumper (cotton – don't tumble dry – reshape when damp) and navy tartan trousers, which contrast beautifully. And flat navy leather shoes, toes slightly pointed. I wear make-up.

The sitter arrives and we go to Relate on a Tuesday at eight o'clock at the clinic next to the library.

In the first session Gloria and we talk about a contract we three make, how much each session costs them and how much we can contribute. Do we want to do it? Yes.

"It's about looking at change, changes in behaviour," says Gloria.

"Marriage is a gift," says my husband.

"No it's not – it's bloody hard work," spits Gloria. *This* is true.

When we go home neither of us mentions Relate. Maybe it never happened? But I start to think. Like *really* think. I've got new information and it kick-starts something in my head that won't leave me now, even when I want it to. It's like a crotchet hook that's got in through my nose and latched on to a bit of brain, tentative at first, then tugging. I don't know yet that it won't leave till there's none of the old brain left.

'If thine eyes offend thee – pluck them out,' it says in the Bible. But also I remember seeing an old Ray Milland film The Man with the X-Ray Eyes where this scientist bloke invents a liquid that gives him X-ray vision. At first he sees through people's clothes, sees their underwear. He increases the dose so it's skeletons he sees, then, inside their minds. Eventually he can't handle what he sees. It sends him nuts. Insane. 'If thine eyes offend thee – pluck them out', he quotes.

So he does. The END.

I know this is the start of something big and different.

My husband has a solo session with Gloria. He says later she asked what he saw in me. He says he told her I was sweet and interesting to talk to. I cry then because I take him at his word and for nearly fourteen years never knew this.

However, the next week he's angry. He tells Gloria we only have sex when I want to.

"Sometimes a person withholds sex to punish their partner." She tells me. Husband one – wife nil. After that we have loads of sex but always with a box of wine. It's difficult to have sex with someone who hates you. More wine. My husband is generous when buying wine, indulges me. Oops, spilling it.

I really look forward to seeing Gloria again. Hungry for information and an ally, I slag him off.

"I think he's trying really hard." She's irritated. "So, Mandy, how can *you* change?"

What? What? Did I hear right? Doesn't she know I've come here so she can tell my husband off, then he'll make it all up to me and we'll live out the fantasy I've always tried hard to squeeze us into? Another point to husband.

I start to feel bad then about the times I've belittled him in front of our friends, the times I've taken the piss out of his dancing. I mean his dancing *is* crap – his arms go everywhere and he keeps his mouth open – but does he need to know it like that? From me. Again. In front of people. And you don't know him so it doesn't count.

It physically hurts to discover I've hurt him. It seeps into my head, grey and slithery. The crotchet hook prods and pulls more. Some weeks it's his turn to get 'told off'.

After a few sessions Gloria makes a suggestion.

"If you think about something you'd like to bring up why don't you write it down?" So I do.

"Mandy," she gasps, "you express yourself beautifully!" PING! No-one's said that before. I'm made up.

"Yeah," he laughs, "but how many spelling mistakes are there?"

"Could *you* do better?" Gloria's eyes snap open as if forgetting she's not in her kitchen with her sons but in a counselling session. Point to wife.

"No, I mean it," calmly, back on track, "And I'd really like to see something you've written too. Will you bring it next week?"

He agrees but never does it. I write more. And more. By hand. And I rewrite it to make it perfect. Then I rewrite it to make it more perfect.

My husband says I made him get married and I made him have the children. I'm full of shame. He seems to hate me so much. I'm frightened when he hates me. I'm getting fatter too with the baby, uglier. We don't make eye contact, me and him. Never did, well, maybe Saturdays. I stop counting points. There are too many.

"I always thought we'd live our lives around me," he admits one day.

Gloria suggests assertiveness classes. We sign up to one evening a week and learn a whole new language and way of being from facilitator Elizabeth, a slim older woman who wears a lot of purple and flat shoes.

I buy books on assertiveness and Body Language by Alan Pease. God, it's so clever. Did you know if someone's lying they can't look you in the eye? That said, if they're *good* liars they make *sure* they do so they're more convincing. We meet new people too. I'm pleased my husband is charming and friendly and the women and the man who's gay find him interesting.

But when we finish the course and no one's looking, the rubber band pings back into place as we get confused about who's supposed to have rights. We emerge like chicks from a distorted egg, me hyperconscious of other's rights, him demanding that his get adhered to.

Gloria talks about expectations. And standards.

Friends come over for dinner. We drink and enjoy ourselves, tell jokes.

"I always say the only good woman is a dead one," says my husband. We all laugh.

My turn. "So as I run out the house, down the drive, he throws a bar-stool at me and it hits my head." We all laugh.

"Yeah, but I didn't mean it to hit you," he laughs. "I just wanted to frighten you."

We all crack up. He's good with people, tops up our glasses, has a charming smile – specially for our women friends. But his face has a darkness. Always.

With all this thinking going on since Relate it gets harder to sleep. Unbeknownst to me I turn into two people. One of me is playing the game that our marriage is getting stronger now that I'm thinking positively as much as I can. Desperately positive thinking and I'm trying hard to change, like Gloria said. But the more I discover, the more the darkness ingests me. It's with me all the time, sometimes it's worse than others. 'If thine eyes offend thee'.

I can't sleep at night so I make a new friend. This friend is there whenever I need comfort and there for me in a way no other has ever been. I can say anything I like to my new friend and there's no anger fired back, no threats or intimidation, overt or subliminal. Only complete understanding, letting me be whoever I am, whoever I need to be. Also, it doesn't call me a slug like my beloved does.

Momentarily my new friend takes away the pain. Sometimes my new friend has a different first name. Sometimes it's called Stolichnaya, sometimes Smirnoff and sometimes plain old Sainsbury's. When I can't sleep at night my friend gives me what I need. Sometimes it only works for an hour or so then I creep back downstairs for another chat and a bit more bonding.

One night I do manage to sleep. Something odd happens around three o'clock in the morning. It's generally recognised that Christ was crucified at three in the afternoon so the opposite then, the devil's hour is three a.m. ...

Something **SNAPS** me awake, fear slapping me round the face while its master creeps silently up my back. Everywhere, it's everywhere. I don't know quite what to be scared of first. Or most. Something's horribly wrong. This room is sinister. Chunks of hate are broken down, smoothed into particles of darkness in the air, the toxic, toxic air, barely detectable to the human eye, nose, lung.

I close my eyes, try to breathe without sound as I realise second by second where Hell comes from. My husband is sat upright, big and dark. He's whispering, hardly audible; how much he hates me, how I make him sick, I'm a slug, how he holds me in contempt. First he leans over me, the poison slurping from his mouth like internal bleeding, over my face, my hair, sliding over my baby's place of safety. Then he moves away, puts his feet over the edge of the bed and with his back to me, continues his diatribe. Wait, though. He's no longer whispering I realise but speaking slowly, gently, his voice low. He turns towards me, slides over.

"I wish you were dead. Why don't you just die!" The ice in his voice smothers me. I try harder to quiet my breath, scrunch my eyes tightly. Eventually he lies down, gets comfortable, falls soundly asleep. He never knows I heard him this time.

Over the months I sleep less and less. The baby's growing inside me and I'm doing two or three hours a night, getting up to look after the other three kids. My eldest son is now five years old, my second son is four and my third child, my beautiful daughter (8 pounds 7 ounces), is now eighteen months.

It's hard to make my husband happy. I book a restaurant table. My fault, I should've known what would happen. If (when) we argue I decide I will be assertive, not stick around. When he takes a leak I leave, taking the car keys. But he catches up with me outside.

"I decided I don't have to sit there and take that." Rehearsed, performed – look no hands – straight from my book A Woman in Your Own Right: Assertiveness and You, in which Anne Dickson tells me I can leave a situation where I'm being put down.

"Fucking whore. Give me the keys or I'll chin ya!"

I know I've got choices. All the books say that. My husband tells me all the time at Relate and in front of friends. So I *choose* to drop the keys on the floor, scared to get too close to my *five-foot-eleven-and-a-half-inch*, normally almost twice my weight, husband.

He throws a tenner at me.

"Get a cab, you slug." My beloved. Father of my unborn child. The ten-quid note floats onto the kerb as the Queen looks at me, refusing to get involved. She doesn't wave, instead looks sombre, responsible. But she's lying. She never cares what she's being used for, whether it's disposable nappies, a couple of albums or a blow-job up a dark alley.

When we next see Gloria my husband first tells the baby-sitter how sensitive he is, how he's just an old softy. He doesn't look at me, obviously. I smile with her.

I dress immaculately in bright colours. Blue, yellow, green and red. Sometimes pink. I wear make-up. I have lots of sex with my husband. Cold, ugly, coming from behind, anaesthetised sex.

I make home-made play-dough. Blue, yellow, green and red. Sometimes pink. I drive the children seven miles to a church school and playschool. I make bread with my Magimix and biscuits using wholemeal flour. Flapjacks. The kids put faces on the gingerbread men. Staying smiley is tough. My husband and my mother and Grace and Tony and Patrick, especially Patrick, take swipes at my parenting skills. Sometimes with my husband it's a mere hint, so mere that others don't hear it.

I listen to reading in my son's class. Mum tells me I shouldn't – having me there will turn him into a right show-off. We go to story-time at the library. Toddler groups. Swimming lessons. Blah-blah-flipperty-fipperty-trying-to-be-a-better-parent-blah.

I go to and hold National Childbirth Trust coffee mornings and meet interesting but posh, clearly happily married people. I start training as a breast-feeding counsellor but when the trainer uses words I don't know I write them down to look up later, go home, burst into tears and don't return.

The NCT holds an evening about child abuse. The speaker is Michele Elliott who will go on to form child-protection charity Kidscape. She tells us that one in ten children is sexually abused.

"There will be at least two of you here who have been abused." That many? I look around at the twenty or so women sitting in a circle, brush a hair off my face so I'm not being too obvious. But which two? Who can it be?

How about the overweight woman with dark-rimmed glasses and spots? She's got an only child, been trying for ages for another. And her sister, but she's not here tonight – does that count? It can't be the woman who's married to a solicitor. Or the person to her right who's a qualified anaesthetist. Obviously. I dunno how to tell really. Could you? Anyway it gets me out the house for an evening, to see familiar folk like Judy. We've had coffee together before.

My husband storms out of some Relate sessions. The first time, Gloria tells me my husband doesn't mind what I do as long as the dinner's on the table. It's a reassuring slap. Still, after each session when we come home we never mention where we've been from one week to the next. Do we really go? Weeks turn into months, like they're supposed to. But they're not supposed to do it so quick. Years unravel in minutes and hours.

Gloria tells me even if I hate Mum I still need her. "She rules your life."

We talk about my being adopted. I say it's never made any difference to me, like Mum says. Gloria knows I've been lied to and I lie to myself as more and more truths are revealed.

"What about your dad, Mandy?"

"Died four years ago – heart attack."

"Did you say goodbye to him?"

"Gloria… I never said *hello*."

I dunno. Perhaps you can tell a lot about people by their telly habits. I mean as a kid I wasn't allowed to watch things I liked. NEVER Top of the Pops. ALWAYS what Mum or Dad wanted – Dad if he was home, Mum when he wasn't. Whereas in my husband's house he was the one who decided what would be watched. Just an idea – what d'you reckon?

In my reading I've happened across two new words. They both relate to my beloved.

Number one – "Omnipotent."

"What? That's it, I've had enough. How'm I supposed to carry on?" He always says that, or that he'll leave or the relationship's over blah blah. Done it since I met him. When he says that I'll forgive him anything. It's one of a hundred little ways of getting me to shut up, be invisible, disappear.

Number two – "Narcissist."

"You can see what she's like! Everyone knows what she's like," he pleads with Grace when she's over for coffee. "I'm sick of giving!"

It's great she oozes sympathy for my man.

Back at Relate Gloria says I've always felt abandoned and that when we finally reach the end of our sessions it's important I don't feel abandoned.

I love Gloria. I write about her a lot. Think about her A *LOT*. Buy her a lily plant.

"Oh, thank you. I like getting presents. Did you know lilies represent peace?"

"No." How would I? But I know I'll buy her more presents.

"No more presents," she tells me one Tuesday. Cringe.

Less and less sleep. Less and less talking. It's as if the rubber band is ageing prematurely, perishing. There's no new energy. It's become frail under the attacks, frail in the face of the truths.

I start drinking during the daytime. Suppose it helps but the aid is real temporary. The gloomy, murky darkness is always there, inside and outside of me. The darkness knows I'm nothing, I shouldn't be alive, should never have been born. The darkness knows that.

I read about Foetal Alcohol syndrome. It's a medical condition that can befall a baby when a lot of alcohol is consumed by its mother during pregnancy. The baby can be born with a deformed face and head and have life-long problems. In about half of cases there's also some mental handicap, says the book.

My snowy-haired son needs collecting. He's been to play with his little friend who lives in this big detached house in a little village. Her posh mum from the posh house comes out to the car as I pull up. She's stood there like she's in an illustrator's impression of a new building development, smart clothes, perfect hair and make-up before a perfect detached house with strategically placed, closely clipped greenery. She was her husband's secretary when he was with his first wife. He's got a new secretary now.

Foot on brake, I stop the car a bit quick and an empty vodka bottle slides out from its hidey-hole under the passenger seat. She glances down. I'm fucked. But luckily she's so posh she doesn't say a thing, just sort of smiles embarrassedly and carries on talking. I hope she files it away in the archives and *doesn't* present her report to the other mums at playschool.

"He's been lovely, your snowy-haired boy."

"Would your little girl with the cheeky grin like to come round tomorrow?"

"Oh, no!" A bit quick. "I've got to collect curtains from Fenwicks."

Something dark, with a red cloak and two horns sticks its red-hot poker up my arse and my body contracts around it, tries to disappear into the heat of it.

Mum's cooked us lunch. Bolognese. Yum – better check it for dog hairs. In the garden she's telling me about the will she'll make one day, though not yet. She thinks you die if you make a will. (It's why she sleeps with the light on – people die in the dark.)

"Want it all to go to Boxer-dog charities."

"What about the grandchildren?"

"Thought of that, maybe give them a fifth. Then I thought… no… it's all for the dogs."

"You not putting me in the will then?"

"You putting me in *your* will?"

"Just thought… "

"Nah, you and your husband are doing alright."

At Relate I read what I've written about how it feels being a woman in my husband's family. How the women are like pieces of china, wrapped carefully in cotton-wool with their mouths taped over, kept in a cupboard, ignored. If a woman is a 'speaking' woman in this family she's ostracised. My husband storms out.

Can you believe his Mum's middle name was May and her maiden name was Dye? Dorothy May Dye. Guess her parents *really* loved her. But before she died and after she was widowed she'd talked more than ever before.

"I never knew my mum could be so interesting," said my surprised husband, just the once.

After he storms out Gloria tells me I see *her* as a mother figure.

"No." I don't always agree with glorious Gloria.

"Where would you put me in your life, what position?"

"After my husband and kids."

"Isn't that where a mother goes?" Fuck. It's true.

I tell Gloria about my drinking, sometimes almost a bottle of vodka a day. I tell her I'm worried about the baby.

"So... even though you're worried about the baby you still do it?"

"Yep," I say. And I don't know how that's the answer that comes. I'm stunned. Somehow it gets round to me wishing I'd been her daughter.

"Look me in the eye and tell me you never wanted a daughter."

"I would have loved a daughter, yes. But I'm very happy with my three sons." She reaches for my hand and I cry. Then somehow we're hugging.

"Please don't leave me," I beg through my tears. She cries too.

I'm repulsed by myself. That I can do this with a stranger? A stranger who presently is everything to me while to her I am nothing.

"I hate you for leaving me." There – it's out.

"I'm proud of you for saying that." She's weird sometimes. But I feel relieved and released.

"I could be anybody," she says.

"No!" But I know there's a tiny, honest, truthful part of me that knows she's right.

"What would you have liked to say to your birth mother if you'd had the opportunity?" says Gloria. The answer flips out like a jack-in-the-box.

"I'd like to go back in time... and say... I'm sorry for whatever I did wrong that made you give me away. Please just give me another chance to show you I'll be good. I promise I'll be good."

I decide to trace my birth mother. The story goes like this. I was supposed to be adopted by the Catholic Adoption Society. But, says Mum, when they find out my father is Jewish they throw me out, won't handle the adoption. So Mum, who's only supposed to be fostering me till the adoption goes through is suddenly off-balanced by a choice.

"Do you want her then?" says the welfare woman, so the story goes.

Mum has her own two 'real' sons but always wanted a daughter. She asks Dad if she can keep me and he says yes. Mum says she nearly fell through the floor then. Anyway Mum, Joan, meets Bernadette, my birth mother, before I'm born. My birth mother's originally from Liverpool but she's now a club hostess in London.

The deal is, says my mother to my mother, you have to get her baptised Catholic. My birth father, George, agrees to pay the fostering money till the adoption goes through. My birth mother visits Mum and Dad's flat, sees the two boys. A nice happy family.

I was born Vivienne Michele (spelt with one 'l') McCourt. At ten days old I leave the hospital and become Mandy Michele (spelt with one 'l') Trent. Bernadette left out the other 'l' by mistake on the birth certificate. They call me Mandy, though it's Amanda on the new certificate. Dad thought of the name but for months he thinks its Hamanda and spells me with an H. What's in a name?

I spend my teenage-hood resenting all things Catholic and Jewish.

At the next Relate session I tell Gloria I've decided to trace my birth mother.

"That's a good idea," she says.

What? No one's said that to me before. I'm twenty-eight and no one's ever told me I've had a good idea.

My poor husband takes a back seat. Yeah, yeah, I know – he loves it.

I tell Grace about the search. The great layer-on of

dinner parties. She told me once she'd done a degree in drama at home in the States. Ha. She *was* entertaining but she lied, made up fantastic stories – that's fantastic as in barely believable. So whatever story you bring into work she's done double, minimum. You broke a leg? She broke three, or knows someone who did.

She's had a child with a man whose wife is her Avon lady. The guilt makes her buy more and more Avon. She's always so well turned out! She's on benefit and the housing association give her a flat, since she's now eligible for it. She's like a really together person. She becomes a foster-carer and runs a playgroup. Luckily, none of this affects her benefit claim. When she has a spell at Relate she tells me the counsellor said he's never met anyone so together as her. She even helps train other foster carers, she's *so* well sorted. Grace's good with my kids, good with my husband. I'm glad he likes her too, that she's a friend to us both.

One day, having dinner over at hers he says he's really depressed about everything.

"I hate emotions – I wish they'd go away," he says.

"I know," she says.

"We were happy till we went to Relate." At other times, times to come, he'll say we were happy till I lost weight. At others he'll say we were happy till we had our fourth child. Is my mind playing tricks? I only remember him saying how *unhappy* he is.

They hug, Grace and my husband with the beard that she likes on a man. It's a decent length hug. He cries and she rubs his back for some minutes. I'm so glad Grace is in our lives. As I watch I feel strange, awkward, shift my weight from foot to foot – me being impatient, I expect, and while we drink our coffee my head's off again.

"Do you think we can ever know everything about a person?" I look at my husband and my friend, hugging.

"Yes," he snaps, fed up with it all.

"Don't know," Grace says softly, looks at my husband.

"You can know all you *want* to know." He grits his teeth.

Grace hangs her head, looks at me like I'm a leper abandoned in a children's home and the electric's run out.

The following week she's in her local library and looks up the name of my birth mother in the UK telephone directory.

I'm three years old and very tiny. I'm standing on a step-stool at the kitchen sink of our two-bedroom high-rise flat in North London. Everyone else is out and my pseudo-brother Patrick is looking after me. Patrick is eleven years old and very tall.

"Do it like this." He squeezes a long worm of toothpaste onto my brush.

He puts his own toothbrush in front of his mouth, baring his teeth, demonstrating. At a regular medium speed, it's back and forward without actually touching his teeth.

"You do it." I do what he tells me. I brush my teeth.

"Now swallow the toothpaste." I do what he tells me.

My older brother, Aijee, is fifteen and leaves home now. He'd make sure I got more cornflakes when Tony wouldn't let me have enough. And he'd whack Patrick round the head when he twisted my arm up my back or break one of my toys.

I start a new school. Mum says I stop speaking properly, saying, 'gis it 'ere' and 'ta' instead of 'Thank you'. *Tar's what they put on the roads.* Mum stops smiling at me.

I'm five years old and very tiny. My pseudo-brother Patrick is thirteen years old and very tall. He pins me on the floor in the front room and tickles me and tickles me. It hurts. So I laugh. It really does hurt, so I laugh more, like Patrick, Mum and Tony do.

"Submit?"

I do what he tells me.

"Yes."

He releases me.

I'm six years old and very tiny. My pseudo-brother Patrick is fourteen years old and very tall. Almost six-feet. We're walking back from my school, alone. Tony's at basket-ball practice.

"Walk faster." I do what he tells me.

"Your Mum doesn't love you."

"But she says she does."

"Nah – she's just saying that. And your real Mum didn't want you either, that's why she gave you away."

"Oh." I shift my duffel bag to the other shoulder. It's heavy.

The more thinking and drinking I do the more I'm losing people around me. Sometimes they choose, sometimes I do. Increasingly there's no choosing. Smiling gets harder, isolating gets easier. I miss Adrian. It's nine years since he died and I've not seen so much of Tony lately, even less of Patrick.

The phone rings. Points at me. Demands to be

answered in that demanding tone that phones have. Now! Get up off that fat lazy arse and come over here. I'm summoned. So I get up off my fat lazy arse and go over there.

"Hello. What's up?" It's Patrick.

"I was going to pop round for coffee." He sounds odd.

"Alright." Tesco's can wait.

An hour later he's towering in my kitchen, blocking out the sun.

"*She's* been on the phone."

"What?"

"She reckons when I took my daughter back last week she was bleeding."

"Well... you know kids... accident prone."

He slurps his coffee. Big noisy mouthfuls, too hot for anyone else. I feel sick. He picks his nose. Like any loving pseudo-sister I don't notice as he rolls it round slowly into that perfect shape, then lets it drop on my kitchen floor.

"After the access visit."

"So... so what? Not your fault if a child has an accident. What, d'she fall over?"

"In her nappy."

"What?"

"Bleeding in her nappy."

"Oh, right."

"She *did* go on the seesaw at the park." Thoughtful.

"She'll be alright. Kids get over things quickly."

"Mandy."

"What?"

"You're not listening are you?" Measured. Calm.

"What?"

"She's saying my daughter's been abused. Sexually

abused. And now she's playing up, making it difficult for me to see her. But it could be anything. Anyone. An infection. Her brother. Tony said I should never have let her get pregnant. *He* knows what she's like, what I've had to put up with."

Investigations go on and Great Ormond Street Children's Hospital is involved. He tells me the police even held him overnight in a cell, took his shoes away, interviewed him for hours doing the 'good cop, bad cop' thing.

When I see Patrick next his face is dark. It's telling on him, all this. The doctor got him a counsellor who told him to look at himself. So he stopped going.

The access visits start being supervised. He takes his daughter to Mum's and to Tony and Hazel's. They have a nice time 'discussing' the little girl's Mother.

He comes to me too with his daughter, who I hardly know since their divorce, though as toddlers she and my two sons played.

I miss her mother too but don't let on. Ruth was like a sister to me. Patrick argues, whereas she's kind, offers you a sandwich, while he'll have a go at you for coming round scrounging his food. He's very down. I sympathise. He says that even when he didn't see his daughter he continued paying maintenance. You can't argue with *that*.

On one visit a social worker comes to my house too. It's awkward. Daddy complains about Mummy to their daughter, to me, to the air. The social worker hardly speaks, just sits there, stony. I make a lot of coffee, bring more biscuits. If only they'd drink more – have more biscuits – have more coffee – how about juice for the little girl?

When we see Gloria I tell her there are three people called B. McCourt who live in Liverpool. One of them's bound to be Bernadette, my birth mother.

"It's best not to get your hopes up. It doesn't mean any of them *is* your mother."

Fuck me, *now* who needs positive thinking?

During my search I join Norcap, the registered charity that helps people in the adoption triangle. I tear open the envelope when each newsletter comes like it's water in the desert.

It's harder still to sleep. I borrow bottles of vodka from the neighbour next door when it's late and everywhere's shut. I write a lot. And rewrite a lot.

I try to tell my husband I've learned something more.

"I realise we're not attached. We're not simply one single person with two sets of arms and legs. I really thought we were, we've been so entwined. Merged. I accept that now and I release you to be yourself."

"There's always something!" Anger – him. Guilt – me.

I tell him something else I've discovered too, though it's a bit shit.

"Without realising it I think we both wanted each other to fail."

That does it. He's outraged at this suggestion. He's like Mr FURIOUS from Richmond who writes to the BBC.

The darkness, however, is with me all the time. I struggle to get through a day doing normal things and I don't know how I do it. I never noticed when we moved in but the house is grey, the rooms in shadow. Specially the kitchen. The living, breathing kitchen. The heart of the house. It beats out a sub-life of darkness, sends a flow of thick, dark-grey and black particles to the other rooms like a diseased cloud that slowly moves across the floors, walls and ceilings. Then it floats down and I inhale it. And it watches. Always watches. It knows I'm a bad mother. Bad wife. Bad daughter. Useless. Should never have been born. I'm in the way and the only good woman is a dead one.

My husband doesn't know I drink during the day. If he knows I drink at night he doesn't speak of it. We don't speak. His dinner is on the table. The rubber band holds together by the finest of strands.

Me and my husband discuss with Gloria ending the sessions. She says again it's important I don't feel abandoned. Ha. I don't know what I'll do without Gloria in my life. Without these sessions. Without the person who helped me unlock the door that now won't shut.

Sleep some nights is just an hour. The vodka doesn't fuzz my thoughts enough, not nearly enough. My brain won't fucking stop. It's relentless. If it's true electricity goes round our brains there's a power station in mine.

The baby is due shortly but I know it won't be born till we're finished at Relate. I couldn't let that happen. What am I doing to this baby, once so invited and treasured? To all my children? I miss my husband though I'm not sure our marriage ever existed outside of my head, not sure he was ever here. Not really. And now *I'm* not here.

We have one more session left. I can't let it end – not now, not like this. What's happening to me? I can't do this anymore. I've had enough. I drink. I think. I write. Then I drink some more.

I still dress colour-wheel perfect in ever-brighter

colours. Outside of my gleeful clothes the world's a slimy, secret, dark place. We continue with the icy conveyor-belt sex. I still wear make-up but dragging out smiles to prove our family's still a happy place is almost impossible.

Chapter 8: Girl Interrupted

I write it and I mean it. There's no way on earth I can stop seeing Gloria. She's everything to me. Another way will have to be found.

"Can't you get from your husband what you get from me?"

I sling a thought over that way but it bounces back. We've come a long way, me and him. Life's appearance is loads better, certainly. But is this all there is?

"You can't just replace people." I can't believe she even thinks that!

We still have an act, me and my beloved, so practiced we've got it word perfect. When we're with people, it's them he talks to. I smile, look on, hover, wait to be included, be good, wish I could be his 'beautiful assistant' and do everything but bring out popcorn and choc ices. Still I try occasionally to catch my husband's eye. Nope. The broken bottle of shame shunts into my gut, twists, and the shards gather with the ever-present darkness, confirming my badness. Naively and insanely I keep hoping anyway.

When we're alone my husband speaks more now, post-Relate. We talk about what we can do to make him happy. I lie. We talk about why he *isn't* happy and when I make suggestions he does that "yes, but..." thing. So I think of more ways we could make him happy. Then more.

I love it when we talk, grateful when he speaks – obviously, as I really love this man – but it's draining as he takes more than I've got, leaving me in the red. It's like living with a sponge as my energy supplies get run **down** and **down** and **down** and down and down.

In every way I'm exhausted: mentally, physically, spiritually. Yet there's this adrenalin that fuels me, keeps me going when I shouldn't bodily be able to.

Am I being unreasonable? He *has* learnt a lot from a year at Relate. Vocab mainly – from the assertiveness course too. It's impressive to the untrained eye, to those he wants to see him that way; an old softy, great with his kids, a husband who 'loves his wife to bits' if only she'd change. He steals my words too. I notice days or weeks after I've come up with a new perception, a new line, he relays it to someone like it belonged to him in the first place, like he's dug it up himself. Maybe it's flattering. But I'm confused when I tell him what I see and he says no I don't, it's not true, I'm being oversensitive and what I've noticed isn't actually there, blah blah. I try hard to explain what I mean and when he doesn't get it I try still harder.

"You know what you're like," he tells me.

"You know what she's like," he tells everyone else: the children, my mother, my best friend. He likes to take what's mine: my dog, my relationship with the children, my best friend, my depression. Maybe he doesn't even realise.

My dog, Leo, was my twenty-first birthday present. First lost to my husband, then to the busy traffic he played with when he escaped through the open back gate.

Some of the others my husband obtains through a slower process, a subtle longer-term plan. *It's all in the preparation.* For now this takeover is a secret known only to himself.

The people we mix with think he's great. (Hadn't Gloria said; "We choose the friends most like ourselves"?) He *is* great, of course, and I'm still proud when my women friends think he's charming, relieved when he approves of my friends. Forgiveness, temporary approval, that's what's in it for me. Don't get me wrong, I'm *glad* we've stayed together. Truly. People *should* when they've had kids eh?

Gloria sets a date for the last session. She's done now with us. The only person alive who cares, the single living soul that knows I exist, have a voice and opinions. The baby's due next week so the last session will be after the birth.

Alcohol, my best friend, holds my hand, calms me like no other, day and night. It's both my fuel and anaesthetic, keeps me going. Does it still help? Maybe for moments but it's no longer a choice but a necessity, a compulsion I don't question.

My brain gallops. I make big juicy discoveries on a daily basis. My head might explode, I fear. Always the fear. More alcohol. I look back, see more and more clearly, wish I couldn't. *If thine eyes offend thee.* In not much more than a few sorry months I've discovered the world is *not* flat. On top of this, other galaxies daily make themselves known to me.

I read books on depression. Postnatal depression. Depression during pregnancy.

"What d'you read so many books for?"

He doesn't read a lot himself. Well, the newspapers with the tits in, plus the top-shelf magazines. Says he likes the stories. He learned to read when he was twelve, was too busy being hyperactive before then. His brother Wayne taught him in the summer holidays, is how the story goes. If he feels inadequate it doesn't prevent him making sure he's the centre of things.

I feel bad for him when Grace tells me he feels outshone by me. It's *easy* to feel sorry for him. He doesn't mind crying in front of people, doesn't mind telling a few lies here and there. Yet if I cry he continues with whatever he's doing, unperturbed. He refuses to make a move to comfort even when I request a change, 'assertiveness book' style. Instead he stays angry. I'm scared when he's angry. He tells everyone he hates responsibility and he's sick of giving. That's all life is for him: give, give, give. Grace also reads the 'how to' books and feels sorrier for him.

"He's not strong like you," she says.

Is it easier for me, like Mum says?

"Your husband's a simple man," Trevor tells me. The guilt drips into me and out from me like I'm a home-made cheese. Is it true I've single-handedly made life complicated for my ill-equipped husband?

There are a lot of people feeling a lot of pity for my poor husband who's such a nice man. See him cry. Hear him speak. Responsibility. His rights. Too much giving. Loves his children, his wife, if only she would…

It takes under two hours for my fourth child, (8 pounds exactly) to travel the length of the birth canal. He has a beautiful, almost black *full* head of home-grown curly hair. During the birth all I can think of is…

I wonder, when Gloria 'leaves' me, like the others did, how will we manage without her? How will my husband cope with his new job at Trevor's office, plus there's the money we've borrowed to fund it! Will I find my birth mother? If I do, will she want to know me? Will she be a dumpy housewife still married to a cabby, my father, who can't wait to cook us all Sunday roast, itching to spoil her newly discovered grandchildren? How will Mum cope? When my husband told me you shouldn't let people know it when you like them, does that mean he secretly likes me after all, has all along, did in the beginning? How did Lillian, Mum's mother, feel when her husband made himself the key person in Mum's life, ensuring Lillian and her daughter were alienated? Why would a father prevent a child from having its mother? What *was* so interesting for Mum and her dad in his workshop? What *is* it about success that so frightens me and my husband, leading me never to finish things; only paint half a window, never complete one scrap of needlework, even my apron at school, even the white felt mouse at primary school when I was seven? I've read it's a type of ending, success. Why are so many people afraid of success? And endings? When Gloria said, "God helps those who help themselves," and I said, "I don't believe in God, he fucked up," was it really his fault? Was it God or other forces that influenced my shit? Did Patrick abuse his little girl? Or is he right, it's her mother being funny? Surely Patrick wouldn't do that, would he? Would he? Would he? Would he? Do you think he would? Why do I worry I'll get a bollocking when hurt has been done *to* me? *TO* ME!! Like the day it rained, years before when I fell off my Honda 50cc. As people gathered round I said, "My husband will kill me." Why did Mum tell us off when we hurt ourselves? Hang on – I *do* get a bollocking when I'm hurt. How can I get my husband to be nice to our second son? I've already asked him, my snowy-haired son, to change when he's around his father so his dad will be kinder, though I'm not sure how he can. And should he have to, is that the way of it? But what else can I do? Why did his dad, my husband, say we should humiliate him when he's done wrong? When my snowy-haired son showed me the knife under his pillow, did he mean it when he said he wanted to kill himself? Why did we have boy, boy, girl – same as my mother did? Does this mean it will all repeat itself? Oh, no – WHAT – *all* of it? Why does my husband have this way with people, this charm, so that he gets away with things? Why's it easier for him to have female friends than bloke friends? When he calls me manipulative is he speaking of himself? Why does he try to prevent me being close to the children? Why must only he be or *appear* to be close to them? Like an unspoken law only *he* can have fun with them. But why mustn't I? Why am I so *scared*? He reminds I've got choices. How can I express myself more clearly so he understands when I try and try...and *try*... to explain what I mean? If I'm blaming someone does it mean I'm not looking hard enough or am I not blaming in the right places? Hang on – what's THAT?

"A beautiful baby boy!" the midwife announces as she hands him over, helps him latch onto the breast. My breast. He is just the most gorgeous... angel, and my husband agrees with the midwife, he's beautiful. Thank God I never have to go through this again. I vomit in a bowl like I did the other times.

"Your body's in shock, dear. It was a quick birth, you're OK," says Comfort, the midwife and she does exactly that – comforts. That's me done, I've had the four children I always wanted. First thing I've ever completed. Will the sky fall in?

He, my husband, father of our baby, leaves after a

few quiet minutes. Nothing to say, like the other times.

The baby lies beside me in his plastic cot. I'm booked in for a day or 'six-hour discharge', though it never is. Get the fuck out of here soon as.

First though, I can't stop thinking about Foetal Alcohol Syndrome. When my husband's gone I tell the nurse I'm worried – will she get a doctor to check my son?

"Please, it's urgent."

"OK."

I remember the book. The black and white photos and the pencil drawings which threaten a life sentence to my son for the crime I've committed. The drawings show a baby with a pointed head. Please God, no.

I'm hot and bothered. The usual polythene cover is underneath the pillowcase so there's no sleep for me even if I *could* manage it. Every time I fall asleep I wake up, my hot face and hair covered in sweat and dribble. Nice. Like I don't already know I'm the ugliest thing ever, ever, ever. And the shittest mother. What's the point of reading books like How to Have a Gifted Child if you're gonna fuck them up with alcohol? Wouldn't you agree? The fault's mine alone. *I've* done this.

TWENTY-FOUR HOURS. TWENTY-FOUR HEAD-BURSTING HOURS. THE LONGEST TWENTY-FOUR HOURS THAT EVER TICKED.

At last a young doctor comes and checks my baby for early mother damage.

"He's fine, lovely," says Mr Young-Attractive-Doctor.

"Oh, thank you. Thank you so much." Tears leg it from my eyes, race each other down my face, hop and skip over the only genuine smile my face has seen in a long, long time. The pleasant young man disappears from our lives, not realising the gift he's just given me. Us. Me and my child.

Right then, now it's time to examine his beautiful toes, and I do. The delicate fingers too, like they were created to make bobbin lace or carry out brain surgery. They curl round my finger like he knows he's mine. And I'm his. How can I make him feel safe when I don't feel safe myself? All I can do is my best.

"I love you precious, precious curly-haired boy."

The good thing about being a woman, or a mother woman is this multitasking thing. At the same time as being a mother to four children, coping with a life outside my body and head, I have the ability to start dying from the inside out. We women can juggle these things.

I'm such a bad person, I hate myself. You know, yourself, I wasn't supposed to be born, shouldn't be alive. Bet even Gloria hates me. Can we hack it without her? Live life without that woman? It reminds me of giving up smoking when I'd wonder how I'd manage normal things like a phone call without a fag. Seeing Gloria, getting new information and being heard – they are my reasons to be.

My husband comes to take us home. When the nice young nurse arrives he glances over at the crib with a big grin for the baby. The nurse carries the baby outside the building, like they do.

Patrick's about again, moaning about his ex-wife. But fair enough if she's doing all this to him. Poor bloke's just trying to do the right thing. I miss her, though, Ruth, who was much kinder than him. But she said she'd needed to take some time for things to settle after the divorce. "You understand, Mand." I said yes…but I didn't.

And now we just see Patrick and not Ruth. At least he's got his own flat now, still sees a lot of Tony and Hazel and Mum too. Mum helped him with a deposit after Dad died but at first, when he'd nowhere to go, Patrick moved in with us. Tony and Hazel didn't have enough room, they said.

"OK, for three months," my husband told me to tell him.

He agreed to pay a fiver a week but when he left eighteen months later he'd not paid a bean. Although…not all men in his position would still be paying for his daughter when they've been accused of something they haven't done. Eh? Now he just comes to see us and stays for dinner. Might as well, since he's over anyway.

"If only I could see my daughter. She's the only person I've ever loved." It's difficult seeing a grown man have to go through this.

I'm still not sleeping. The thinking is driving me nuts. I wonder if it's like being juiced up with chemotherapy – you know it's necessary but you wish there could be a different way. If this is the only way I'm not sure I want it.

Judy from the National Childbirth Trust comes round. They do this, these posh people, come round when someone's had a new baby and the support helps prevent them from cracking up. Ha. Judy was a social worker before the three children but she's still nice. Does loads for the NCT as well as runs the toddler group where we met when my daughter and her son were both at that stage.

I make us coffee. The house is tidy. Make-up on. The baby is five days old. My burly, thoughtful eldest son is five years old and at big school. My snowy-blond full-of-questions second son is at nursery. My daughter, in pink corduroy dungarees with rabbits on, runs, jumps, skips, bounces off the wall, shouts, screams, reads, sings, tries to whistle, then sleeps. With a periodic, gentle foot on the bouncy chair containing the baby I pace between the kitchen and front room, fussing over handmade biscuits, juice, coffees and being a new mum who's chatting brightly. I'm proud all the ironing is done. My thoughts blend as, with the shiniest smile I can muster, I tell Judy I'm finding it harder having four than three.

She frowns, not unsympathetic and looks so far into my eyes there's no hiding.

"I find it helps to have a good cry," she says. So I do. Blimey, do I? I'm sat on the arm of the chair opposite Judy and out comes the crying. It goes on and on and busts open another door that maybe wasn't supposed to open but it's the door that links reality to fiction and threatens to allow more truths in.

"Have you noticed how me and my beloved have this banter thing Judy?"

"I've always found it rather immature." Ouch… but.

The thinking won't stop. I feel so unsafe. I've started smoking again after eight years – eighty a day like John Wayne. My beloved starts again too though not as heavily. Like he says, he's not as bad as me.

I spend hours on the phone, specially calling Grace. But the dinner always makes it to the table on time. I lose weight, down to just over seven stone. Food repulses me. It's for fat people, and I like the way I can feel the curve of my ribs, my flat stomach. Simple.

Lean. Clean.

Next morning I look out the bedroom window. It's just after six o'clock. To the right in next door's back garden there's a large square that's been cordoned off. A sly wind creeps through the window, leaving me cold. I know then they've found me. The game's up. They know that by day I'm Mother Teresa and by night I'm Myra Hindley. They've found where I've buried the bodies of all the children that I've *killed*.

So, I was wrong – I *didn't* give birth to a baby last week. That was all a dream, vague now and soft round the edges like a Doris Day still. I shouldn't be wearing this pad, which I throw away since I won't be needing it. The reality is I'm a murderess and I'm going to prison where I'll be safe. At last.

Downstairs, I wonder who this man is. He's relaxing in the armchair, comfortable, territorial, says he's my husband.

"*What's your name?*"

When he tells me I grab this address book by the phone. Quick flick.

"*Who's this person then with the same first name?*"

Friend he worked with, he tells me. Obviously in cahoots with this man who's here to keep watch on me, collect evidence, make sure I don't kill anyone else. Or run away.

Looking through the address book I instantly spot addresses where I know bodies have been found by the police: Bristol, Reading, Sussex. I obviously do it at night, go visit these areas and kill people, adults and children. That's it! The man sitting here knows my crimes and exactly how bad I am. He's always known and his friend with the same name in the address book, his colleague, is in on it too. He's obviously working with the police. There, what did I tell you? The doctor's here now – he's in on it too. It's all been one big undercover job.

The doctor speaks with me and I talk, talk, talk. I tell him I know I've been put here to have children for the men. My husband's abusing me and the children. He's part of a gang of men who are the organisers and my mum and dad run a paedophile ring. I keep talking and talking with the doctor and eventually I come down, down, down and realise what's happened, where I am.

None of that was real. I *have* had a baby and I go get him from his crib. He's here now, safe in my arms. The cordoned area next door is where the neighbours have re-seeded their grass and want to keep the birds off.

My husband looks past me to the doctor. Lighting a fag he tells the doctor he doesn't know how to cope with this. The doctor gives my beloved the attention he needs. I'm worried too about him coping with it all and feel bad about it. He makes the tea while the doctor speaks to me.

"You swear a lot, don't you? Are you angry?"

"No." What's to be angry about? Best to stay positive, like Gloria said. I know he means well.

"I've come back to save the children," I tell the doctor, during my descent to earth. He nods his understanding.

"The reason this has happened is my ideal self is so far removed from my perception of myself."

"When people intellectualise at me I suggest they say how they're *feeling*."

There's a gap then where the words should go so, duty-bound, I fill it.

"Is it puerperal psychosis?" I've read but never heard the diagnosis spoken out loud so I pronounce it wrong.

"It is," says the doctor, gently pronouncing it correctly. He talks about medication.

"But would I have to stop breast-feeding?"

"Let's say I make the decision and take responsibility for it."

This great blockage, like a flow of sewage, whacks its way into my throat from nowhere and the tears come, working their way around the turds and piss of life, with loud, can't-be-stopped sobs. This is so bad. How can I not breast-feed my child? He'll suffer. I really am a shit mother.

"We're trying to prevent you being hospitalised. It's better if we can keep you at home."

"It would be helpful if you can try not to be angry with her," the doctor suggests to my man as he walks in, tuts, then agrees.

I'm seven years old. I'm sharing a bed with mum and as I face her back I'm desperate for her to make the bad stuff go away but she doesn't. What am I going to do? What will happen to me? Crying doesn't help, doesn't take it away. I'm supposed to finish making the white felt mouse at school but I just can't. Everyone else has more or less completed theirs. It's to be done by tomorrow and I've hardly started. I can't do it. It's too hard. *Impossible.* I can't tell Mum, she'll kill me. She knows how bad I am. I can't sleep. It's like worms fill my body, pumping, pumping, trying to burst through the skin and nothing will make them stop. Please, someone, help me.

I learn how to make up bottles of formula milk, first time ever with all this sterilising shit. It means, though, my husband can give the baby his milk. One hand bottle, one hand fag. He wears a suit now he's started the new job, well, shirt and tie. Handsome, very smart, more ironing.

When we talk in the evening he tells me how hard all this is for him. His new job is exciting and I envy him being able to get out there, get good at something, chase and win work, run the work, get paid for the work. He's scared and I try to soothe him, think positive.

The pills the doctor gave me make me feel odd. The thoughts remain but float unattached to each other while I try thinking positive.

It's decided that Grace will be the 'middle man' who will contact the three people with the same name as my birth mother. The first two are blow-outs but the third B. McCourt is Bernard McCourt and it turns out he's my mother's uncle, the one she was named after. Grace writes to tell him her name is Vivienne Michele (my birth name) and she's an old work mate of Bernadette's from years back in London.

I phone Trevor and ask him to give his brother, my husband, lots of support. He's going through a tough time and needs it but best not say I phoned, better if it's come from Trevor so he's not offended. He agrees and the minutes slink into the hours of another day.

One of the bedrooms is being decorated and it's out of bounds. The next evening I hear men's voices coming from inside the room. Frightened, I put my face to the closed door. Yep, I can hear their low murmurs... and realise they're making plans to *kill* me. And that my husband is in their gang, part of the plot.

Back in the kitchen I place the Sabatier knives neatly in a line, side by side on the draining board. Next thing I know the doctor's arrived. And Judy – I'd phoned her.

I tell them both my husband is trying to kill me and there are other men in the bedroom upstairs, all part of the same gang. I go up first and, trance-like, take the phone off the hook in our bedroom.

Judy and the doctor check the bedroom. It's hard getting them to believe me as they clearly want proof.

"Check the wardrobe. *Please* just check it."

Judy sees I'm terrified and does it.

"There's nothing in there, just an empty bedroom being decorated."

Back in the kitchen I point out the knives, lined up, menacing. I tell them it's a message, a threat from him that if I tell he'll kill me.

They look confused.

"I bet you can't phone the police either. He's cut the phone off so it won't work. Go on, try it, try it."

Judy looks first at me then at the phone in her hand. Nothing. No dialling tone.

Someone makes coffee. Me and Judy are in the kitchen. The men, doctor and husband, talk in low murmurs in the front room.

"I've been locked in so long I don't know how to get out. There's no key, no lock and no door." As I say it my husband walks in.

"It's important to get out sometimes even though you've got the children." She's sweet Judy, thinks I mean it's the house I can't get out of.

My husband agrees we could go out then talks about his distress. He looks at Judy, pleading, eyebrows furrowed, puts effort into it.

"It's hard for you with a new job." Judy tells him. "It must have been like living with a time bomb."

We get through that day and zip onto another. Nice

crisp ironed shirts and packed lunch for my husband. On the way to school I scream a long one. The passenger seat's empty. Oh no! Where's my daughter, where's my daughter, where's my DAUGHTER? She was here when I just looked. Now, nothing but the empty seat! Oh, no, oh, no, oh, no… After a few minutes I realise she's back at the house with her dad, who's off work this morning.

Later that day there's something I need to do before I collect my son from school. I drive fast to the doctor's surgery, run up to the reception desk and ask for my doctor. He's not there. Panic shrouds my body, makes me sweat though my hands go cold. What will I do?

I whisper at the receptionist, "Please give him this note?" It's too dangerous to say it, gotta write it down. I grab a leaflet and pen from the desk and scribble away in the bits where there's white space; above the meningitis, below the rash. The receptionist looks at me strange, then looks down where I've written "It's my husband – it's HIM".

Next stop, school. I collect my son, and, shaking, I tell his teacher my husband is abusing me and the children. With the other three already safely in the car I drive to Judy's. There's hubbub there too as her own three bundle in from school and playschool.

"My husband's abusing me and the children." Eyebrows scrunched, Judy makes us coffee and we sit at the small round table in her kitchen. She offers me a plate of homemade peanut-butter biscuits. It's soothing here. A safe house.

"I've got to call social services and your husband."

I nod. Whatever she thinks is OK. It's OK. It's OK. It's OK. Isn't it?

"That's why I picked you – you're a social worker. Were." She's puzzled but puts a hand on my arm.

Two people arrive from social services – a man and woman. Then my husband. They keep him in the front room away from me and the children. They talk in low voices. I smoke, lighting one fag from the other from the other from the other as I pace round the kitchen. The kids play quietly with play-dough. (Judy makes it too – blue, yellow, green and red, sometimes pink.)

The door bursts open. It's him, looking for matches, he says.

"Get him away!" I can't face him – he'll *kill* me for telling.

"This is ridiculous, keeping me away. You're being stupid. I just need a light." His face is dark.

Judy gives him matches and escorts him back out.

"That's it, the matches!" The fear, visible, I know it, strikes through me like lightning.

"What?"

"When he strikes a match! It's a warning for me not to *tell*."

"Why, though?"

"Matches, matches, never touch; they can hurt you very much."

"Sounds like a children's rhyme to me."

"You don't believe me, do you, Judy?"

"Well…"

"I understand why you wouldn't but can you understand how frightening it is not to be believed?"

"Yes." She asks me questions and I get 'talked' back down, realise what's happened. It wasn't real. Again. But the fear is *screamingly* real.

Judy explains to the man and woman from social services and they leave. My husband drives home and I follow him.

I'm seven years old. It's dinnertime at school. When I get my pink semolina something's wrong and I don't know what. I should be glad it's not tapioca, with its dollop of jam on top. As a child Dad, hospitalised with tuberculosis, told the nurse tapioca makes him sick. She made him eat it anyway and when he puked it back up she made him eat that too. Maybe nothing's wrong – it's just me. The wet on my face surprises me as tears plink down my face before my mouth gets busy with the semolina. Looking round it's like someone took out the lights. The colours have seeped away leaving the huge room all over the same shade of grey, grey, grey.

Late that night I call the police. I tell them my husband and a gang of men are trying to kill me. Then I go to sit in the front room and watch telly with my beloved.

The doorbell goes. As my husband answers it I creep up behind him, curious. On the doorstep there are four policemen. What do they want? They immediately surround my beloved, don't let him go anywhere. I'm not sure why. But they let him talk and he tells them I'm having problems, tells them to call the doctors, they'll back him up.

So much for the tablets. Another flip. Next day the doctor tells me I'm to be hospitalised.

"You can go in voluntarily. Or otherwise."

"What if I don't want to?"

"I'm a gambler and a con-man," he says. "There are ways of getting you in there."

The good news is I can breast-feed again because I've come off the (fucking useless) tablets. The bad news is the baby has lost the reflex and can't do it anymore.

He's got used to the bottle and I'm gutted. I cry buckets. Buckets.

Pacing. I do a lot of it. Then I curl up on the floor, gas fire full on, in the front room. The June sun shines fifteen-tog rays through the window but still I need the fire.

The NCT send other mums round to bath the children. I phone a few friends as well as Ruth.

Sometimes Grace stays the night and does a night feed. She talks into the night with my husband. Opposite sofas. I don't always sleep so I join them, listen and watch from the chair, feel guilty I'm putting them both through this. He takes a turn with the baby, hand on bottle, hand on fag. We laugh as I tell her that on my last flip, pacing the floor, I felt like I'm gifted. She's straight-faced.

"What?" I laugh.

"I think you are!"

Me and my husband laugh again.

That day, later, pacing from room to room, something comes back to me. Not this, though. NO, PLEASE, NO, DON'T BE THIS. I'm not ready, don't want it in my head but the thought does its own thing, balloons, battles its way through, won't stop till it's HEARD. It will be HEARD. OK, OK, I hear it but I don't like it and it proves how guilty and bad I am. I carry on doing normal things. Dinner is on the table at the right time. But instead of remaining like an old film I once watched, the thought comes to the fore of my mind, fresh, like the blood of a sacrificed lamb.

That night when my husband arrives home in his shirt and tie with his empty lunch box I sit in the kitchen with him. I need to tell him this but I'm scared he'll kill me.

"Promise you won't get angry if I tell you something?"

He tuts, watches me arrange mashed potato on his plate.

"Depends what it is."

Here goes!

"Patrick…" And I tell him what happened.

"You angry?"

"Why didn't you tell me before?"

"I only remembered today."

He starts on his dinner. He's home a bit later today – he must be famished.

"When I was little." I can't see properly, my head's gone somewhere and I don't know where. But life's moved a degree on the compass, like being in the same place but in a different dimension. Life can't be the same again now it's out, now I've snitched. No-one wants to be a grass.

I'm seven years old. And very tiny. I go upstairs for something. No one else is home. Patrick calls me into the boys bedroom. I do what he tells me. My pseudo-brother Patrick is fifteen years old and very tall. Over six feet tall. He's lying on the bed with no clothes on. Oh.

"Shut the door."

I do what he tells me.

"Take your clothes off."

I do what he tells me.

"Get up here." I do what he tells me. Is he angry with me? I want to please him.

Afterwards he sends me away. Have I disappointed him?

"You'll sleep well tonight now you've got a clear conscience," says my beloved.

And I do. I'm right to worship my beloved – he's got all the answers.

I can't bear this waiting for a hospital place though. It's driving me mad. Ha. The local mother and baby (post-natal depression) unit is full. Overfull. Instead I'm booked into the psychiatric unit at the local general hospital. I tell the doctors what I recently remembered.

"Do you remember what Patrick told you, about not telling? What was said… it can be significant." Despite the doctor's nudge nothing blips into my head.

"No."

My last day at home, I'm in bed sleeping. Just as I'm going off I swear I see the bedroom door swing open. In walks Patrick – he looks dark. And see-through.

"Don't tell your Mum, she'll *kill* you."

I sit up quick. Something cold runs up my back. It's daytime but I can't believe how dark it is in here. Large clouds join up, become one, swish round the room, and gently, gently release themselves lower, lower onto me until I'm fully covered. The darkness penetrates my skin, oozes round my body. I can't get comfortable. Nowhere in the bed is safe.

By the time I'm due to go to hospital my body has changed. My mouth is so dry it's weird, difficult to speak. I no longer walk but shuffle. I'm only fucking shuffling slowly round the room like an old, old woman. And my hands have turned inwards like from real bad arthritis. It's frightening because I look like a proper insane person, a genuine inmate from One Flew Over The Cuckoo's Nest. I realise then, seeing myself like this, that once I go into the insane asylum I won't be coming out. Nobody, anywhere (till I ask the staff, days later) tells me it's the side effects of the drugs, which luckily I'm stopping.

At the hospital, in my room, I'm straight onto the bed and curl up in its centre. Safe. But I'm not allowed to stay in bed, have to join everyone else in the day room.

It's like something off a scary documentary. I'm locked in this ward with a bunch of loons. No one's coming in or out of here, let me tell you. In the toilet, there's a pretend mirror on the wall, plastic with a pink tinge and it doesn't show you back what you give it. It's like those fun mirrors at the fair but not quite as fun.

Some of the staff, specially the big fat one, Jim, shout at the patients to get up, to wash, to tidy their things, answer when he talks to them. I phone my husband, whisper I'm afraid I'll be raped.

The patients are weird. Nutters. There's this young woman called Jasmine from Greece. She's really tall and she talks to herself. She's always walking. Big strides. You'll be looking at her and she might look back and swear something in Greek. Or, more likely, she seems not to notice you looking, then she puts her hand under her waistband, brings out her two 'fag' fingers, wet, draws them up to her face and inhales deeply, appreciatively, like a wine taster. Perhaps she's starving and thinks she's just arrived at the fish-and-chip shop. She doesn't give a fuck who's there – visitors, whoever – nor does she mind where she does it as she moves across the dining room atop her long, long legs at meal times. I can't eat anyway and when she does it I just stare and stare at the grey and white plastic salt and pepper pots. Well, okay, I've shouted at her to fuck off a couple of times but I'm not at my best, am I? The staff have a go at her. Sometimes she shouts at them, other times she'll laugh. They say she can't help it.

But I settle in, get talking to Pamela. She's an alcoholic and her boyfriend's violent, as is she. In a farewell gesture of love they knocked seven bells out of each other. Tells me all her problems and I listen as well as I can as she goes round and round with the 'yes buts' of her own dark, heavy life. I try to make suggestions but I'm fucked by it. My head! I can't take any more in. Please! When I tell a member of staff he says, "Don't do it. Don't take on other people's problems." It's Jim and he doesn't rape me. Or shout. Not at me.

Next day my baby joins me but still won't take the breast. They put us on twenty-four-hour watch. At all times there's a member of staff with me and my curly-haired boy in case I hurt my son but I don't hurt him, why would I? He's meant to be here, it's *me* that never was.

When my husband visits he tells me Bernadette has phoned. First she thought Grace was me until Grace explained and put her in touch with my beloved. Bernadette's still with my birth father, she said, *and* they went on to have three more daughters. Yes, three. Which they kept. They work from home and she can't wait to see me so a visit is arranged.

My husband tries to contact my psychiatrist to see if he thinks it's a good idea for me to be told about the birth parents but by the time he gets back with a 'no' it's too late and I already know they're coming.

In the nut-house I get a timetable and have to go to groups. Sewing. Art. In the sewing room I make *and* finish a white felt mouse and leave them the cardboard pattern in the sewing room in case anyone else got stuck when they were seven.

At the weekends we have to fry a breakfast. Wow, I've never done this before, four kids and married a thousand years – such an experience. Occupational therapy, they call it. People, inmates, keep coming up, ask me if I'm a nurse and I don't know why. It's the same in shops, people often think I work there.

After breakfast I'm allowed home on a visit for practice at living in the normal world again. So Grace baby-sits and my husband phones Patrick who's staying at Tony and Hazels. He arranges for him to meet us at Mum's. I'm doing what the books tell you to do.

Before Patrick arrives I tell Mum what happened when I was seven.

"Well, it's obviously had no effect on you," she says.

I think of my comfy bed at the psychiatric unit.

"I was hoping you'd stick up for me."

She softens like a Rich-Tea biscuit, rubbery, as it falls into an old lady's tea-cup. "If I'd known I would have cut his cotton off!" She laughs. It feels good she's on my side.

"Makes me think now… when one of the foster kids… she was bleeding. But the doctor said it was nothing."

When Patrick arrives, me and him move to the dining room. My husband stays in the front room, Mum's in the kitchen. I start talking to Patrick, remind him what happened in that bedroom that day when I was that seven-year-old. When I tell him what I know Mum goes out the back door, off up the garden.

"But it only happened a couple of times." Did it? Or is he mixing me up with someone else?

He's upset though. Says he's sorry. Cries.

"What have I done to you? You're the only person I ever loved."

"I'm here for you Patrick."

I can't bear it, seeing him cry like this. I've never seen him so upset, ever. Poor Patrick. Somehow we get on to the subject of his daughter, who's been like family to me and my children.

"You *do* believe I didn't do it?"

"I want to." And I can't give him any more than that.

After my visit to the insane asylum that's my mother's house I go back to the sanity of the psychiatric unit where it's easier to make sense of things.

Some friends visit including Tony, with Hazel trailing behind him. And Ruth, who comes alone. I say to her we should have some ground rules about who not to talk about – like guess who. She tells me it's going to court, this thing with her little girl and Patrick. She says the doctor at Great Ormond Street told her Patrick has sexually abused their daughter. I remember our ground rules... then tell her what I just remembered about me and Patrick when I was seven and he was fifteen.

"Tell me this," Ruth says. "Would you let him babysit your little girl?"

When I don't answer she says it confirms what she's to do.

"Will you give a statement to the Court?"

"Don't know if it'll help."

"My solicitor says we can have you subpoenaed. This is my daughter. You'd do the same to protect your children."

"Oh." She also tells me he's *not* been paying for their daughter. Oh, again.

You'll never guess who else comes to visit me. Gloria. Gloria in Excelsis. There's a case conference with a whole group of people gathered, doctor, social workers, Gloria, blah blah, the whole bit. Just to talk about me. Blimey. And after this meeting she visits me. She hands me a book Families and How to Survive Them by Robin Skynner and John Cleese. A book about the meaning of life – or families anyway.

When I tell her Ruth wants me to give a statement she wonders why I'm protecting Patrick.

"Didn't know I was."

"What about protecting any other children?"

"I'm frightened. What if he didn't do it?" Though the words leap out they topple back down and crawl across the floor, wounded. The game's up.

"At what price do you want his approval? Believe me, after you've made the decision you'll feel better, you'll feel relieved. It's much worse this side of the decision."

I feel so heavy with it all. I look down at the book.

Inside she's written a message to us both – "If John Cleese can do it so can you two!" I wonder if the authors' families are like mine.

I phone Mum, see how she is.

"I can't come and see you Mand. I can't stand those places, make me feel funny."

When I tell her I've been in touch with Patrick's ex, who she hates, she says I'm to promise I won't say anything about Patrick and me. When I was seven.

"You know you're not thinking straight at the moment, what with being in that place. Patrick was a teenager. He was only experimenting, after all."

"What about the foster child who was bleeding?"

"Well, she was dirty, yes, but the doctor said it was nothing." But now I'm wondering about his own sisters blah blah, the one's he 'didn't get on with'.

When I see the psychiatrist it's two things. It's depressing because of what we talk about but it's also such a buzz speaking with someone with great intelligence and it satisfies a hunger I didn't know I had.

I talk to him about what happened with me and Patrick and about Ruth wanting me to give a statement for court. I don't know what to do. I'm so scared. Patrick could get into trouble, couldn't he? And it'd all be my fault.

"You're not responsible for what he did to you or his daughter. He is."

"What if he does it to other children? What if he does worse than that?"

"Not all child molesters go on to murder children," he says.

"Mum says I'm not thinking straight."

"You're expressing yourself very clearly to me."

"I'm scared it means I'll abuse my own children."

"No. I think that's your worst fantasy."

Well, thank God. Dear, dear God, thank you. I've read up on it and driven everyone nuts obsessing I either will or have, without my knowledge and theirs, sexually abused my own children. When the darkness sends the thought back to punish me over and over I remember what the psychiatrist said.

Chapter 9: Meet the Fockers

My beloved tells me he's sick of it all. It's so depressing for him. And I'm sure that's true. Despite this he kindly buys me a new outfit for the big meet with my parents tomorrow. A longish turquoise dress, pleated skirt, polyester. He likes Maggie Thatcher. Was he thinking of her when he bought the dress or the peach plastic bangle with matching clip-on earrings for my pierced ears? Ah – I love his little boy-ness.

The hospital lends us a room. It's small, square and lined with orange and grey plastic chairs. I wonder how dumpy my mother will be. I can't wait to discover the things I've always wanted to know. Twenty-eight years in the waiting and OH GOD – like an apparition – here she is! In walks this tall, blonde, glamorous, slim woman who looks like the actress Kate O'Mara. High heels. Giorgio perfume.

She throws her arms around me. My mother, Bernadette. At last. This is the safest I have ever, ever felt. Nothing can touch this. Nothing. There's simply no substitute for being liked by your mother. None. Going from being Most Wanting to *most* wanted, well, bliss.

"Not a day's gone by that I haven't thought about you." Never mind the clichés, this is my Mother! M-U-

T-H-E-R of mine. Motherrrr. We both cry and she absorbs my tears with a tissue, pats away my past with a smile and another hug. My father, George, joins in with our tears.

"I've never seen George cry," she says.

She's lovely. I'm so proud of her. He's handsome too, a bit Michael Caine but not a lot of people know that. She calls me her sunshine and knows my favourite colour is green because the other prime colours are covered by the girls. Yes. It's true. I really have got three sisters too! I always wanted a sister and now I've got three. This is *some* fairy tale. Oh, and they're millionaires. It's good to know I come from successful stock.

They tell me they live in the biggest house in the best road in their town. When Bernadette told my husband they work from home, from the garage, I naturally thought… Well, you would, wouldn't you? What's funny and rather lovely is that my husband has gained a new respect for me since meeting his new millionaire in-laws. I've not seen him like this before and he's specially like it in front of them. He includes me, smiles, asks questions – even waits for an answer.

Maybe he was always this way and I just never noticed all these years. He's making a real effort, truly cares about the marriage and I do appreciate it. Can it *get* any better?

"I'll think of you like a son," George tells my husband, his arm round the shoulder of the taller, younger man. George the property developer talks of giving my husband thousands of metres of ceiling work in an office block.

I stare at the photos they've brought. A big smiley one of them in a restaurant in Eilat where they go every

January. MY FATHER puts their phone number on the back, says to ring any time. There's a picture of MY GRANDMOTHER who can't wait to meet me and two of MY AUNTS: Marge (who told MY MOTHER not to tell their mother about 'the baby' as it'd kill her – ha!) with Vivienne Michelle, who I was named after. Except she's got two 'l's. She's my mother's favourite baby sister and she's Vivienne after Vivienne Leigh because their mother, my Grandmother went into labour watching Gone with the Wind at the cinema.

There's another photo of three beautiful young women in a garden, dressed up really posh. Ball gowns. They're called ball gowns and it's as if they've stepped off a Disney screen. My very own sisters wearing their very own ball gowns.

I'm so happy and keep saying so. They pay me lashings of attention, Bernadette and George and notice things about me.

"I'm proud of you," says George. Oh my God, imagine having a parent that's proud of you. Fuck.

"Swear a lot, don't you?" says Bernadette.

Yes, but I keep my children.

"Do you like my dress? My beloved chose it."

"Is that what you normally wear?"

"I love suits."

"Me too." We hold hands, the three of us. Then with both hands I hold my mother's slim, elegant wrist. She's beautiful, truly. Special. Fantastic. How could I ever choose anyone better? I couldn't, nobody could. Not if I'd had first pick out of the box.

"That's pretty." It's three-colour gold, her bracelet.

"George says you shall have an allowance like the other girls." Gets me thinking, maybe I could get Mum some counselling. She's had a rotten time of it.

"George flies. We'll take you to Le Touquet for lunch. And take the kids to Disney World. We could all go – a big family holiday."

Gosh. My father! And he's doing his night-flying licence. Would have thought you just switch the lights on, but no.

They think my baby is beautiful, which he is.

"He looks like George." Maybe the eyebrows.

They agree with most of the adoption story I've been told. Bernadette says for three months she couldn't bring herself to sign the forms. She and George were both with other partners at the time I was begat. Interesting but then how does she know who the fa..? Anyway, she wanted to keep me. He didn't. He being him who's definitely my father.

"I was a young bloke with everything going for me. I was engaged to someone else and didn't want to be… encumbered… with a baby."

"I basically chased him for two years before we got together."

Someone pinch me. There's more smiling going on in this room than at a hyena's wedding. When they leave my mother says she'll come back tomorrow on her own. My beloved leaves too after a bit but not before he reassures me how much he loves me.

Back at the day room I clutch the photo of my smiling PARENTS looking tanned and gorgeous. I'm still looking at it in the canteen. I can't eat my sloppy fish pie anyway so when Jasmine walks by, sniffs her fingers and shoots her arm in the air like she's conducting her favourite Tchaikovsky I really don't care. My baby sleeps through it all.

Pamela's really pleased for me, writes a poem about how special I am. Lynne's pleased too, Lynne with the gammy leg.

"You deserve this." She's warm, thoughtful. A young woman in her early twenties, she's depressed. They gave her a council flat but she 'can't cope' with it so keeps coming back into hospital.

Do we ever *really* know why others get depressed? How many are willing or able to dig to the bottom? Is it easier to call it 'clinical' and bung some medication at it? It's a miracle some people *don't* get depressed, I reckon. Lynne acquired her gammy leg five years ago after this cabby raped her and as she tried to get away he slammed the door on her leg. She's not told them – well, I think one doctor knew – and she hates her leg. It's twice the size of the other one and bandaged up all the time. On its way out too, not long for this world. It's going to get amputated. Lynne can't wait, bloody useless, sticking out in front of her wheelchair like that.

Then there's Mary. She's not pleased about my parents or anything else. She's neither here nor there and can't hear other people when they speak about their own lives. Mary has 'clinical' depression and a 'miserable fucker' husband. She's booked in for another lot of ECT. She's had it before and her husband says it helps. Mind, after she has it done she doesn't seem any happier to me. And she's still married to *him*. The marriages some people put up with! Be worth going on Old Sparky if the husband got buzzed away too. That'd really cheer you up, wouldn't it? To wake up and find your 'miserable fucker' husband has been fizzed by the machine and isn't coming back, like a fly on a butcher's shop zapper. I wonder if that would help her 'clinical' depression.

When Bernadette returns next day she's wearing a suit.

"I always thought if I stayed with George you'd come back to me." That's George the millionaire (now), not the other man she was also seeing, Dan, the one who drives a van. Yep, yep, I know, Dan the man with a van.

She has *the* most beautiful, huge smile, this woman and she keeps telling me how clever I am! I am so on cloud nine. Imagine having a mother who tells you you're clever. This is so good it's cry-worthy, though I'm smiling loads. More even than on my wedding day...but then she likes me.

"I've brought you a present."

It's a three-colour gold bangle.

"I tried to get one the same as mine. It's similar."

What can I say? It's not about things. Never was. I'm floating to be so liked. I've found the bit that's been missing for so long. Small yet enormous. Is this all it takes to want to live, to know someone cares about you?

It's strange being adopted. In life whatever you do you know your mum still wants you. So if even your mum doesn't want you – well – there must be something *seriously* wrong with you...me.

Bernadette's had years of therapy, sorry, analysis. She says it wasn't till she'd done twelve years that she admitted she'd had a baby adopted. I wonder how it affects the next child, children?

"Every time I think of leaving my analyst that's when I get results." (Does her analyst worry he'll lose something... his hold... some income?)

"All I saw were your eyebrows. One eyebrow. I knew if I looked at you properly I wouldn't go through with it."

Was this the start of my invisibility? We hold hands

the whole time she's here. I feel like I've come home, slung off my shoes and put the kettle on. Bernadette asks would I like to come and stay on my next weekend home? Would I? Do the starving want food? Do the ugly want make-up? Would Robinson Crusoe fancy a five-night cruise, including Friday? Yes, I'd like that very much.

Next visit Bernadette and George bring MY SISTER, my very own sister. She's twenty-one, tall and beautiful, like her (our) mother. Both women are wearing suits. My sister's is a Prince of Wales check and – look at that! – gorgeous high heels. Her legs are so long. What happened there then? I quickly glance downwards.

My sister immediately hugs me, cries and whispers, "I love you." Perhaps I misheard it or she mis-said it?

Since I've been in the psychiatric unit I've not flipped. Course I miss my husband. And look, no, over here – no pills! It's weird being this 'high' when what seems like moments ago I was so low. Am I enjoying a manic phase?

Bernadette wants to bring me 'home from the hospital' like she didn't all those years ago. My beloved comes to get the baby first. Then she does it. My Mother brings me home from the hospital in her bright red Mercedes sports car with its squished-up back-seats with pygmy room only. And the roof's off!

The house is impressive. Once through the big electronic gates I spot the Rolls Royce heading a line of other cars, snaked in front of the house underneath tall, thick arches atop strong pillars. It's like something off Dallas. Is Bobby Ewing upstairs in the shower, ready to rejoin his life at the ranch? Are we both about to wake up from a long dream?

No one else is home except the two fuck-off German

Shepherds scanning the yard, with the freedom to roam the house. Great. I'm terrified of these dogs ever since one bit me on the mouth as a teenager, leaving my lip hanging off. Luckily Mum didn't kill me, wasn't even too annoyed! I know that dogs can smell fear so I try not to smell of fear but it's quite hard, it's a place I know well. I look over my shoulder, see if they're sniffing more than usual. Smile. See, I'm not scared of you. See how naturally I'm acting. Head-fuck!

There's a double staircase spiralling up, up, up from the floor, Cinderella-like. Goes all the way to heaven, I suppose. And this great marble floor in the hallway, acres of grand elegance. I'm expecting Scarlett O'Hara to dash downstairs in her swishy skirts and beg Rhett not to leave. There are loads of rooms so it's easy to get lost. I should feel guilty being here without my beloved but I feel so free, so *liked* that, frankly, my dear, I don't give a fuck.

Suppose I'm a big fat liar because when I was looking for my birth mother (parents) I said I was curious but *not* looking for a mother replacement. That's ever so slightly rubbish. I can see that now. This 'having a mother-that-likes-you' thing is something I could get used to. Delicious.

Bernadette shows me round the house. Some of her books are the same as mine. Exactly the flippin' same. Specially books on assertiveness. Look – A Woman in your Own Right!

Dark wooden cupboards surround us in the kitchen. There's a fat-bastard fridge-freezer and when you place a glass in this hole in the door it vomits out juice – then ice-cubes! And there's this special tap next to the sink that pours out near-boiling water so you can have coffee straight away, no kettle. Ta-dah!

George comes in from his office in the garage. Then the girls. My lovely blonde sister again who, at twenty-one, is seven years younger than me. She's the next one down. As soon as Bernadette and George married she fell pregnant. Why do we say that – 'fell pregnant'? Is it like you're walking down the road towards the Co-op, trip over, skirt blows up and along swims some sperm being chased by terrorists and in need of cover? Nothing to do with the adult humans involved at all. Not their responsibility!

My next lovely sister is nineteen. She's sweet, short and dark-haired – like me. And she's quiet – not like me and I feel a bit protective. Here's my youngest sister, the 'baby'. Like the others her face is similar to mine but again she's tall and blonde, reminding me of a younger me. She's fifteen and teenage shy or I want to think so.

"Everyone knows I think 'the baby' is the best thing since sliced bread," Bernadette doesn't mind admitting. Fancy having a favourite. Is it a gift or a curse for my youngest sister? And confessing in front of others too! But the three girls are fantastic. Utterly. And we've all got the same flattish noses; my mother, me, the three girls and ALL my children. Ha. Something of my very own at last. Mine. A bit of identity though ours is a lesser version of the original.

My beautiful next-down sister works in the business. Her days consist of bombing around building sites in her Jeep, swearing at the blokes where necessary. She doesn't always like her job she tells me, but it's expected so she has to do it. It's a job I would've loved.

She's louder than the others, like my own bouncy daughter.

"You *have* to like my dogs," she says. Oh dear. I

smile, say I'll do my best, remember the eight-year wait for plastic surgery. Well, they *are* her pets. It's better if we all like each other. Life's about compromise – so say my assertiveness books.

My sweet dark-haired sister is clever and taking a degree that's property related. She's to spend a year in Arizona. She's friendly, gentle, a tad invisible.

Then my youngest sister, who's still at school is talking about going to the Lucy Clayton finishing school. Why? What has she started? Should I have gone too, learned how to finish things? Maybe my husband should go to 'starting' school since he's got a fear or a something of starting things though he pretends he hasn't. I don't think it's that he's thick and lazy – he's *always* mowed the lawn and done all the overtime. I remind myself that Trevor said he's a simple man and I feel bad for expecting too much. Confirmation again of how evil I am.

If you woke up one morning, realised you've now got three sisters (when you always wanted a sister) you couldn't fault this set. They're a great collection. But it's my Mother I've wondered over for so long, though my father's of great interest too. Specially now I don't have one.

Dad died three years before I met my father. He nearly got what he wanted too. "When I go," as he'd snatched his fag from his mouth, exhaled, "I want to be sitting on this stool at the bar."

That's the bar at the Post Office where he and his postmen mates spent hours guzzling their way through the overtime. If his shifts hadn't been changed around that day that's exactly where he would've been. Instead he was at home in the front room. He and Mum had just had a big fry-up, even had a cuddle, she said later. She was in the kitchen and heard a roaring sound, came in and saw he was slumped. Over the phone the doctor told her to try getting his heart going. She'd been trying that for years and it never worked. Now too she had a go but it was a massive coronary and Mum couldn't change its mind. He was fifty-seven. My Dad. He who taught me how to whistle, how to have a laugh and through his stories how to fail at school in a way that entertains. We went over to the house later that night, me and my beloved. There was a wet patch on the floor where his body had been. After a life full of laughs I guess that's where he pissed himself.

My beloved's obviously missing me. During the afternoon he phones the house of his new millionaire mother and father-in-law to let me know there's an interesting program on telly tonight.

"That's not why he phoned." My Mother smiles. She's quite knowing. Suppose the twice a week analysis helps, along with the books.

"He wants to be here too." She so understands. Everyone should have a mother like Bernadette. Right here and now I feel sorry for those who never will, envy those who always did.

In one of the rooms there's a wooden and brass plaque. The words written on it are by U.S. President Calvin Coolidge: -

> *Nothing in the world can take the place of persistence. Talent will not; nothing is more common than unsuccessful men with talent. Genius will not; unrewarded genius is almost a proverb. Education will not; the world is full of educated derelicts. Persistence and determination alone are*

omnipotent.

A few sentences that can change your life forever. If you get off your arse and do it. If you think you deserve it. If you're not afraid of success while believing you're afraid of failing and don't choose people who'd rather you didn't succeed either thank you very much.

Will I be able to use these words now I've read them? Me and my 'yes, but' husband together? Will we strive forward in life and be successful like my birth parents? He's being so lovely now, I think we've finally cracked it, turned that razor sharp corner. Of *course* we can do it. United we stand! Or will it take me another twenty years and a miracle to realise I deserve better? To get over that last big hurdle, stop holding myself back by choosing people who hold me back? Hark at me being negative!

Bernadette and George take me into the TV room. A cosy room with sofas, plain white walls and Tudor-ish beams.

There are framed photographs on the wall. They're mostly black and white, some older – sepia, some newer. Bernadette and George talk me through who's who. George's Great-Great-Grandfather who was tailor to the King. Forget which King or how many Greats. George's even got a cousin who's head of Psychiatry at the Tavistock in North London. Am I ashamed Dad was a postman? Or that Mum rarely gets off her arse unless it's on an errand for her bossy, demanding, spoilt, fractious stomach? A bit.

Mind you Bernadette's cousin Anne is on the dole, does some sessions in a pub. Bernadette used to give her money but it didn't help Anne look for work so she stopped. Bernadette also gave her Mum, my

Grandmother, money but found out she gave it to Anne so stopped that too.

Funny seeing the photographs dating back so far. And not so far.

"Who's this getting married?"

"That's me and George." She smiles at me. I look at the date. I was seven years old.

"So... while I was being abused you were getting married?" Silence.

I lose interest in the other pictures. The three of us snuggle up on the squishy print sofa and watch telly. They've got this huge satellite thing on the roof and get telly from all over the world!

Dinner's at the local Indian. She's took it in, the assertiveness books. When she gets her masala she asserts her culinary rights, "Are these peas frozen or tinned?"

Likes what she likes. It's good we're finding out about each other. She likes wine a lot too, like I do.

"Wish you had long hair." How quick could it grow? Silly to get it wrong over something like that. It's good spending time though, she's chatty tonight.

"Shame your name's not Amanda. Mandy... it's a bit..."

Bernadette tells me she was her dad's favourite but when Vivienne was born his attention shifted onto the baby. Says she felt abandoned then, still feels insecure.

"Her insecurity, Bernie's, it gets me down," George says to me, "I tell her if she wants to be miserable she'll have to do it by herself. I've decided *I'm* going to be *happy*."

Bernadette tells me about a secretary they had. Their number plate on the Roller has Bernadette's initials on it and as they're talking The Secretary says, "That's really nice of George to let you have your name on his car."

You hear that? The sound of a squidgy thud on concrete – it's The Secretary dropping a bollock. They've got a different secretary now.

"I keep telling her." To me, "Don't I Bernie?" To her.

"You need to sort your insecurity out. I'm not a bad looking bloke, got a few bob, drive a Roller. I'm a good catch… could go off with other women," grinning, "but I'm with you!"

Her turn. "People ask me how George became successful. I tell them it's because he's got me!" We have a laugh then.

They talk about when George drove a black cab by day, ran snooker halls by night around Shoreditch, late fifties. The Krays were looking for him at one point but he says it got sorted out. Bernadette was a club hostess when I was born, I assume they met at a club but don't get round to asking.

He got sick of working eighteen hour days so he learnt bricking, took on a gang of blokes. In the seventies a development site came up, they got a loan and went for it. Been property developers ever since.

Is this where I got the bug for doing 'the bags' albeit tiny by comparison… but is it in the blood, liking business? Feel a bit sad about 'the bags.' It's like a baby that died. But my beloved went on so much it was easier to stop in the end. Afterwards, he tells everyone he didn't want me to stop – just to cut down. Pin Money rules! Pin Money's OK. Yay – we love Pin Money! Down with proper success. Boo Hiss. We hate the 'S' word.

At bedtime we fly up the curved staircase with its

huge wide steps. If the kids were here we could stand side by side wearing curtains and go up together singing 'These are a few of my favourite things'. I'm in a spare room with its own bathroom – like the other five bedrooms.

Bernadette sits on the side of my bed and tucks me in. Holds my hand, says she's glad I found her. It's the most *wonderful* thing this. Ok I know, I know, I'm twenty-eight and not a child but there's a bit of me at the moment that feels very young. I hope everyone has this for at least one night of their life. To be tucked in by a mother who likes you, says kind, warm things. And smiles.

That was probably the best sleep of my life. Now we're hanging out in the garden, the sun blazing down on the patio. Bernadette bought a paddling pool for when my kids come over tomorrow. And the gardener's already built a sand-pit for them.

"Where you going tonight?"

When my Mother speaks to my youngest sister I can't believe it. She's so different to Mum. It's nothing like *Oh – you're not going out AGAIN! Shouldn't you stay in, fucking going out all the time? About time you did more around the house.*

"Might wear my new dress." *You're not fucking wearing that! You look like an old scrubber!* Or plain old…*Tut.*

"Yeah, looks lovely on you."

"Hair suits you like that, curly."

I can't bare my hair tickling my face like that, those straggly bits, drives me mad. Pin your hair off your face. Never fucking listen to me. Sick of the sight of you.

It's hard being a parent when you've got no maps, working blind. My learning's come from books and watching other people do it right and do it wrong. I'm still shit but I read books like The Good Enough Parent which I'll never be, obviously but it's useful anyway. It's by Bettleheim who survived the Holocaust. Parenting must be a piece of cake, piss-easy, after that, surely? Suppose a starting position could be not to hate your children. Hate. There's a lot of it about. I love my children and would both kill and die for them and it's difficult when your map is one of hate, like climbing a mountain on one leg, no arms, no assistance.

The evening brings a crowd. Grandma, who cries. Vivienne Michelle and her two kids. My beloved and our kids. We're gathered in the enormous 'best' front room. The carpet's almost white. There's a silver bucket keeping the wine cool. And a white Grand piano though no-one plays. I'm proud of my charming husband who's making an effort and getting on with everyone.

Next day there's a barbeque. The kids love the sandpit.

"You're not very affectionate with your kids are you? Me and George noticed." I smile and look at my husband playing rough and tumble with our eldest three. He looks over. Yep, everyone's watching so he keeps going for a while longer. He's clearly a good parent eh?

Our snowy-blond son bounces over. I gently pull him to me,

"Gorgeous kid, come sit on mummy's lap." Then immediately...

"Where's my soldier? It's rough and tumble time." Instantly distracted by his dad, again, the magic of mischief lights my little boy's face as he runs off, full of laughs back to the fun parent.

"Mummy are they rich?" My eldest son, who's five,

plods from the cloakroom pulling up his shorts.

"Why, beautiful boy?"

"There's gold everywhere," He points at the taps. "And there's two torlets in there."

My parents are not only successful but titled too and I'm not talking Mr and Mrs. They're a Lord and Lady, bought the title. Understandable. I wish *I* was someone else too! George tells me they checked with their solicitor whether I could make a claim on their title, which goes to the eldest child. Nice. He reassured them I can't.

Back in the garden Bernadette's chatting, "What road does your mum live in? I used to know someone in that town."

So I tell my mother where my mother lives.

When Bernadette accuses, asks, me why I didn't trace sooner I explained Dad never wanted me to. I didn't feel I could while he was alive. He didn't even want mum to tell me my mother's name when I turned eighteen but she has this thing about doing what she says. Usually it works against but this time it didn't and as she'd already promised we'd played this round-about-guessing-game where I had to guess each letter of Bernadette's name.

The drive home is a happy one. I even don't mind going back to the hospital, me and the baby. The psychiatrist said I'm vulnerable. But what about my poor husband at home with the kids, having to put up with people all over the house from the NCT, social services and my friends? Bernadette told me to ring if I'm having a 'down' day. So I do. Trouble is I have a few what with being in the nut-house. And I ring a lot.

After I phone my mother, I phone my mother, tell

my mother how it's gone with my mother. Explain how well it went.

"Is she slim?" Should I lie?

"Yes… and nice…and they're millionaires." She's always made me tell her the truth catholic style but I both hate and enjoy this bit.

"*Proper* little Cinderella story *isn't it*!" She spits. I hate myself then, kinda, for rubbing her nose in it. But I'm torn because I'm glad I've found a mother who likes me.

When I phone Patrick he says my statement didn't do any good. The Judge had said it was too long ago. (Ruth later told me the Judge said it didn't help that I wasn't there at Court to back up my statement). Patrick said he worries it's getting more difficult to see the little girl, his daughter.

Back to groups. Back to staring at photographs and showing my new friends.

"I'm so happy." And it's true I am. I'm walking round a psychiatric unit professing my happiness – a permanent Cheshire slapped across my face.

"You definitely deserve this!" Lynne's gammy leg is getting on her nerves. It's hot June weather and the weight of her leg's annoying her, as yet still attached.

Mary's gone home with her slightly happier 'miserable fucker' husband escorting her out. She's a bit more docile now there's less juice in her brain battery.

Pamela's become a day patient. Sober too, her and her beau. And me and my baby are going home. It's been a long month.

Chapter 10: Gas Light

Soon after I'm home from hospital it's like I've never been. Other mums from the NCT still come round for the first week, mostly to chat. Social services lay on a cleaner, which we pay for, as well as two times two hours per week of baby-sitters – so I get to kip or shop.

I treasure every moment with my new family, the restaurant meals and driving back in the Roller, George's favourite Chas and Dave blaring out the stereo. When they come back to ours we huddle on the settee holding hands. My mother listens when I speak.

"I feel like a little girl. It's stupid."

"I do too sometimes. I like George to treat me like I'm a little girl."

I meet my next-down sister on her own a couple of times, go out to dinner and she comes to ours. Thankfully my beloved's friendly to my svelte and beautiful sister. I can't fault him with people, and though he's saying he's depressed it's more obvious at certain times with certain people.

Me and my next-down sister speak a lot on the phone. Will motherhood in years to come turn this thinking young woman into one of the kindest you could meet? One day there's even a postcard from my sweet dark-haired sister. She's on holiday in New York and writes that she was thinking of me. Precious, precious words. Words are… only things that last forever.

Me and my father George, Lord George, talk on the phone too. He tells me Bernadette's getting stressed about having contact with me. She's finding it hard to handle. Bad cop.

"It's between you and your mother, nothing to do with me. I want everyone to get on with each other and be one big happy family." Good cop.

Sometimes I get a visit from Gill, a social work assistant with big bouncy hair and matching body. She's chatty. Likes a fag. Her boyfriend committed suicide, she tells me and she's doing an Open University degree. I try to talk about the Patrick thing.

"You've *done* that one now."

"Oh."

"Your problem is other people. Friends are temporary – a bit like passing ships. Then we move on and meet others." She's interesting, friendly, cheaper than a social worker.

"What's it like living with someone who's depressed?"

My poor husband, he's been through it with me. I've heard (read) it's almost as hard as being depressed yourself.

"Pah! You just get through it. My life's good now, I don't regret any of it." As she rolls a fag to go with her coffee her body spills over the sides of the kitchen stool.

I'm down to sixty cigarettes a day now. My beloved, who's not been working is on rollies, and he's wearing dungarees. Cool, man. And getting cooler. He's giving out a message of laidbackness, openness, good fatherliness.

"Women like a bloke on his own with kids," he tells me when we're alone.

It's decided he won't go back to the office. The hospital set up some sessions for me with a clinical psychologist.

"He lost his nerve," Sarah says.

Surely he wouldn't bottle it? She's good but what she does is non-directive, doesn't make any suggestions. She's clinically silent – somewhat of a head-fuck if you're married to someone who pretends he can't hear, ignores you, bypasses your existence. Once I commented on the sunny weather. Nothing. Occasionally I say something two or three times and press for an answer if I really need one from her. But I like the gentleness of the therapy. With no pressure it goes where I want it to go, wherever that is. Apparently.

I tell her how worried about him I am, worried about his future.

"You and he both concern yourself with his happiness."

I worry about the kids too. A lot. While I was in hospital the teachers at my eldest son's school arranged for my snowy-haired son to start big school like his older brother. Overnight he went from playschool to big school. The teachers thought it would help (my husband). Nobody let on he was so distressed he hid under tables for days (my son). Four years old and we're doing this to him!

"Why didn't you *tell* me?" I ask his teacher.

She speaks kindly but I feel like we've betrayed my son.

"We didn't want to worry you."

I hate that my son's been through this – though he takes to his teacher, thank God.

"I love Mrs Smith," says my snowy-haired son. He makes me smile. My throat squeezes in on itself.

"I love you Mrs Smith," he professes to his saviour. She who loved him when I couldn't.

I've got a 'women's' thing that needs doing – a small procedure. The doctor gives me a letter for the hospital, telling them to treat me sensitively as I've had 'severe psychological problems'. My husband reads the letter.

Over the days he tells us all how depressed he feels. Tells Grace and me he's got worse than 'severe psychological problems'. I love him but it's hard not to laugh as his games and some of his intentions become more transparent. As well as wearing denim dungarees, using the new lingo and sporting a beard, he cries a lot, usually when there's an audience. I do feel for him though my head, body and spirit can hardly stand life a'fucking t'all. I feel like a chamois leather that's been used to clean eighty-six mini-cabs then left in the bottom of the bucket. Forgotten, dried up, crispy. I try still harder to be there for him.

"There's no way out,"

"How about a holiday?" Here come another ten mini-cabs.

"We'll have to end our lives and take the kids with us," he tells me over his shepherd's pie. Only he calls it cottage pie and it so isn't. How frustrating, why won't he see it for what it is!

"What?" Yes, he really did say that. I don't answer.

Is he right? I ask Grace later.

"No Mand that's *sick*! Wanting a *suicide* pact for you and the children?" And when he repeats it over the weeks I still don't answer. It rolls over me like some of the other unusual things he says, don't realise how what he says has become normalised. I don't recognise the denial, don't realise the extent of my own ill-health which covers up the cracks, don't see how hard I'm working at making this square peg marriage fit into the round hole of alrightness. Things must be OK if *he's* said them.

He and I both believe his truths. I've taken his lead for so long – seen the world through his eyes no matter how injurious to myself or others. Accepted I'm the baddie, he's the goody. Promoted it, surrounded myself with others who agree with us. And I've withheld the truth from those who don't. No truth, partial truth, anything but the truth so help me God. This despite much of what my beloved says is inside out and upside down while he uses silky subtle hooks to catch you with. Me with.

I'm guilt-ridden by his accusations and criticisms of me to others; how selfish and manipulative I am, how much I exaggerate and how I always get my own way. So I try still harder, as I wonder what I can do to help this poor *sick* man who tells everyone of his pain. Maybe if I'm more loving…

He cries when Amy and Den visit. My poor beloved's distraught.

"Our troubles started when this baby was born."

They nod. Especially ordinary Den, who's prevented from holding his usual chat with my beloved: "All Tories are bastards," "Thatcher's wrong, hasn't a clue," "Join the union, workers will never have equality.."

Normally me and Amy, Den's equally kind, beautiful, intelligent, wife watch or talk mother-things. Den takes the red corner, backs the little-guy.

My beloved disagrees in the blue corner, banking down a smile. But not today.

He's incredibly understanding of Amy not learning to drive. Amy, his beautiful blonde, intelligent, interesting wife, who does though instead, learn to stodge out and quieten down during her years of marriage to short, ordinary Den.

"We can't cope with an extra child," says my poor beloved. "Will you take him from us, look after him and bring him up?" Centre stage now, he peeps through his tears, eyebrows meeting like old buddies out on the piss.

As I watch this play out from the stalls, my happy, thinking-positive smile slides down my face and plops onto the patio. It's a lovely bright day and we're making the most of it. But you can never count on it, can you, the English weather?

"No, we won't." Den refuses outright. But later he explains to me, the *Mother*, the reason he'd said no. It wasn't that he didn't want to help or didn't want our curly-haired boy but thought if he'd agreed and took the baby my beloved might 'give up'.

I'm worried about my beloved who's not improving despite lots of attention.

"Maybe you should see Elizabeth?"

"Beth, your school friend?"

"No – Elizabeth who did the assertiveness course."

He agrees but when I ring up she says he needs to make the appointment for himself.

"She's alright," he says, "but not really like a therapist. More like a little old lady." But he goes anyway, learns more lingo, calls everyone 'guys' in the laidback way of an old softy. She's good for him, still wears a lot of purple.

My birth mother, who's not let a day go by without thinking of me starts blanking my calls. Says she needs to work through it with her analyst who, she's said before, is 'all' for me. Me and my father still talk on the phone as well as my next-down sister.

This is almost too much for my poor husband. "I'm unbelievably upset. I feel so rejected by them."

Grace gives my bearded husband a hug and pats his back. He's taking it bad about my parents.

It's like something's slipping or being stolen away and I don't know what. But somehow I've disappeared again and we're ALL, including the doctor, concerned about my husband's happiness. Or his depression. He wants something from the doctor who's reluctant to give in.

"I want to go into the psychiatric unit." He almost jumps up and down.

"That's not necessarily best for you. It wouldn't look good on your employment records."

"I need to go in, though. Anyway, you know my dad was depressed *and* I've got worse than 'severe psychological problems'."

In the end they get him a place in the unit I was in just over three weeks ago. Most of the help that was at home for my husband gets sucked down a drain – I must've left a tap running somewhere. The drain's a dark, stinking, slimy, putrid vessel that catches and disposes of all the good. It sucks out the energy and leaves it at the bottom of its pit. Empty, useless, forgotten. I shouldn't moan – it's easier for me than it was for him – I'm *already* at home with the children!

But he *does* like taking my things. Do I step aside and make it easy for him? It's not like I don't have a choice, right? Hush my mouth! He means well. *Such* a nice man, everyone says so.

Anyway, I'm alright. I just keep going like many women do. But there's a surprise the first day my husband is hospitalised. For one thing my birth mother comes over, wants to talk.

She looks gorgeous as ever in matching denim jeans and jacket and her huge gold chunky chain reminds me of Mr T from The A-Team. We get talking about our families. Mine.

"I don't want the whole package. Only you. Not your kids. Not your husband." It's nice to be wanted but… and it's good she's assertive, says what she wants. We also talk about her husband, my father.

"It's not easy seeing him hug a grown woman sitting on his lap. I don't even know if George *is* your father."

"Thought you said you '*just knew*' it was him?"

"Well…" Shrug of the shoulders.

"And I don't like you talking on the phone with him. Or the girls. This is about me and you."

Is it? Or is it about her? Just her? Wasn't it always? A Cinderella story? The Fairy Godmother before me speaks deep and cold as she turns into the Troll from Billy Goats Gruff.

I look over at my sensitive eldest son's black A-Team van then at her gold chain. Van – chain – van – chain – van. Get a grip, Mand. Then she says, "I don't know what I want." *It's not you it's me?*

"I thought you wanted to spend time?" My voice leaks out the pathetic truth that is me. I'm feeble. No wonder it's all going wrong. I'm nothing, never have been. She probably thinks I'm stupid, ridiculous, ugly, bad, should never have been born. Faulty goods fit for rejection.

"But what if they want to stay in touch?"

"George and the girls – I shouldn't really say this… but they're puppets on my strings."

A pattern seems to be emerging with my mother, who didn't want me first time around, pursued and stays with a man who didn't want to be encumbered with a baby, *her* baby. My mother, who was replaced by her baby sister, feels like a little girl with her husband and doesn't like him near another woman, even his 'own daughter'. With a husband who reassures while reminding her what a great catch he is to other women. If he's not my father it explains a fair amount as in neither of them want me any more now than they did then.

"It was alright for you. At least you had a *replacement*."

"What?"

"You had Joan. Taking you to their flat, nice family, two boys – it was like taking *my* kids to Buckingham Palace!"

Her kids? Why do I not say she had THREE replacements? Why the *fuck* do I stay nice? Smiley, positive, mustn't offend her. Don't want her to leave me, that's why. That's always why. George said before, "And what's this 'please don't leave me' every-time we hug?" Lemon juice on a cut.

The little red sports car like Noddy's, shrinks away down the road carrying my mother away from me until eventually it's small enough to fit into one of the kids' toy-boxes. Toys. Fun and games. If life is a game I've just lost one of the main pieces. Fancy a drink. Good old vodka will never leave me.

Oh, no, it's the phone. *Come on, oh parentless one. Get off your skinny, lazy, unworthy arse. Do something right for once in your life, come answer me.*

"Your mother phoned me this morning!"

"Hello mum. What did she want?" Didn't know she had the number. Then I remember... *What road does your mum live in?*

"Asked me if you had a happy childhood."

"What did you say?"

"Told her the truth. Told her yes, you did. Thought she might have thanked me for looking after you all these years. But *oh no – nothing*. Ungrateful cow!"

Another surprise. Who should turn up? Yup. My husband. Said he doesn't like it in the hospital so he's walked home. It's a good two miles, poor bloke.

"Drive me back later, they'll never know." Giggling. He's a laugh sometimes, my beloved. He only does this every single day he's supposed to be there!

My husband decides the problem could be he's got an allergy so he stops eating wheat for a bit. Tries rice cakes. Yum – polystyrene. From behind his beard and inside his denim dungarees my man, love of my life starts drinking herbal tea. Camomile.

He listens about my mother, his new millionaire mother-in-law, hears me out. But he's furious. He looks like the marzipan green dragon birthday cake I made our snowy-haired son – more sneery, less sweet. Like an actor de-roling he stops waiting for me to answer. With Relate nearly ended and no millionaire in-laws his audience dwindles. The witnesses who provided some safety all but disappear. The ones who remain are the more malleable non-seeing witnesses: best friends, mother, etc. My 'parents' are virtually gone and it looks like so have I.

Friends and neighbours can't believe how selfish the woman is.

"Can you believe how selfish the woman is? Turning up like that without so much as a bag of sweets for the kids."

"Said she'd got them presents from Miami, teddies, but my youngest sister got jealous so the kids never saw them."

Grace can't believe what this woman's like.

"I can't believe what this woman's like."

"Gloria reckons the girls are spoiled. Guess what else Gloria said?"

"You've got a wonderful husband (with a beard), fabulous kids and a lovely home?" She's a good friend Grace – always sees the positive.

"Not exactly. She looks at me and she said… "

"I'll say to you what I say to my own children… while you're here with me I love you and…"

Kerpow – a flash of brilliant white light blotting out the less important "when you leave here you'll go off and have your own life…"

The room really did go white and I couldn't hear or see a thing. It was the most profound moment. Well, *obviously* my beloved loves me. He tells others he loves me to bits. So does Grace. She also said it to her good friend Heather; before, during and after the seven years that she shagged Heather's husband. I'm sure she meant it at the time…

"She said she loves me!"

"No she didn't," my beloved husband informs me and Grace, "Don't know where you got that from."

I assume then I must've misheard her. Maybe she didn't really say it. Makes me think I'm going mad – hormones, probably.

On the drive home my beloved brings the subject up.

"What you said about Gloria saying she loved you? She did say it."

"Why did you say...?"

"Maybe I didn't want you to think she did."

You ever seen that old black-and-white film called Gaslight? About a man who psychologically tortures his young wife into having a nervous breakdown. She becomes full of insecurities and thinks she's going mad, scared she'll go into an asylum, which he threatens her with. Even the doctors are involved. He makes the lights flicker on and off, says she imagined it and other things she's seen, heard and done. Can you believe someone could do that to someone they're supposed to love? Still, it *is* only a film. It's not like it would happen in real life. No one's really that sinister!

I remember some of the times my beloved said things to others, acting like he'd mentioned it before. Like telling people when we already had four children that he'd only wanted two. Truth is he'd not mentioned it before. Same when I gave up doing 'the bags'. *Then* he says he hadn't wanted that. Again – not said it before. In a session with Gloria we talked about his lack of support over 'the bags'.

"I offered to take direction." He'd suggested he take over and run it for me? Nope! Not a sausage. Really makes you feel like you're going mad. Ha.

In our final session with Gloria it's strange saying goodbye. So much has happened this past year. Too much. Gloria tells us we're over the worst, it won't be this bad again and that most people only have this many problems over a whole lifetime.

"Usually with my clients I suggest they keep in contact and let me know how they're getting on. In your case I won't" – looks at me – "I think you'd abuse it." Great. But I say nothing, shamed as I officially now am. Obviously she's known us for a year, knows just how bad I *really* am.

Me and my husband go for a pub meal afterwards.

"I'd rather say goodbye to your mum than that lady."

"Yeah." He's complained about my mum and the rest of my family since we met. To me, friends, his family, anyone. I suppose it makes his family look like clergymen against the even darker foil of my family. And creates distance between me and them. But Gloria…how will we fare without this outside witness?

The food's good – well, average cheap, chewy, pub steak. But there are no words. There *is* nothing to say. Better the devil you know, eh? Ping! Ah, yes. The rubber band is back.

Chapter 11: The Great Escape

Since Relate, life's changed. My man increasingly demands his rights and his space. Vodka's still in my life – such a special relationship I couldn't let it go but only in the evenings, usually. It's a social thing. I drink on my own but I'm real friendly about it. Life is run on fear: fear when he's in the room, fear when he phones, fear when his words come to me via others. With a few seemingly innocent yet carefully chosen words, days and weeks of my life get destroyed. Outsiders don't notice the secret language.

His therapist, Elizabeth, phones.

"You might want to see someone."

"Why?"

"Your childhood may have been worse than your husband's."

I file it away under 'People who Might Give a Shit One Day'.

The love of my life has become real open-minded and goes out more. He tells me he's got the right to see friends. So he sees mine. Why would I mind? It's nice he gets on with people.

Specially Valerie. We met at a toddler group. Valerie goes to church, a Christian, but she's still nice. She depends on God a lot. A *lot*. When she doesn't know what style to have her hair she and her Christian hairdresser pray for inspiration. Flat broke as in completely skint, living off social security since she birthed her son after a non-Christian-like indiscretion with some bloke who just appeared one day in the congregation. He wanted to do the right thing by God but, well, you know how it is, their love was far too special to see in human terms so he did the off. Never paid jack! Her mum bought everything, including the buggy which Valerie keeps spotless, even dries off the rain and cleans the wheels. It's an immaculate contraption.

"I'm praying for a car."

"I'd be lost without mine. Course..it's not brand-new anymore."

The more I think about it the more I don't mind my beloved taking my good friend for a drink.

"God will provide if I keep praying."

"Why not get a job like everyone else?" She *is* good with money, only person I've ever known to save a fiver a week from her social. The fridge is empty, obviously, plus she spends her evenings watching telly in the dark.

So she keeps praying. Preying? Sometimes she sticks a notice up at church asking for prayers for money and instead gets back envelopes with cash in. She wants a husband but no luck yet, and I don't mind a bit that she's seeing my husband tonight. I make Valerie a cuppa while he gets ready. Being Mandy never worked that great so I tell Valerie my news. I've grown my hair too, give it a whirl.

"I've changed my name back to Amanda."

"I like Mandy better – I'll still use that." She's got the right to express her opinions.

"But I prefer Amanda."

"Tough!" says my Christian friend Valerie.

But she likes my husband and he likes her so that's nice. They're both really modern-minded, going out for a drink like this.

The kids asleep, I settle down for a companionable evening with EastEnders and vodka – my best friends all in one room.

"She's nice – I never realised!" Sounds like they had a good time. Strange I don't hear much from her again.

He sees Julia too, my other friend from work. That's Julia who liked to play at boxing with my beloved, straddle him. Remember? His gloves are off now, though and he tells me he's seeing her because he needs to talk to *someone*. She fills me in when I ring.

"You don't understand him. Why don't you be spontaneous – have sex in the garden?"

"We did."

"Well... he's such a nice guy – I just know how much he's hurting." Funny I only see the anger...the sighs.

If I love him harder, better, different, will it be alright? Am I over the top, like he says, exaggerate, too sensitive, can't take a joke and not as sensuous as some women? He likes that word. Sensuous. Like the actress Jane Seymour and some of his page-three girls.

I read Women Who Love Too Much by Robin Norwood and while I'm at a weekend workshop based on the book he goes out.

Later I press redial on the phone. Julia answers... click. Ice cuts through my head like I've been bottled in a pub ruck.

"I'm having a shower." He disappears and his sports bag beckons. Swimming around the bottom of the bag, muffling giggles, flipping their tails and waiting for action are several condoms wearing life jackets.

"We talked, you're paraonoid! I've got the right to see people. How *dare* you check up on me!"

"Condoms?"

He laughs.

I'm on the Mother Teresa phase of my life. Maybe those with money do tread on the little people on the way up, like my husband says. He's back on the tools, self-employed, working for others putting up ceiling tiles. When chatting he'll tell you he's got a construction company.

I've decided to do my GCSEs. Crazy I know – in my thirties. I sign up for English and Maths and have this idea I'll do a degree afterwards. GCSEs must be easy if fifteen-year-olds do them? Wrong. I'm scared but take it all in, do all the homework – a lot – and being as stupid as I am I need extra help, obviously. So I do a revision workshop in London run by David Lewis the psychologist who wrote How To Have Gifted Children. A real writer stands before me. An actual writer who writes actual books. It's good of him to come, yes, well, I know the ticket wasn't cheap. My friend Judith's a Maths teacher so I swap her some child-care for extra tuition. At the local secondary school I pay this English teacher to give me some time, help me out. Once I get into it I absolutely love it. In the months before the exams I get up at four a.m., tick off the boxes on my revision timetable. You won't believe this but I only get top marks. Yep. A's. Me!

I want to be a social worker so in preparation I become a bereavement counsellor. People ask if it's depressing but no, it isn't. After the training I visit this old bloke who was married for over fifty years, nursed his wife at home for the last year of her life while she slowly, slowly disappeared with the cancer.

"Mustn't grumble – there's other people worse off," he says, every week.

Maybe there *are*. That's such an English 'mustn't bother the doctor' thing.

I get offered a place on the degree course, can you believe? Me!

My husband's furious.

"You don't care about the kids. You're never satisfied. Why can't you just get a little job?"

"I need your support."

"No, I won't support you," he yells, big, puffed up like a bear. The killer kind.

"Financially?"

"Can't afford to financially."

"Practically then, with the kids?"

"No – not practically either!"

My words jump from the assertiveness books but my body shrivels. It's hard for him. He doesn't like change and I'm trying to change the rules of the relationship. I'm frightened and gutted. It's probably a combination of PMS, my childhood, the way I look at things, me being selfish, manipulative, controlling and having my own way, like he says. This is the worse thing I've ever done to him.

"When we lived with my mum, you wanted to be the one that ironed my shirts," he says. Twelve fucking years ago. And he says it's *me* holds on to things!

More holes appear in the doors. It's getting hard to stay positive.

My part-time job as a residential social worker means I cover shifts at different places in the evenings. Working with adults with learning difficulties is OK.

They're nice, some of them and anyway I've been married for years. But the children's home is out of this world. The young ones *are not* angels. Some have seen horrid shit and I feel for them but what they need is 'discipline that comes from a caring place'.

There's a little boy of six and I know strangling won't help. The youngest of three, he jumps from bed to bed when I try to settle him for the night. Generally he wipes the floor with me. As do the scary teenagers who run rings around most of the staff. They're forever running away. I'm sure it's for the crack, the buzz. But gradually I realise I'm shit at this job. I try covering it up, have a laugh, but like rabid dogs they smell the fear on me and give me shit, really take the piss till I'm running round in circles.

My beloved decides to take a mate with him when he's invited to join Trevor on his family holiday to Florida.

"Why can't I go?"

"We can't afford it."

What's the point of arguing? I still do the bills but he says I'm controlling and manipulative, that I do it all wrong. He's furious that it's me who chooses the food when I do the shopping. Did I ever have confidence? He and Mum tell me I'm very confident. It's said that having kids can affect your self-esteem. If I've had four that's four times low self-esteem. Pretty low I reckon.

I'm gutted the night he leaves for the airport. At the door, he turns.

"I wish you were coming with me." Me and him know he doesn't mean it but he needs to hear himself say the words. I slam the front door the hardest I can. Screaming and crying, I run upstairs to the newly decorated bedroom and throw a hammer at his beautiful walls. HOORAY – I've made a small tear in the paper though I know I'll be too scared ever to confess.

I know that deep down – and yet to be acknowledged to myself – is one cold truth about my husband, the man I've loved since he was a boy: This man has never loved me. Though he refuses to admit it in a cruel trick to keep me ever trying, ever hoping, doing the work, taking the blame, carrying the guilt, I'm being backed into a corner where the marriage is an impossible place to stay. Me the baddie, him the goodie, publicly wounded while subliminally presenting me with a fait accompli. This is the moment I give up hope.

I've been losing the weight I'd gained in an effort to become the wife he wants, get his approval. I've tried everything he wanted or said he wanted. I've got a bit fat, bit slim, bit ugly, stayed in a lot, stopped talking and shagged more. But still, *still* I can't make him happy and I certainly can't make him love me.

While my husband's in Florida I finally go clubbing with friends. I end up celebrating reaching my target weight over dinner with a tall dark stranger. Different from the tall dark stranger I'm married to.

He still sees Julia. Grace too. Once I call him at Grace's but he doesn't replace the receiver and I hear them speak.

"You *know* what she's like," he tells Grace who agrees, joins in the mumbling and moaning about me, feels sorry for him. I can almost hear her head nodding on her neck bone like those dogs in the back of a car. My best friend.

Vodka keeps me company the nights he's not here. And the nights he is. It soothes rather than hurts, doesn't attack me, takes me wherever I want to go.

Toxic...No More

"You want out of here, girl?"
"Can you do that?"
"Trust me... I'm a vodka."

I get other part-time work as a Weight Watchers lecturer. Unbelievable, the excuses people give each week for gaining weight. Honestly, some people just lie to themselves. The other night I'm at the scales eyeing the queue, smiling, staying positive, helpful and supportive. One by one each spits out their excuses.

Woman 1: "My husband's got a collapsed lung."

I knit my brows, nod, sympathetic, like they taught us in training.

Woman 2: "Been a bad week – my son's first birthday. But look how slim you are! It's *easier* for you."

"Don't be hard on yourself – have a good week this week."

Woman 3: "I've had a cold." Fucksake.

"Must've been a heavy cold."

Rituals, rituals – we've all got them. Some people can't eat till they've washed up, can't shop without a list or have to wear their lucky knickers on an interview. Usually I drink and drink till I don't care, vomit, then go to bed. That's my little ritual.

But I'm missing him tonight. It's so painful, this huge crater inside me, full of what? Something toxic, alive, writhing, ready to kill. If only he'd come home, be with me, put his arms around me, love me.

I phone him at his friend's.

"What d'you want *now*?" The humiliation of his public boredom. Rather than tell him I love him and miss him I replace the phone.

I take in more and more vodka without clocking it. One drink follows another. They're confident as boomerangs, know they're guaranteed a return showing.

Without realising it, I go to the bathroom cabinet. Woss this? Anything will do, so I grab whatever's there and wash it down with a drink, thassa girl, thassa girl. I don't care what it is – paracetamol, suppositories, aspirin, cough mixture. Fuck knows what I'm doing. I sit on the side of the bath, slide off, giggling, float downstairs, miss some steps.

"Oooh – skiing."

Somehow the phone works.

"Julia… just phoning to say goodbye."

"What?"

"I took some tablets."

"That was childish!" I suppose *he's* more sensible, calm, collected, in control. Ha. Why am I phoning her? I don't see my cry for help, don't see my needing someone, again, who's not my friend. Will I feel closer to my husband? Julia was married to a solicitor once. Violent, he was.

Keep drinking. Damn it, no more tonic. Ah – kids' orange-squash. Damn it, no more of squash. Ah, milk. No more milk. Just do it, gel.

The door opens. S'good he's back. I hover towards him, collapse, giggling, slurry-worded.

"Mand, fucksake, NOW what've you done?" He sighs then tuts.

The ambulance zooms seamlessly to hospital where I get my stomach pumped. First they give me this dark green liquid in a plastic shot glass. Then tube down – yaaaah – watch out, here it comes. DO NOT TRY THIS AT HOME. It's not good. There are electrode things on my shoulders and chest but what takes me over completely is the vomiting. Vomit, vomit, vomit, then no more vomit. Just the dribbles of yellowy liquid. The bile is vile. I'm clean out of vomit but my body searches for more. The retching, the racking, as my physical self tries to turn inside out in earnest, confessing something it knows not what.

Next day it's sunny and I'm in the hospital garden when my beloved arrives.

"Why, Mand?"

"I feel so peaceful here." And it's true. Look at that, he's almost... no, no, he's looking away again. False alarm.

"I'm so depressed, I feel suicidal," he says.

I don't understand why I feel soothed here but at least I tried to pay my dues for being so bad.

He walks away, oblivious of me sat there, instead displays his depression. No kiss, hug, affection, just more of the same darkness, poison and hate infecting the good air swirling around the garden.

I speak to Sarah at my next appointment.

"I'm glad you brought it up," she nods. "The hospital informed me. It might be useful to look at your impulsiveness."

I'm so blinded to it, this part of my behaviour. I'm a complete knee-jerk person. Press me here – see how my arm raises. Now press me here – see how my purse opens and money flies out. See how I shout, get mouthy when you put a knife in my side while no one's watching.

Nothing's different at home and the incident is forgotten like the milk from an empty bottle.

One night he doesn't come home, but turns up next day after the kids have gone to school.

"I needed some thinking time."

"What's wrong with thinking at home?"

"I needed to be alone." Wistful.

"Where?"

"My mum and dad's grave."

"Isn't the crematorium locked up at five o'clock?"

"Yeah, yeah, but I was so upset I climbed over the gate."

"The whole night?"

"Um, then I came outside and sat in the car, thinking."

"The whole night?"

"I felt so alone and *you* don't care." There it goes, slicing into my stomach and piling onto the *thing* at my centre, the one I know so well, the chunk of glog that confirms my badness. This is going somewhere I don't want – like a roadblock that's waiting for me and my brakes have failed. Everything's failed. Whatever's happened I don't want to know this. The pain of it *is* physical.

I pretend it's no big thing but my guts spill out in stew-sized lumps onto the dark red carpet. Warm, bleeding. One for each year we've been together. At the same time I *have* to know what I don't want to know so I keep on and on asking questions. I always said if he cheated on me it would be over. But then I've said a lot of things and each 'rule' got bludgeoned through. Or worse still, voluntarily stood aside, sometimes at a mere suggestion.

"Just admit you've *been* with her." There's a smile on my face and I can't believe it, can't believe I can make it stay there but it's the only safe way of asking – asking as if it doesn't matter. Ha. Make it a game or he'll get *angry*.

"OK, yes, I have." He's laughing too like he's been caught eating sweets before dinner.

"It doesn't change anything." And I mean that. They say relationships are hard work but believing that has kept me in something I shouldn't have kept myself in.

It shouldn't be *this* hard. Life with this man is continuously painful and whether he's shagged Julia or not doesn't change that. When I'm with him I don't like who I am. As well as my dinner with the tall, dark, stranger, I too have had anonymous *indiscretions* since Florida. Anonymous even to me. It's over.

Yet when he thinks I'm not going to end the marriage he doesn't celebrate and stupidly there's another slice into my belly as I'd hoped he'd be pleased. He's not.

When I tell Sarah, she shrugs her shoulders.

"Think I want a divorce," I say.

"He elicits sympathy from people... you want to change each other. Sometimes it works, sometimes it doesn't."

"This time it hasn't," I say, glad for the permission I needed.

Are therapists always sorted themselves? They must be. They're the therapist so must be *really* together. Though today when waiting for my appointment I could hear two voices from behind a closed door, Sarah's and the receptionist's. When it gets to Sarah's turn she screams like a two-year-old. Then, "I AM NOT HAPPY WITH THIS." What a turn-up for the books! I suppose it shows she's assertive, happy to express herself.

"I can recommend you a solicitor, someone supportive of women's issues," she tells me now. She really is so together.

The solicitor fills in a load of forms, using up volumes of legally aided minutes. I'm barely listening, can't take it in. I gabble but don't know what I'm saying. He'll kill me. No matter – it's done. Fear. Adrenalin. Fear. Adrenalin.

My husband is still not happy. The anger, the hate, always lying in wait have been there for years, their first stirrings there right in the beginning of us. Or before. I thought he might want to try at the marriage, give me a reason to change my mind, but no. Instead takes his sports bag to Julia's.

Next day after EastEnders, the kids are in bed and I grab the moment.

"Can you please sit down? I need to talk to you."

"What, now?" He whips me with a big sigh. Instant guilt, always the guilt. He's good at this.

"There's something I've got to say that might upset you." I grab his hand, try to limit the damage, *feel* for him. He's looking and listening but it's too late and for the wrong reasons.

"I've started a divorce…"

That's it – he's off. He jumps from the chair, FURIOUS. He may well write to the BBC. Strange, he's not happy when he thinks we'll stay together and not happy once he knows about the divorce – almost as if he *wants* me to be in the wrong, take the blame and all the responsibility.

Next day after school we tell the kids. All six of us are on the bed, hugging and crying, with the grown-ups spilling their sickness onto the children. Insanity. My daughter looks at her little brother, laughs, quickly turns back and cries again. He, my youngest, my curly-haired boy, is four years old and my bouncing, too streetwise eldest boy is nine.

Over the weeks I start my degree course but it's hard to concentrate. My head's fucked.

"No! I ain't budging," he blasts, tenor, when I ask him to leave.

"You can leave if you want. But the kids are staying *here*."

Instead he sets about a mission of his own to prove his parenting skills and rubbish mine. He keeps a little black book, notes everything down. My solicitor tells me what he's doing.

"Making a case for himself." She says it like she's seen it all before.

I'd just thought he was angry with me but maybe she's right. He starts getting home early from work. I'm in the kitchen doing the kids' tea and he leans across me and with his body, sweeps *my* body away from the worktop. For years he's refused to help – now he takes over the kitchen.

"No! I'M doing their tea."

Outsiders don't see any of this and I don't think to tell them. With them he acts differently and like a compulsion, I can't *not* react. He prods and I scream or embarrass myself in a hundred different ways. I make it easy for him and my reactions make me look insane. Like magic he hints or suggests something and then I do it, believe my own press – written or conjured up by him. I'm still heavily glued to his wants and I don't know how it works but somehow while I'm stabbed in the side he distracts witnesses with his grin and oozing charm. Slick.

"Who wants a story?" I herd the kids into the other room as they bounce up to see what's afoot. On the surface they're oblivious. Who knows, underneath?

After college a young, bespectacled, fellow student brings his washing round, his own machine broken. My husband's in the kitchen when my friend goes to his car. The kettle putt-putts to the boil as my husband lifts it.

"Get rid of him or I'll pour this over you." Quietly.

"Shall I leave?" He walks back in during this marital tête-à-tête.

"Washing's nearly finished." I smile, like this is the normallest house in the world. Square peg – round hole. Although terrified I'm furious at the injustice.

Next day I empty a bottle of blue Quink into a wash of my husband's white shirts then spend forever undercover in the High Street finding a suitable dustbin for the evidence – the empty ink bottle hidden in a bag. The shirts? They come out Daz white. Luck of the devil, that man!

When I first start the divorce I think my husband might need support so I get him details of a fathers support group. He attends their meetings in a London pub.

"Really nice guys. One of them said I should kidnap the kids," casually, smiling.

There are so many gems like this I'm rich with them, don't clock them as threats. There's been too much hate for too many years and the part of me that wants him to love me hates the part of him that won't.

His solicitor writes that he's not convinced the children are better off with me though my husband wavers when we discuss finances in the downwards direction he seems to like. That's the unspoken agreement: I keep the kids if the price is right.

The fear keeps me awake at night, often falling asleep just before wakey-up time. On Sundays I set the alarm so I'm up before the kids, afraid of what he'll do on his mission to put down my mothering and promote his fathering.

"Come on kids, time for school," I say in the morning. But – oh no look! I *can't* take them.

"Come on kids, time for school." He pounces from somewhere and the kids bounce off with their fun dad to his car which is blocking mine in, like the cross-stroke on a 'T'.

"Have a lovely day kids, go take a risk!" Ha. Big snap, crackle and pop smile from Mummy. Fucker!

One evening, fairly civilised, we have a coffee in the kitchen.

"We could have the kids one week each." I say it quietly, glad he ignores it.

"If I get custody I don't think I want them to see you," he says.

"Well, I'd want them to see you!" I say and shiver, hoping he wouldn't carry out the threat. Although I've never wanted to abandon my kids, even to Buckingham Palace, I still want them to see their dad.

He stops me having access to any money, won't let me shop. He does it all. I pay for childcare and my own food from my student grant.

Bit by bit he monitors my every move. I know – I'll phone the father's support group! This kindly, intelligent man suggests I contact a group called MATCH – Mothers Away From Their Children. Nuh!

"We advise our members against using little black books. It makes him look like an obsessive who won't let go." Ha.

How does this work? He's never wanted me, yet *now* look! There's an edge to this. The attention's tempting but the fear's a high price to pay as he towers over me, close, then tries to eliminate me with his 'I'll fuckin' chin ya's'.

I find respite on the phone to Grace.

"GET OFF THAT FUCKING PHONE NOW."

I don't. Grace hears this unusually public outburst.

"If you don't get off it now I'll pull it out the FUCKING wall."

"I'd better go."

"You be alright, Mand? I'm frightened for you."

Where would I be without her friendship?

He spends a lot of time at the school, suddenly. I don't know what he says but they start asking if my daughter's eating right. Someone gives us a hand-me-down coat for her, but the buttonholes have gone sloppy so the buttons keep coming undone. The day she has a school trip I forget to pack her wellies. She refuses breakfast and I can't *make* her eat it. She's a strong, bright, bubbly, vulnerable, fascinating and vivaciously gorgeous, determined five-year-old.

Bit by bit he prevents me taking the kids out of the house. He wants to know how, where, when, what, who. But not why. Never why. He doesn't let me cook, won't let me take the kids to their doctor and dentist's appointments but makes a point of doing it himself, creates opportunities. Only *he* can do this public service. I want one of the kids to have a tutor. I've always attended to anything school related. But he arranges a tutor then tells everyone, especially the school about 'his' decision, makes sure he's the visible one. It's like he's killing off my spirit. The subliminal pressure to conform to his desires screeches at me. It's like being caught in a web and, compulsively, asking the spider for advice and I can't stop myself, can't keep myself safe.

College is impossible – I just can't think straight. Money's a mess. House is a mess, four lots of toys strewn about. The linen basket spills its guts. ALL four kids get nits and I don't fucking notice, for fucksake. It's the childminder who requests their removal, the nits'.

"Mummy, I can hear the eggs cracking," says our daughter.

"Do you think I'm a bad mother?" Terrified, I ask the childminder whose six stone overweight.

"Bit scatty, maybe." Yet when her son burns my daughter by holding a light-bulb to her skin we both say nothing about her scatty childminding.

Their father takes photos of the mess and updates his black book. Calm, measured, he goes about his day-to-day usually hidden agenda, depending on who the audience is.

I go clubbing. Love the dancing, the drinking, the attention. Vodka soothes and removes my head from my head. It helps me forget. The night-time attention is mind-blowing. My perfect size ten arse gets noticed but it doesn't do me any good. I'm playing to his tune and I don't know how to stop. He's publicly looking the good parent and I don't know how to stop living down to his expectations and suggestions. The compulsion to do what he wants is strong, like I've been trained by a cult. His cult.

One morning I find my brand-new little black dress cut up in strips in the bin.

A rare occurrence: my husband's working so I get to cook for the kids. Ha – what's this? The little black book speaks to me. READ ME, READ ME.

Sunday: *She came home with love bite on neck.*

Monday: *Only said hello to three of the kids, left one out.*

Each word written in poisonous ink. I'm a bit pissed off when he arrives. I go to close the kitchen door as he enters but he bursts in anyway, then lifts and throws the six-foot breakfast bar at me. ROAR! Like the hulk.

Daddy throws Mummy to the ground and straddles her.

"There's more of this to come, you whore."

"Daddy's hit Mummy," my little girl spreads the news to her brothers. After he's left the room I comfort the kids, try to absorb the darkness for them.

Coffee with Grace brings momentary relief. He's out and it's fantastic when all the kids are with me. Safer.

"Yes, I do think he'd hit you but I don't think he'd hit anyone else," she justifies.

My beloved sees her a lot too.

"I know I could have Grace if I wanted but I wouldn't do that to you," he reassures. When I tell Grace she cries. I'm confused but then I'm always confused. Probably my hormones making me over-sensitive.

The psychotherapy at the hospital keeps me going.

"You could go to a women's refuge." Sarah says it with a straight face. You're right – she says *everything* with a straight face.

A refuge never occurred to me. Do I qualify if I'm not black and blue all over, no broken bones?

"And… it's bad timing for you but I've been promoted – I'm leaving in three weeks."

The only real sanity in my life and she's going.

Next day Mum makes lunch. It's barely possible to eat there now, the state of the place. They should make a telly programme about houses like hers, call in Environmental Health. There are boxes everywhere. And filth. The grime on the kitchen floor, round the sink, inches thick of dog hairs on the carpets, settees covered over with piles of clothes where she hasn't bothered with a wardrobe for years.

I have to eat without thinking about it. Takes an act of bravery just to go round, like jumping from an aeroplane: risk my life every visit, pray the chute opens.

"You can stay here a couple of weeks with the kids, if you like," she says, now the only occupant of her three-bedroom house. She's got another suggestion too.

"Why not let him keep the older two and you keep the younger ones?"

"I'm not splitting them up."

"Just thought it'd be easier for him, what with working."

"It's like you're on his side, Mum. You always defend him."

"I don't! I just think he's having a hard time of it. You know what you're like. I think he's frightened of you."

"You seen him lately?"

"Brought me over some cheap pâté from the warehouse."

"Mum…"

"Huh?"

"Did you tell him I'm a bad mother?"

"Wasn't like that. He was talking about things so I told him about that time you didn't change your eldest boy's nappy for ages when we worked the market stalls."

Bollocks. That day was nine years ago – and I still feel bad.

In court I apply for an injunction. He represents himself.

"It was self-defence, Your Honour." Butter wouldn't melt and it's a blow-out in court as in the Judge doesn't ask him to leave the house but instead grants a Non-

Molestation Order, which bans him and his agents from entering the marital bedroom where I'm hiding out. Or from hurting me.

This woman comes up at the end, sad-smiling, head to one side.

"No one believes me. It's like the whole world thinks he's right," I shudder, crying, ashamed, powerless, feel such a twat.

"It's not that. He can't be removed without *physical* evidence. These are difficult times, but there is something you could try…"

"What?"

"Relate." Oh, nice lady. Bless her.

He no longer allows me to take the kids out of the house except to school. I try anyway, once, just the once, and he snatches my curly-haired boy from my arms. I hold on at first then release him, don't want the child scared or hurt.

At school pick-up my daughter's teacher has a word.

"I'm worried about your daughter not eating. She says she doesn't have any breakfast, then tells me she's hungry."

"She refuses. You try making a five-year-old eat when she doesn't want to." I'm still calm. Good.

"It's about nutrition." She says it like I'm stupid.

"Don't tell me about nutrition," I'm not so calm now as I grab my daughter's dead lunch box, hold up the remains of, firstly, yoghurt:

"Calcium", then apple:

"Roughage", and bread-crusts with cheese slivers:

"Carbohydrate and protein. DON'T tell me about nutrition. I *know* about nutrition. I was a WEIGHT WATCHERS LECTURER."

"Well…she says she's hungry so I give her a drink

and a biscuit."

"What about the rest of the class?"

"I sit her behind the curtain so they don't see."

"I feel like you're singling her out."

"Ooh, no! I treat the Traveller children the same way."

I wonder if she's a little-bit prejudiced and a large-bit thick as shit.

I'm running out of ways to carry on so think hard about going to a women's refuge. It's not ideal. Choices, choices, choices. The assertiveness course said we have them. My husband tells me I have them. Choices. Hobson's choices. If you don't know you've got a choice do you still have one? Or if you think or you're told you've got choices but it's not safe to administer them, do you still have choices?

I'm at the solicitor's office. She knows we're off to the refuge the next day. It looks like I won't ever be a social worker now as I'm leaving the course. Probably just as well – I can't imagine myself in a tweed skirt.

I have loads of questions from and to my solicitor. Delay, delay, delay. It's an emergency, this, but I'm getting later and later for school pick-up. It's too rude and scary to hurry a solicitor and these details *have* to be resolved today.

I'm an hour late picking up my daughter from school. A fucking HOUR. Naturally the new headmistress is angry. She – no-one – can make me feel more shit and guilty than I already do, maybe always will. She shouts and shouts which makes my daughter cry. It's impossible to explain in less than ninety thousand words what's happened over the years between me and this man whose charm plan I've colluded with, how he's slithered into the school, into their hearts and others'. Her friend. But she's yet to play her best card.

In the morning I call social services for help with a place at a refuge.

"I must just tell you," the woman is kind, sensible, "the school have been on the phone this morning. Said your daughter comes to school not properly clothed, her coat flaps about in the wind. Also that she doesn't wear suitable footwear and isn't eating properly."

So I tell her the 'coat, wellies, lunchbox' story, the 'attitude towards traveller children and my daughter' story and 'my husband's friendship with the school' story.

"Well…I'm not too interested in the prejudices of people like that. The most important thing is to get you and the children to a safe place."

I cry then at the kindness I'm not used to. Like velvety hot chocolate or a foreign language I'd like to hear more of.

So it is that on Tuesday, 11 February 1990, after retrieving black sacks full of our belongings from next door's under-stairs cupboard we do the off. Me and the kids go to the women's refuge in my now old blue Ford Fiesta. The snow only adds to the adventure I try and turn it into for the kids.

"We're going away for a while," I say, trying to concentrate on the road.

"Where?" I always tell the kids it's good to ask questions, good to be nosy.

"Just away. You'll see when we get there."

"Did you bring my teddy?" My eldest son has had it since a baby.

"No, darling, I'm sorry."

"Doesn't matter, it's only a toy." But sat in the passenger seat, he doesn't turn his head quick enough to hide the tear that rolls across his nine-year-old cheek.

As arranged we meet the refuge worker in a pub, handily, so I get a couple of glasses of anaesthetic down me before she arrives to escort us.

In the house it's another world. Safety – I can't *tell* you what it's like! Settled into the refuge, five of us in one bedroom, we're squashed but it's delicious. There are two sets of bunk beds and a single for me. No matter that we've left a big house and everything behind. Huddled in one room like this, knowing he can't get me, knowing where the kids are, they're safe and I'm safe. No matter the black sacks are everywhere, filling every space on the carpet. No matter I feel like I've lost my past, my present and my future. We're safe at last.

It's the *best* and gradually life feels better. It's like learning to breathe again after long-term suffocation. The kids miss their dad so, against the advice of the refuge workers, I/we phone him. It's not like I miss him too, obviously.

He gets to our daughter first. He cries, so does she. Me too. I feel sorry for him then as always. Sorry too for the kids. Break the hold, Amanda. I phone Grace.

"He's changed the locks, Mand."

Bollocks. Next I ring the woman who's done our cleaning since my stay in the psychiatric unit. She agrees to get some of the kids' toys, including the teddy bear.

I collect the toys from her then go back to the house. The older three are at their new school near the refuge. They hate it – hand-me-down uniform, shit free school dinners blah blah.

The police meet me there and help me break in. It's

illegal to change the locks or prevent me entering as it's my property too. Ha. Once in I get essentials and food from the cupboards. Once in I see the black book next to a Dictaphone. Once in I can't resist a listen.

"I've returned home. No-one here. Can't find them. Kids' clothes been removed. No note." His voice is scary, robotic, sounds like a Dalek.

Coming to the refuge meant leaving behind most of life as we knew it, the bad and the good. We settle in with the other women and their children.

Patricia has multiple sclerosis and a six-year-old daughter. Her husband slept with her best friend but she and Patricia stayed friends.

"I wasn't going to let a man ruin our friendship."

She doesn't give exact details of what he did to her but it's something violently sexual and involved her arse, which didn't help with the illness that's already left her frail. Whatever he did though, it was bad enough that the social workers told her he should stay away from their daughter. Patricia's quiet and perfectly behaved. She does all her housework immediately – even the ironing. Irritatingly good. Would imagine she got all her Brownie badges straight off. And she has a quiet, demure, Brownie-badge-getting daughter. I feel bad resenting her though when she's got MS.

Janet's an older woman with no children. Just long, straggly, greasy hair and glasses. She's not the prettiest hat in the shop. *Shh – I think she might be a drinker!* We've not been here long when she finds somewhere else to go and leaves.

It's easier to relate to Liana who has three kids. She's attractive, a bit younger than me at twenty-five and altogether more fun. She spends all week phoning different blokes to borrow money to pay off this one and that one. We go out together a few times and Patricia baby-sits. One night we're at a nightclub and suddenly Liana drags me into the toilet. She's only nicked some girl's handbag! I feel sorry for the girl but don't stand up to Liana, only listen 'eagerly' to her stories about other times she's done it, compelled to be her audience.

Liana has been in a refuge before but went back to Steve just like loads of other women do. Incredible. Why would someone go back into something that hurts them? This time she's determined to stay strong and ignore his pleading, his tears and promises to change. Liana says she's so scared of Steve that sometimes when she hears his key in the lock she wets herself and worse. But she becomes a good friend over the weeks as I give her lifts to view some of the places the council offer her. We have a good moan about perfect Patricia.

Liana's making toast one afternoon and doesn't notice my eldest son sneaking out the back door to play the cruellest joke ever. I walk in just in time to hear him putting on a deep voice.

"Liana, it's Steve. Open the door – I've come to get you."

I quickly open the door and drag him inside where I make him apologise. Liana smiles, says nothing.

There's a meeting in the house which the manager attends, or the house-dust police as I call her. I'm not too worried as I know we all get on quite well. Patricia speaks first.

"I don't like it that I'm supposed to baby-sit their children."

"And I don't like it that her four children swear so much."

Liana points at me and when Patricia agrees I realise

they've been talking and I don't have any friends here. I look over at Liana's three, their bottles filled with sweet milky tea, and I remember the handbag and the easy usage of my petrol.

I'm glad we've moved here but it's hard trying to do normal things. Strangely, I miss him. I'm off my head with the grief of withdrawing from him, my *addiction* to him even though I tell myself it's love. The pull is phenomenal. *Physical.* But I carry on with my voluntary job as bereavement counsellor. It's only right, isn't it? It's not the old man's fault but when I drive near the town where my beloved still lives, the fear of being in the same vicinity freaks me. It's like he has power over all the buildings which watch me as I drive past. Don't be stupid, don't be stupid.

I've had to go counselling on a Saturday this week. Trouble is he seems to think it's sort of a date. Bless – he's in his late seventies. Along with the too-weak tea he brings out a box of chocolates. They're old with white bits of something that looks like dandruff settled comfortably on the dark chocolate.

"I nursed her that whole year, the year she died." I know this already – he's said it a dozen times. "Course, what would you know about problems eh?"

I nod, smile a bit, try to look my stablest. It must be working as he carries on.

"Bet you've got a nice life, young girl like you. Got no problems at all, I bet."

And I carry on with the nodding. How I don't burst into tears and pour out my troubles to this gentle man who's eager to please, I don't know. I want him to be my granddad, pour me more cat's-piss tea, pat my back and listen, tell me 'there, there'. It's a miracle I pull it off without giving in to the almost overwhelming yearning. I could so easily slide down onto the floor. This life is exhausting. I'm so very tired.

We've talked about me stopping the visits within the next couple of weeks. It's been a year. Wait till they hear about this in supervision group. Ha. Trouble is, I won't be telling them jack. How can I? Would anyone, would you tell this middle-class bunch of people that despite living in a refuge with your kids and the future's looking hopeless, you're still making yourself useful to this poor old man whose wife of fifty years died – because it's not his fault? Mind, at least he's had a fifty-year marriage.

Anyway, what would the supervision group know about problems, eh? In their nice little middle-class lives full of husbands who like them and food from Waitrose. Got no problems at all, I bet.

Guess losing everything reminds me of my birth parents. Despite the lack of contact they agree to meet up in this smart hotel not too far from the refuge. They've replaced their blue Roller with a new burgundy one – I see them pull up.

We have dinner, the three of us. Me, Bernadette and George. The restaurant is swish, overlooks an indoor swimming pool. As the evening gets darker, lights appear around the pool.

I hope my mother likes my long hair. She says she does. George tells me they bought my next-down sister a house. She was upset at the break-up with her fiancé. Me and my mother drink wine. The restaurant's almost empty as it's a week night. They play gentle music and me and my 'father' dance. My mother doesn't like it and they bicker but she says it was me she's annoyed with, not him. They dance then too. We talk about the circumstances around my birth.

"Abortions weren't legal when you were born. And I knew someone who'd died from a backstreet abortion, so I wouldn't do that," says my mother.

"It was different in those days," says George. "When you were born it was just like having an abortion." Could I feel shitter? But I sit there smiling.

"Do you know anyone who deals with mortgages?" Dare I ask them this? I've not asked for any favours before but I need to find a way out of this, get a home for the kids.

"No, we don't know anyone like that." I guess it was an unacceptable request, like it says in the assertiveness books.

I had said I didn't want to talk about going to the refuge, about my beloved, but drink loosens my tongue and then I speak of it and regret it. What don't I regret? Why do I always break my own rules? It's like I'm programmed to tell all just because someone's asked. Or not, even.

Their car leaves as smoothly as it arrived and I know I won't see them again. My mother, who all those years ago strategically withheld the truth of my conception from George, her future husband, knowing my real father was her then boyfriend Dave Young. A plan truly hatched.My mother, who holds the power to put it right but chooses not to. And a 'father' who – who what?

When we're at the refuge gradually we phone the kid's dad more and more. He gets nicer so the gaps between phone-calls get shorter and I agree to take the children round. I don't see the manipulations. When I pick them up from his, my curly-haired boy runs across the hallway behind his dad.

"You nervous of Mummy?" Then to me: "Horrible

being rejected, isn't it?"

"I don't *feel* rejected! What's going on?"

"KIDS – MUMMY'S HERE."

With this horrid eerie shit crawling up my back, my neck, into my ears and down my throat I drive back to the refuge. I'm doing the right thing aren't I, taking them to see their dad? And they love the steak, the fizzy drinks, the sweets that I can't afford to give them. So everyone's happy. Right? He admits later he deliberately gets the kids these things, knowing I can't.

Somehow driving the kids to see him over the weeks turns into me and him talking about things. It's nice he's talking to me. Is that what it needed, this break, for him to realise he does respect me after all? Certainly he says he misses me. I've wanted to hear him say something nice for so long. I take the kids over more often till they're seeing their dad a lot.

At the refuge they wonder why me and him are talking so often.

"I think he's changed." And I do. I really do. It looks like all we needed was a bit of space. Ha.

After a month at the refuge the manager does me a letter and the council re-house us in a bed-and-breakfast. "Me and him have come so far," I tell everyone – Grace, Mum, anyone. Drinking's easier here. At night, the kids asleep, I lie in bed with a bottle of vodka or wine. The kids, if they notice, don't say anything. In a practical sense life is easier than it's been for years. Although my head is all over the place with the trauma of it all, my only responsibilities are to get the kids fed, clothed and to school. This I can do.

I phone my college tutor and spill. Have I been trying to become a social worker when what I really needed was one myself? He's lovely, though. More kindness.

"You can come back for next year's course if you like." Gosh – where are the men like this? Fuck do I choose the ones I do? That said, my husband's being so nice. We've taken to having coffee in what's now 'his' kitchen or soon will be – we both act like it already is. Perhaps always did.

One day we're talking and he agrees he'll buy me out of the house. He tells me the price he's decided to value it at and what he'll give me – less than half of the equity. Bit awkward, me not working and with the four kids to re-house but if I say anything he threatens, "Don't have the kids then."

"Will you help with legals?"

"Can't afford it – and they won't give me more mortgage than that." What can I say?

Fear stops me from saying I think he's talking bollocks but can we just get on with it. I want the kids to have a home as soon as possible. One woman stayed in the refuge for eighteen months and I don't want that for them.

With keeping seeing him and him being nice, I'm missing him and the pain of that is difficult to cope with. The following night after a drink, I phone him. He agrees to meet us in a working men's social club near our bed-and-breakfast. He buys me drinks and the kids get cola and crisps. Lovely. We're so broke it's wonderful to have a treat. He's not all bad is he? He even treats us to MacDonald's. Can't fault him there. And now we've agreed the money thing, he says he'll drop the custody thing.

'Misdirection'. That's what Magicians call it. It's their most powerful tool for pulling off a trick. They get you to focus, concentrate on something, while they're doing trickery somewhere else. Oh, look! While I've been terrified of losing the kids he's got a fantastic deal over the house and maintenance. Hark at me being cynical. I read later that it's not uncommon, threatening to take the kids in order to get a better financial deal. He said he's keeping all the contents of the house too.

He wants to stay the night with us in our ground floor room at the bed and breakfast, wants to see where we've been staying. I don't know yet that I'm not the first woman who does this but I point out the refuge to him. He's being so soft, gentle. He tells me what I want to hear, alludes to us getting back together though, as always, 'doesn't know what he wants'. How can I resist this man? He's the father of my children and I've loved him for so long. I only ever wanted him to love me. After a while we consummate our talk in the sack. Cats piss on their territory, don't they? He had a cat as a boy.

Despite too much vodka last night I wake up to the alarm with a hopeful feeling. Let's get the kids ready for school. Hang on. I remember last night, my beloved becoming my beloved again just before we had sex. Where is he? What's this note?

"I don't think I can do this," it reads. That's it? A thousand years of my life and four children and that's it? *I don't think I can do this*. Fuck is that draught coming from? The net curtains billow into the room. Oh look! He's only left the window open after he made his exit!

Drop the kids off at school, explain that Daddy left early for work. On the drive to 'his' place I play tapes – sloppy, mushy, cry-my-heart-out tapes. Relationship replacement music – has been since I was a teenager. That's how I've always used my music, to create a relationship that's not there much, to fill in the huge gaps. The fantasy relationship. The illusion. The pretend. The square peg in a round hole. The covering-up to others but more importantly to self. The maybe's and what ifs of …a hundred million things.

He answers the front door, a small towel round his waist.

"I need some space." he shakes his head, looks over his shoulder.

"What happened?"

"Sorry… you'll have to go. Someone's here." The new girlfriend, Suzanne. My body freezes, immobilized by his words. I don't understand what last night was about. Surely he loves me? Surely it's best for the kids if we can sort it out. This is gutting. Once I'm back at the bed-and-breakfast I snuggle up with my bottle of vodka and just about wake up in time to get the kids. Struggle. Luckily leggings are in fashion so no one notices I sleep in the clothes I walk around in. The truth is my soul's in bits. *I'm* in bits, broken, and I don't know how to fix things. Some people like revenge – surely not the father of my children?

"It's not tit for tat," he always says that after he's done something that hurts. Actually it's often revenge for something he's imagined so I can't prevent it. But that's the whole point, isn't it?

Eventually, after several prompts, the lazy fucker/carefully-controlled/purposefully-obstructive man gets the paperwork done so we can buy a house. A little ex-council house, I suppose like the one he always said would be nice to have, though curiously not for himself. I get one in the hope of getting his approval, not reading it as the suggestion it is. It's hard getting a mortgage with no income, but… Right, then. Where's this single life I'm to make the most of?

Chapter 12: Dirty Dancing

My New York adventure is only for a few days so best I make the most of it before the money runs out. I've decided to try to meet some Mafia – have a go, anyway. I enjoy the long flight over, the free drinks.

My friend Tim, who moved back here from London, meets me at the airport and I check into the Marriott Marquis. It's deliciously posh. Huge, with brass and glass elevators.

Later me and Tim have dinner in this rotating restaurant. The vodka gives me a snug warmth albeit briefly. Then it takes me to a place I don't handle so great – which doesn't combine well with the moving floor. Bloody jet lag. Luckily Tim goes back to his life while I can still see properly. He's lovely. I met my friend Tim, who's gay, in London a couple of years ago. He's quite posh and clever, works high-up – director – for some elegant shop, sorry, stoarre, on Fifth Avenue.

I think of myself as an alternative tourist, not too interested in the average touristy attractions and I've a thing about meeting some Mafia. They're sexy and exciting – or they *were* in The Godfather.

When I go back to the Marriott Marquis I decide, or Tim decides it's too expensive so we check me out of the hotel and I go to something much 'lower' on West something Street for a third of the price. I reckon I'll compromise – I'll stay here but drink at the Waldorf Astoria so I'm still having a treat.

Forgive me. With drinking and that the days have this habit of getting sort of mixed up, but my trip goes something like this.

I meet a bloke. In a café. He seems intelligent, a decent type, and we get talking. He's a podiatrist with his own practise and it's his lunch break. He's got silvery hair, bit Steve Martin-ish but he's not as old, about late thirties. The 'settling down' type rather than the 'shag you once without a condom' type.

We agree we'll meet up for dinner later. But he gets real wary, reserved, when I ask him questions about the Mafia. We walk back to his podiatry place but when I call him in the afternoon to confirm dinner arrangements he's got to work late and can't make it. Awww that's a shame. He seemed really nice.

I get a cab to Little Italy and walk round for two hours in the cold looking for signs of the Mafia. All I see are shop workers and smart tourist couples with smart shopping bags walking in and out of smart restaurants. Disappointing.

Grabbing a coffee – sorry, cawfee – is a real treat though. I shift in my seat, staring at a smart couple with smart shopping bags. The man listens while she talks, even laughs at something she says. Then he talks and she listens while he touches her fingers with his fingers, gently. They both smile and neither shouts.

How would that be? I bet they even drink tea in their garden together. I'd *love* that. Someone to drink tea with me in my garden. Someone to talk with, who didn't talk facing the other way so I struggle to hear, and if the winds going the wrong way I hear nothing, nothing but the wind and someone's irritation that I didn't hear their (purposefully?) quiet voice. It's getting darker so I go back to the hotel.

I meet a bloke. A very thin, bespectacled man. In a cab. He's the driver. He's a bit like Norman Bates out of Psycho but with glasses. We get talking. He doesn't say he has mother problems so I tell him I want to go to a comedy club and he says he'll take me.

He picks me up from my hotel and we go to a seedy comedy club. It's very dark and the wooden floor's slippery with alcohol. Wasteful. The comedy's crap. The company's crap. The drinking is good. I let him buy me drinks but return to my cheap hotel alone. Remembering the evening I have a shower, shivering, then fall into bed.

Most nights I drink at the Waldorf. The drinks are expensive – I shall have to be careful. The people are posh, mostly suits on business except for the odd prostitute. And me. What am I?

I try a martini. It comes with salt around the glass and green olives – proper James Bond style or so I'm told. Repulsive but I can't waste it. I look around the impressive art deco bar, glad I'm having such fun. The dark wooden bar and dark wooden furniture are perfect in their stillness. They keep watch like royal guards on surveillance. This is the life, eh?

The huge, aching, painful, dark hole in my stomach and my head and my legs and my feet pops up and screams to be soothed. I wriggle my toes but there's no solution. Never has been, never will be – will there? It's been there so long I accept it as part of life. I drink up – that'll help.

I study the prostitute. I study the suits. Could they be Mafia? How can I tell? It's not like they're carrying violin cases or wearing trilby hats. I wonder if the hotel is owned by Mafia – the prices they charge are criminal.

One suit tells me there's a lot of Mafia with interests in the construction industry. And there's a load of them here tonight for some convention tomorrow. They all look immaculately similar in sharp black dinner suits with bow ties and crisp, white shirts with the frilly bit down the front. And clean fingernails. How does that work – construction workers plus clean fingernails?

The toilets or 'bearrthrooms' are so luxurious it seems a shame to return all those Bloody Marys. But needs must, eh? Shame to let the red liquid swish back up through my throat – it tastes almost the same the second time round. Wonder if anyone re-drinks theirs? You'd have to strain it, separate the chunks of food from the drink. Or would you? Two birds – one stone?

I go exploring down a corridor. It's quiet. I find these double doors and gently prise one open. It's a huge banqueting hall thing. Looks like some kind of conference or business award ceremony. I sneak in, inch my way to one of the big round tables near the doors. There are white linen tablecloths, mostly empty glasses, people wandering around like it's all almost over.

The thing is I collect salt and pepper pots – got loads at home. But the ones they've got here are so elegant, tall, slim, plain white china. I wait for the moment everyone at the table's concentrating on another speech. Suddenly into my head pops this prayer we used to say at infants' school before we ate our school dinner. *For what we are about to receive may the Lord make us truly grateful.* In a simple sliding action I put one then the other pot into my bag. I leave soon after, hoping I look suitably bored, chuffed with my 'purchase'. *Amen.*

Back at the bar I study the prostitute. She's wearing a fur coat. She's got company but I can't tell if it's business or pleasure. A punter, a 'john'… or is she chatting with a fellow guest? Hmm. I wonder if I could do it. Can't be that hard –surely? What's the harm? No one will ever know, being so far from home. Sod it, why not?

So when this bloke opposite, a bit chubby, notices me giving him the eye he comes over, smiling. He's about mid-thirties and, of course, wearing a posh suit. But with ginger hair and a moustache. Pulleeze. I absolutely DO NOT fancy this man but he'll be good to practise on. I cannot get to grips with a moustache on a bloke so I try to think of something nice like balloons (the gas ones, not the cheap type that burst in your face as you're blowing them up), cocktails with Malibu in (mmm..rum and coconut) and a silk scarf from Paris. I've always wanted a silk scarf from Paris. Maybe when I'm rich and famous…

Mind, he's pleasant enough, friendly. My Bloody Marys are going down a treat too, but then I have to rush to the 'bearrthroom'…

"Where were we?"

"I was telling you I'm in sales. And I'm from Charleston. Remember? My girlfriend and me, we live together and we're very happy."

After the bit where I ask him if he'd like to pay me for sex and he says no but thank you for asking, we have a sort of heart-to-heart and I tell him it's good being single and yes, the kids are with their dad while I'm away, no, splitting up hasn't affected them at all because we've stayed good friends, he was the love of my life and when you've had kids with someone the love doesn't go away just like that does it if you know what I mean yes please a large Bloody Mary yes please same again yes please same again yes please same again yes please same again well yes we did go to a women's refuge me and the kids but like I say we're friends again now me and him well yes he did keep the house but I bought a small ex-council house round the corner for me and the kids don't ask how I did it he always said it's nice to live in a little council house so I got one but it didn't cheer him up oh well I never could make him happy yes please same again it's best for the children if we stay friends don't you think I don't wanna turn into a bitter ex-wife person well if that's okay yes please same again but first I need to go to the bearrthroom that's better I've made room for the next drink and now it seems like a good idea to go back to Mr Salesman's room in the Waldorf Astoria and I let him do certain things to me well why not a woman's got needs too but I don't let him go all the way and I'm indignant just because I've come to your room and I've let you do that to me doesn't mean you can have sex with me I'm not that type of girl who d'you think I am and he says he's really soarry.

I leave early the next morning. I'm repulsed by him but more repulsed by myself. It's quite dark in New York. But then it *is* November.

The next night I'm back at the Waldorf. It's okay because Mr Salesman has gone home. The prostitute with the fur coat's back. She's quite attractive in a black-dyed-hair-God-knows-how-many-bodies-have-laid-on-top-and-underneath-her type of way. It's like those almost but not quite invisible lines on her face are a tally. A shagging tally. I've had a few to drink and someone asks me if I want to go to a club. Awww, it's nice to be asked so I agree I'll go. Next thing I know, a gang of about eight penguin-suited blokes (can't tell if they're Mafia – they're not telling and they're not wearing hats) and the prostitute and me are getting into a white limousine.

We go to a club called Tattoos. The entrance is cordoned off like it should be a crime scene but it's not. It's just the entrance. The men pay for the limousine and for me and the prostitute to get into the club which is really sweet of them. And it turns out the doormen only let the blokes in because they're with me and the prostitute. So that's lucky.

Almost immediately I'm on my own, which is how I like it. It's dark in here, with small coloured lights, red ones and blue ones, dotted about on the bars. The dance floor is big.

I get a drink then get on and dance – squished up as there are so many people. It's different from a club back home. Here it's a bit more 'everyman' and there's a weird psycho in the corner dancing on his own. Dancing on his *own*. What a freak! I look away from him, pathetic creature.

It seems like quite soon I spot and am spotted by a gorgeous man who slides over and starts dancing with me. He's Italian-American and the gorgeousest bloke I've ever met close up. He buys me a drink and we dance and chat. I talk to him about my search for the Mafia.

"Come here," he grabs my arm.

"What?" God, he's gorgeous. He pulls me over to the wall. I think we're less conspicuous here. I bet he wants a snog. God, he's gorgeous. And a quick worker – not a problem. God, he's gorgeous.

I stand with my back to the wall looking up at him. I'm smiling as English rosy as I possibly can. He stands over me with his arm against the wall above my head. I am so ready for this. I hold my stomach in.

"I wanna show you su'mnt." Here it comes.

He bends down. No – not here surely! Even I would draw the line at cunnilingus on the dance floor. I'm just about to suggest we kiss first when he pulls up the hem of his trousers. On his ankle there's a holster. And in the holster there's a gun. This is *so* exciting.

We leave the club and sink down into his black sports car – a Corvette thing – which is parked a block, sorry, a blahk away at an underground car park. He drives us back to my (cheap shit) hotel and somehow I get the key to fit the door of my room. It's not so easy, what with the walls moving away from me, then up-close to me. Away. Close. Away. Close.

This man is stunning, late twenties – early thirties.

"Can I see it?"

"Pardon me?"

"Your gun – can I see it?"

"Sure." He takes it out of its holster and empties the bullets onto the bed. I hold the gun in my hand, stroke it, giggling.

I think he likes me as much as I like him. He tells me his uncle, who lives over by Westchester Racecourse, works for the Mafia. Job done.

Oooh no, hang on, I won't be a sec. I rush to the bearrthroom and vomit good and hard, emptying a fair bit into the toilet. Oh, please God, no, never again. While I'm in there I hear a firm click as the door meets the frame, determined. Shit shit shit!

The next day I can't reach Mr Italian-American on the number he gave me. Oh, well, I must have written it down wrong. I feel like I've more or less achieved my goal to find the Mafia. It's a laugh all this, isn't it?

One last treat on my final night. I've done a few tourist bits like Wall Street and for tonight I've booked to eat at the restaurant at the top of the World Trade Centre. I'm wearing a khaki-coloured woollen coat-dress I treated myself to from Hampstead, natural tights and black high heels. I *know* I look good. I dressed really carefully. Oh, I wish someone would say, "Blimey, you look gorgeous," like I do when my kids are dressed up special.

As the cab pulls up I look up at the Twin Towers. This is the life, eh? My birthright – I just never collected till now. I reckon my birth family does stuff like this all the time with their million-dollar apartment on Miami Beach. But who needs it? Who really needs all that? Eh? Eh?

I go up in the otherwise empty lift. It's not long till the wind whistles around the lift. It feels like any moment it'll take off. Up and up, the whistling accompanies me respectfully, my arm on its arm till we arrive at the restaurant on the billionth floor. I'm here – Windows on the World.

I'm shown to a table over in a secluded corner, up a couple of steps. It's not a small table meant for one – more like for six.

I can see the view from here though. Before the waiter returns I go back down the two steps and stand nearer to the window for a closer look. The powerful lights from the city out-do any darkness. From up here the lights are bright, hopeful.

While I eat my meal I look around. There are a few couples but the restaurant's not full – it's a Monday. Tonight it's a lonely place. A few drinks later I find the familiarity, cosy and warm. But the dark, dark gap, the hole at my centre, screams for my attention, bringing the fear with it. More drinks settle it slightly.

Oh well, guess I've completed my adventure, achieved my goal. This is the life, eh? I'm back home tomorrow, back to my life. I miss the children, must pick them up some Hershey Bars. I leave the table and move my feet extremely carefully down the steps. Funny, it's like they don't want to move.

Chapter 13: Return of Dracula's Bride

The kids see their dad more and more often. Sometimes the whole gang, sometimes in ones or twos. I've read it's better for children to maintain good contact during a break-up so I make sure they see him. A lot. Encourage it, promote their relationship as always and never say no. So much do I do this that my eldest boy notices.

"We want to see you *too!*" he says, which never occurred to me. Sweet that he says it but why? Why would they want to see *me*?

It's awkward saying no to their dad. Since assertiveness classes he tells me 'we've' got the right to say no but is it true? It's an unspoken secret we keep to ourselves that I work with his rules even when I don't know what they are. And still if there's something I don't like he'll convince me otherwise.

Often he turns up unannounced and whisks them off with him, the kids, usually to stay the night at his. Even on school nights. They're late back in the morning but he refuses either to drop them at school or bring them home earlier. When I take them into school late I never squeal that it's his fault. Who wants to be a grass? I tell everyone "You'll never get me to say he's a bad father". Even in the refuge I said it.

I'm struggling with the balancing act of running a home like a normal mum and trying to be a nice ex-wife while still enjoying singledom. I'm right into the habit of clubbing now, usually at the over-thirties clubs. 'Grab-a-granny' or 'Jurassic Park' as they say. Or should it be shag a shifty over-fifty? Love the dancing. It's that rather than the vodka, which I can drink anywhere, obviously. The dancing and the attention. I don't take it too seriously myself – just have a laugh, a dance and a drink.

It's Friday so tonight is clubbing night. Here we are. I manage to find a space in the crunchy gravel car park, which is full of holes that knacker your heels. The doormen here are gorgeous, with towering, muscle-rippling 'give it to me gently' bodies. Mmm. Bloody five quid to get in! Still, it's an investment if I achieve the three dinner dates I've set myself. Obviously I'll have a few drinks, who wouldn't?

There's a nagging voice in my head – my pain-in-the-arse invisible friend. Sometimes he moans about the drinking. Even worse, he gets all moral when you're busy trying to pull. Starts tutting, says things like "Conversation should come before condoms."

Condoms. As if!

Myself, I think safe sex means 'WHEN SHAGGING IN BACKSEAT ALWAYS ENSURE HANDBRAKE IS ON'. But only in drink and on the odd occasion when things can run away with you. Me.

My friend Andrea's here already with some friends. I always feel awkward like they're looking down on me. Well, some of them are. Specially the gorgeous tall blonde woman who some of the blokes call the Ice-Maiden.

I'd love to be tall, not the short arse I am. Five foot

two. Okay, one. One and three-quarters. At the moment though I'm pleased with my body which I work hard at, intake wise. I work out how much I drink then deduct it from food consumed or to be consumed. If there's too much to deduct or if I eat something I regret I shift it in the toilet. How else can I expect to keep a flat stomach and an arse like this? Your tits get a bit empty, like saggy elephant's ears, though no one's complained. As they say, there's a price for everything. After years of being ugly and repulsive I'm like a kid with a new toy. I love the attention, flattering. Last time I saw my beloved's brother Trevor, he noticed I'd started to dress different.

"Why d'you wear these... short skirts?"

"Takes the attention away from my face." Silence.

Andrea's new bloke, Lenny, turns up. She's chuffed – it means they're back on. He's ten years younger than her. Go, gel. She's a laugh, Andrea. She likes a drink, like we all do, but this woman, she's like two completely different personalities. Can you believe how drink changes some people? The rest of the week she's Mrs Perfect: perfect house, perfect dinner on the table, ironing all done, her kids' shirts bright white – like they're Germans on a camping trip. She does several different part-time jobs, including Avon and she's one of the top reps in the country! She was one of my managers when I did the bags and we've been friends ever since. She's perfectly organised, remembers everyone and all their children's birthdays. She missed yours? No! Must've been the post.

But get her out, get a drink inside her...

Usually I start off with the group then drift, spend the night dancing and 'mingling'. Ooh look! That trainee barrister bloke's here. I do like a bit of smooth.

I can't believe my luck when he asks me to dance but then he starts asking me all these questions about some woman at the bar, thought she was with 'us'. Fucksake. Ladies' room time, I think. Wanker! Some women in here are older, fatter and uglier than me. There is a God, then! Why's it so easy to feel inadequate? What's that about?

And why do us women spend forever in the toilet trying to become more and more gorgeous? The state of some of the blokes out there! Saturday is couples night but on Fridays there are a lot of married men whose wives don't understand them. We reapply and reapply and reapply our make-up. For what? Some of the blokes are repulsive, sleazy, slimy, balding frogs – and on a bad night they're just the *good* ones!

Make up refreshed, the women go back into the club looking for the man of their dreams but will probably end up with nightmares. Not me, though. Don't take it seriously, like I said.

A few drinks later – good old vodka, my old friend. It reminds me I've never been to bed with an ugly bloke but I've woken up with a few. Feel a bit sick. Ooh, no – I'll go outside. Stomach in, that's better, deep breaths as I go round to the car park. I can hear a woman's voice. And a bloke's. The woman's got her little black dress hitched up though it doesn't take much hitching. She's slammed against the brick wall with some lorry driver who's always here. Looks like she *has* found the man of her dreams and he's making-promises-of-a-great-future-and-he'll-leave-his-wife-and-it's-definitely-her-that-he-wants-to-be-with-and-isheonthepillandthistimeit'sdefinitelytruelovehe'sneverfeltlikethisbeforeandhe'lltellhiswifetomorrowand… Aarrrggghh.

"Wow babes," he pants, dragging on his fag.

"What about my turn?" She tugs on her dress.

"Typical woman. Self. Self. Self."

He storms off, zips up, tucking his flapping shirt inside his trousers.

Cheeky trucker! Unseen, I puke up behind a car then go back for more dancing and a top-up. Luckily I already achieved my 'three dinner dates' goal.

After everyone's danced and drunk and danced and drunk and crunched and snivelled and tripped over and I really love Andrea – like sisters an' bess friends – oh you're so funny you and Lenny – iss time to go. I drive myself home.

Next day I notice something on my car. Up close I see the dried vomit along the side, starting from under the driver-window. Tornado super-vomit. Liquidy bits and bitty bits. Honestly, the kids on this estate! I remember then opening the window on the drive home. What? No, I know it's not ideal but I wouldn't vomit *inside* the car would I? That would be disgusting! It's all a laugh, though, isn't it?

With the kids' dad seeing them so much we also see a fair bit of each other. He's still in touch with Grace too. Sometimes she and her son go round to his for dinner though she doesn't always tell me – it's the kids that do.

Grace always worries she's dumpy but others hardly notice. She's a lovely person, that's what counts. She really cares about people. Fosters teenagers, which pays a lot more than younger children – hundreds each week. Keeps her in a brand-new car. Not bad for someone on benefit, working part time at play-group eh?

One day we're talking about our friendship.

"I love you. You're my best friend," she says and I'm

chuffed she feels like that.

She's still here when my husband returns the kids and stays for coffee, has a laugh. It's nice, this, in my home, grown-ups relaxed, kids happy.

I look down at my fake nails. One of them is super-glued back on, the index finger, the one that's supposed to point things out. I wriggle in my seat with my perfect size ten arse. Life's good. Hand-me-down table but brand-new cups. Matching. A perfect show. It's so perfect maybe I'll be forgiven.

"Why does no one ever just phone up and say they fancy a shag?" He's funny. We all laugh.

Later that evening I have a sudden brainwave all my own, pick up the phone.

"Do you fancy a shag?" The kids are in bed and it's a bit of harmless, grown-up fun eh? Kitchen table. He leaves afterwards without looking round. The 'no kiss' goodbye mirrors the greeting. It's like business but no money changes hands. What's that old saying? Not all business is good business.

Stood at the open door I call out…

"Do you like my little house?"

"It's alright. Needs decorating."

"How d'you feel about it when you're here?"

"Territorial." It's nice he feels a bond to our new home which is in a road off his road. Not far at all. Share the same bit of sky, same rain, same clouds. I float in the essence of him, father of the children. And through the mist of too much wine I slide as if on a silken escalator up to my bed. He was here for less than thirty minutes.

Sometimes I take the kids to the pub or working men's club. They get to play in the garden, have cola and crisps. On Sundays I take them to a karaoke pub.

They like the singing and dancing. We have a good drink and a dance. The kids enjoy it.

But life isn't just about having fun. Why's there so much paperwork with running a house? Normally I like it but it's piling up so this week's goal is to sort out the bills, etc. Bank charges. So irritating.

I tick off my to-do list. With the others at school, me and my curly-haired boy head for the building society. The queue! Why did I come on a Monday? My curly-haired boy runs under the rope the grown-ups are hiding behind, like we've been called in to see the headmaster. *What is it this time?*

He pings the rope against an old lady's shopping bag on wheels. When she smiles at him he does it again. And again. And again.

"Come and stand with Mummy."

"No!"

"Come on, darling."

"No!"

"Have a story when we get home?"

He throws himself onto the comfy thick, thick blue embossed carpet in the middle of the building society. The queue parts in waves like he's really important – Moses at *least*.

"Wanna go to the pub, wanna go to the pub."

A tall man in a raincoat looks at me, his face neutral. Snidey fucker think he's looking at? I grab my child's hand, smile at a woman I recognise from the NCT and try to avoid the gaze of the building society worker peering over her glasses.

"What, darling? You want to go to the park?"

"Pub. Wanna go to the pub."

"Shh, now, we'll go to the park later. Come on, give Mummy a hug."

He whimpers as I pick him up, shh-shh him and there-there him. I smile like life's a great place to be.

When I get a regular boyfriend or two, my beloved's interest in me gets rekindled. They say that, don't they? You never know what you've lost till it's gone. He tells people, specially other women, specially his new girlfriend, "The first cut is the deepest." It's strange because it seemed shallow for him at the time – not deep at all. Almost as if there must be a reason why his current woman, whoever she is, doesn't feel good enough about herself.

It's Sunday and we've brought the kids to Walton-on-the-Naze for the day. I like it here, where we went as kids, first with Adrian, Tony, Patrick and the foster kids. Then without them once they'd all disappeared.

The usual plan for Walton-on-the-Naze is: beach and paddling under the pier, fish and chips then onto the pier as in funfair. As young as four I remember going back to the caravan at the Martello camp in the dark but warm nights. The excitement that came with the crackling of Radio Luxembourg on Mum's radio. We knew she was happy, *they* were happy, Mum and Dad, because she wore perfume. Topaz by Avon, with its yellow-fake-rectangular- glass stone on top of the bottle. The haze of happy days. The bliss of simple memories. So I've always taken the kids.

After the day on the beach we do fish and chips. Then it's pier time. Then. Now. There are still the same fun-fair rides as when I was a youngster; same horses on the merry-go-round, lick of paint, that my dad went on with me when I was four. Three, even. Same helicopters that rise and fall as you move the metal bar in front. Same boats that go round and round on the dark mysterious water, daren't put your hands in where it doesn't concern you – NO, DON'T! Same toy monkeys in the brass band, bashing symbols to tunes they've played for thirty years like they're pop-pickers' new releases. A whole day of laughter, kids happy. Then. Now. Busy making the illusion fit into the day. Then. Now.

My children's father makes to hold me upside down over the edge of the pier after we discuss the two blokes I'm seeing.

"Choose me," says their joky Dad. "Choose me!" he keeps on.

I love the attention, scream with laughter. How can I resist him, father of my children?

"OK, OK," and our little kids laugh to see Mummy and Daddy having such fun. And the dish ran away with the spoon. Onlookers watch like we've escaped from the asylum. Ha.

I get rid of the other blokes and he gets rid of the girlfriend, Suzanne. They're due to go to France next day but he tells me he drops off a note saying he can't make it. Payback – except I feel bad for her. He tells me it was to be her first time abroad. But he goes on his own instead, he says. Phones me with stories of the beauty of the Bayeux Tapestry. It depicts the story of the Norman Conquest. It's over seventy metres long, did you know? Must've been a long battle..

Over the weeks he stays over more and more. I cook nice things, put them out prettily on the new crockery, new everything because we had nothing. Well, he gave us the kids' old bunk beds and they topped and tailed, head to foot till I got extra second-hand beds. He needed the other beds for his lodgers and decided he'd keep for himself the double bed my dad got us for a wedding present. Fair enough, just me being picky.

The kids like it when he's round. It's all you want, isn't it, to be with the father of your children? Gradually it's like we're becoming a couple again. This time my biggest concern is being even more perfect, looking good, slim, available, make-up, try and keep his interest up. King Husband.

In his house there are three or four lodgers but he stays with us, mostly. I've taken to staying in more. His hair permanently in a ponytail; he works weekends behind the bar at a nightclub. Sometimes he doesn't come back afterwards. I never ask why but assume he doesn't want to disturb us when he's back late, assume he goes to his.

I don't expect him to pay for anything, though it'd help. Anyway he says he can't afford it and it's just nice to have him here with us. My money's run out now. I lent him some for a car but he didn't repay it so I borrow to buy things for the house.

For my husband's thirty-fifth birthday I've planned a surprise treat. We're picked up by a white limo. Scotch for him, vodka for me. Fleetwood Mac for him, Madonna for me.

He's wearing his suit – double breasted. And I'm wearing a white sailor dress, big square collar, drop waist, pleated skirt and a navy-blue linen pill-box hat. White hold-ups – lacy thigh-highs. My friend Jan did my hair and make-up – *even* eye liner – and lent me her sexy strapless basque.

I make an early start on the vodka. Can't stop once I start on it, that's the trouble. And if it's in front of me, well. Is it a compulsion? Like doing what he wants is a compulsion? But the drink allows me to tolerate life by seeing it through a veil. It protects me, sieves away the truth like pebbles in the soil of a seed-bed.

That's me depending on things. The drink, him, it used to be the fags. I loved it once I gave up smoking. The cigarettes were no longer telling me what to do. Hate being told what to do, rebel me, so they say. So I say! Rebelling against what and why? Do I wear it like a badge? Does it make me more fun to spar with – the entertaining shag? Does that make me a person with more energy to give away or to be taken by the energy stealers? Am I a better notch on a belt?

Or just a tart with a heart, as my neighbour once said, the one who hid the black sacks pre-refuge, for us. My eighty-year-old neighbour who I'd chat with over coffee or vodka when his wife was away till the night he grabbed me, told me he loved me. Fucksake – I thought he was a father figure! *Grandfather* figure!

By the time we get to the opera, Pelléas et Mélisande in London, I'm a goner. Do you know they only put all the words up above the stage in English. They do!

"Oh – it's just like watching EastEnders!" Hard not to giggle. A little one hops out, bounces off the horribly expensive programme and hits the seat in front. Mrs Beautiful Red Velvet Dress wriggles her elegant bare shoulders.

"Please don't spoil it, Mand." He's got his sensible hat on. I'm fucked, sleep through it, mostly. Weeks of planning gone in a vodka bottle. Whoosh. But I come round enough for dinner at the Ritz, back on track.

I tell him, get a cigar if he wants one. Twelve quid! Jesus! But it *is* his birthday. During the meal it's like something's missing. Can't fault the meal. It's glorious. Nouvelle cuisine. Lamb chops to die for, which the lambs *did* of course. Can't fault the surroundings. It's all so ornate and the ceiling is beautifully painted, with flowers fluttering against the palest, fluffiest of skies.

Conversation – that's what I can fault. It's conversation that's missing. Or interesting conversation. We have a dance and he looks round, as if to see who, if anyone, is watching or can be watched. No one is so we just have the one dance. Why's it so hard to get his attention? Get him to say anything that means anything? When we're alone it's like he's an empty shell posing as a person. I try then give up, let the silence settle. It's peaceful here at least.

After the meal I pretend to visit the ladies but instead pick up the room key as arranged. He approves of the surprise. Before we came I wrote to the Ritz, told them how special it is that we're back together, what it means to the kids, blah blah. Voila! There's champagne in an ice-bucket, a rose on each pillow and chocolates. Special. We're both impressed.

There's a balcony with a view of Piccadilly. All that energy: lights, lights and more lights. The buzz. It's exciting watching people together who look as if they like each other, the traffic, the taxis honking.

Great night, cost a fortune but it's been worth it. *He's* worth it. He always wanted to go to the opera so now I've made sure. And I love most classical music. So.

When it's my birthday I'm not sure what he'll do. I try to act like I'm not excited. He's not good at good surprises. Tentative, he enters the house, goes into the kitchen, sits at the white melamine hand-me-down table. Ceremonious.

"Happy birthday." He's hiding something in his hand. Is it a huge pink diamond, sparkling with his love for me?

"What is it?"

I can't help but smile as he grins. He holds out his hand, puts something on the table. Look! There it is, my birthday surprise. It's a pack of Wrigley's chewing gum.

"Happy birthday."

What do I say?

"Don't look at me like that."

He's pseudo-offended, half smiles at my reaction.

"Like what?"

"It's a big thing, me giving you that. It's my *favourite* chewing gum – the one I buy all the time. And I'm giving it to you… so it means a lot."

The drinking's not good. I say that but it *is* quite good, the actual drinking. It's *living* that's become the problem. I'm sick and tired of being sick and tired, as they say. I've tried different things like changing drinks, buying smaller bottles, drinking after a certain time, watering it down, blah fucking useless a hundred different ways of lying to myself blah. I'm not an alcoholic, obviously, because I keep being sick. Alcoholics can *hold* their drink!

But I've had enough. So, shit scared, *bricking* it, I call up AA. Yes, yes, as in Alcoholics Anonymous. This woman tells me I'm welcome to come to a meeting. She's lovely, doesn't have a go or anything!

"See what you think," she says. So I agree I'll go, I'll be there. I don't tell anyone what I've decided. It's embarrassing. Not your average night out, is it? Hmm, let me think… Pictures? Restaurant? AA meeting? I know – I'll go join a roomful of drunks.

There's a meeting of Alcoholics Anonymous on Tuesdays and Fridays at the community hall. Today is Tuesday. First I go to the pub for possibly a final top up. I look decent, mustard-coloured leggings and a matching cowl-neck jumper. Good ones, Marks and Sparks. Nails done. In the pub's 'ladies,' the mirror lies for me once more.

You look fresh as a daisy.

"You sure? Only it looks to me like if I poke something sharp into my cheek neat vodka will pour out."

Maybe a bit tired, bit run down that's all.

Best I keep my nails to myself in case I puncture my body.

At the first meeting I don't remember much about the huge room; kettle, tea and coffee on a table, assortment of biscuits, loads of people, lots of kissing and hugging shit.

I'm struck, however, by the warmth that's here. It hits me as soon as I walk in. Bamm! Like stepping off a plane at Gran Canaria – whooph! It's a shock but a welcome one as I sink into it. Heaven on Earth. Someone hands me a coffee, thank God. I don't remember many words, just the BRIGHT WHITE LIGHT that blocks out everything like that time at Relate when I thought I heard Gloria say she loved me. Just the same.

Someone says it's a chip meeting so I look round expecting someone to take orders for the chip shop. Truth is I'm a bit nervous to eat. But no. They hand out a chip for differing lengths of sobriety. The chips are like counters in a Snakes and Ladders game but this is more serious. It's a life-or-death game: heads you live, tails you slide into the snake pit and die. Which way you gonna play it?

"Anyone here with the desire to give up drinking?"

I raise my hand a little. It's like one of those posh

auctions where someone with hay fever twitches half a nostril. Next thing they know they've paid a million quid for a dirty, mouldy, cracked vase.

My hand's obviously connected to my tear ducts because droplets push each other out through my eyes like they're on distressed space-hoppers. Or wait – is it the vodka getting out? No. It's tears.

This woman hands me a blue plastic chip. Everyone smiles and claps. Am I that clever then, that unique? I've never been so rewarded for crying. Mascara's had it!

It suddenly seems like a massive step even to have come here. Then something I barely recognise – relief, it's relief – washes over me like a huge Hawaii Five-O wave.

As I look down at the chip, the size of a large coat button, the woman gives me a hug. Hugs from an adult. For me? I feel a bit awkward then, as I don't get too many though I've seen them from my husband to Grace and vice versa as he holds her firmly, tells her she's safe now. There, there.

They all do it here. It's as if people in this room like each other, say kind, encouraging things, keep quoting from 'the big book of AA.' Strange, because it's not that big, just the size of any other completely life-changing book. Dark blue, the book matches my chip. It's the book of Alcoholics Anonymous and contains every bit of magic needed to live a sober life. Everything. Abracadabra – just like that!

The words that filter through to me here and there from these sober-drunks are also on posters round the walls: 'Easy Does It', 'One Day at a Time', 'Keep It Simple', like they're starring in a sit-com and trying out catch phrases. There's some talk of a Higher Power –

yeah, yeah whatever.

And the Twelve Steps. Got that right because there are twelve or thirteen steps on an average staircase, did you know? How perfect. After completing the Twelve Steps do you get to the bathroom, bedroom or even the loft? What's up there anyway, way up there, beyond the steps? Is it possible to get that high? Will I get to meet God on the landing?

Though I only 'hear' a few words I do notice it's a big, big room full of people sat around tables, joined up in a quadrant and they 'share' round the room. At the end of the meeting soon after chip giving I scarper lest I get pounced on. I'll probably come back, though. Yeah, I reckon.

My new yet old beloved won't move in properly. Though I tell everyone I know that we're back together, he doesn't. Won't tell his brothers and he goes to see them all without me.

"But you've got lodgers at yours," I say. "Can't you move in here, give it as your address, let us be a proper family?"

"No. I can't afford it." I don't ask how he did it for all those years. I do, though, tell him I went to AA.

"Don't be silly – *you're* not an alcoholic!" He smiles down at me. But I keep going to meetings anyway. Haven't had a drink since that first Tuesday.

Life's different without a drink. Blimey, is it! More painful, for one thing, without the shield of alcohol. Whoah! Where did *they* come from? All these feelings rush in and swamp me. Life's unbearably dark, crippleing, and it's fantastically hard to think positively – to think at *all*. What are those things again, the long things kids have when you look through the end and see all the colours jumbled up? Kaleidoscope – that's what it's like. Life before me is mixed up together, broken bits covering over other broken bits like a child's collage and I can't make sense of it. Even if I try to turn the pictures round several degrees they're still not clear. Nothing fits any more. I can *see* the crisply angular corners of the square pegs, the smoothness of the round holes. And it ain't happening. They're not fitting together.

The new wave of self-respect – I like that part even if I'm not sure I like what I see now. Crying is easy specially when I go back to the meeting, that one and others in different dingy church halls. No way do I open my mouth to share, say, "I'm Amanda and I'm an alcoholic." I can't do that bit.

I used to think alcoholics were those people you see on park benches with string round their coats. Truth is I haven't seen anyone anything like that yet. Some *have* lost jobs, families, driving licences, been to prison and psychiatric units – no, wait, be fair, that was different! Well, not me. And it's not *for* me, this Step malarkey. I will read the literature, though so then I can convert people to be like me. Come live your life the way I do, everyone, do it the Amanda way. I do this for a while. They call it two-stepping. People suggest I go to Step meetings and get a sponsor. Nah – I'm alright with the books!

Most appear to be decent human beings. There's a lot of talk of 'being on the programme' or 'working the programme.' Bit boring, that side of things.

I do read all the literature. And I get rid of my fake nails.

We're going camping in France. Wanted to go for ten years but he always said no. Ten years of collecting camp-site addresses in the address book. It's decided – Camp Benodet in Point St Gilles, Brittany. At last. Hope it's worth the decade wait! It was exciting when we first booked but over time and now sober I start to see things differently.

I think we're taking food with us, been planned for ages. But the day before we go, after I've bought it all he tells me, no, we're not doing it that way.

There's a build up. Without the drink I notice it's about sex, making him nice dinners, sex, providing a comfortable home that he doesn't have to pay anything for… and more sex. Smiling, looking good for him. I start to see how I'm still ignored, realise how hard I've tried, concentrated on being the perfect size ten, holding in my stomach, having just the right size and shape arse for him. Though *why* when he doesn't say he notices? Only notices when I'm too thin, too fat, too this, too that, food's too salty. Blah blah a hundred fucking criticising put-downs blah.

In one hour's time we're driving to France with the four kids for a fortnight in the sun. A decade – a whole decade of waiting for this. My eyes are opening real wide. I think they might pop out my head like those dogs who look constantly surprised. I can see that he does nothing in this house, won't contribute financially or to the 'relationship'. Won't mow the lawn but spends hours doing his at his big house that he kept from me and the children. His own children. And I'm starting to think it's not okay any more. It's just not OK. If thine eyes offend thee – pluck them out! There's a few more bits of ironing, then that's it, me done.

"Can't pack mine yet – got some more ironing."

"About time you did *something*," he sneers.

In crack-second timing I realise France will be two

weeks of arguing or, more likely, being ignored while he makes a public fuss of the kids and ingratiates himself, oozing charm over total strangers he'll never speak to again.

I pounce over to the plug, switch off the iron.

"That's it. I'm not going. I'm NOT FUCKING GOING!"

So my four children – our four children – go with their dad to the car. Five minutes later he phones from his house.

"You coming or not?" Romance isn't dead, then.

"No."

I find out later that he stopped off to see my beautiful, young, sexy friend Jan. He invited her to bring her kids to France. All paid. Just as friends. She refuses.

I don't regret not going. I *do* regret not going with the kids. They phone me from France on my birthday but I don't let them hear me cry. On their return me and all four kids hug and hug and hug like it's a harmless game of ring-a-roses. Their father sleeps on the settee.

It's only been a month since I started going to AA meetings but already without the vodka spectacles things look massively different. I know now that if I lied to myself about the drinking I lied to myself about other things too. Many other things.

I'm furious at how stupid I've been, at what I've let him get away with. I'm ready. Ready to do what I've got to do. It's taken five years since starting at Relate and the Gloria thing. A protracted ending indeed. Time to have a life. Time for that grown up talk. I prepare myself to speak to my beloved next morning.

"FUCK OFF out of my house and don't come back!"

And that… is exactly… what he does.

Chapter 14: Second Chance

This time I don't have contact with my soon-to-be-ex-husband. Partly I know I'll be magnetised back into something that will hurt – without offering anything he'll make me an offer I can't refuse.

I keep up the AA meetings. I meet some good people, do all the reading and spout it to anyone who'll listen but don't bother to get a sponsor or work through the Steps. I've read them. That'll do.

I'm driving for a living – executive car service – but it doesn't pay well, so I decide I'll get a lodger. I advertise in the newsagents and some bloke rings up.

"Must just tell you I've got four kids."

He laughs.

"Not a problem. The woman I've been lodging with had two husbands die on her. Talks about death and illness all the time."

He's such a laugh. The kids love him but he's not my type AT ALL. He's three years younger than me at thirty two. Was in the RAF, went to the Falklands and lived in a sheep shed for three months. Farmers slaughtered sheep while Our Boys ate their sarnies, the blood running and the sheep heads rolling down a gully in the middle of the room through to the outside. We'll speak of it later once he becomes My Lodger.

"Did you see any dead bodies?" I know, I know, but I'm not the only one who asks!

"Just kids they were, the Argies. The worst thing was the noise – loud bangs, artillery, bombs – never knew when it was your turn to die." My hero. "When we came back, you couldn't relate to anyone. They hadn't been there so how could they *know*?"

Now he does security work at the BBC where they make Top of the Pops, EastEnders and the teen school drama Grange Hill. Grace's round when he comes for coffee.

"Doughnut?"

He takes one and tells me later that when jam splodges onto the floor he places his foot over it and it stays there the whole visit.

He agrees it's a good idea when I ask for ID. He's security-conscious and radiates warmth like a jolly visiting uncle. Always smiling. Always, always smiling. It's September '93 and my husband left last month. My *first* husband.

Going clubbing is so different without a drink. I feel like I'm in another dimension in the same place. I notice different people, different things. It's like if you're a waitress in a restaurant it's the staff you notice first then the diners. But if you're a diner you notice the other diners then the staff – if you notice the staff.

Sobriety doesn't affect my pulling power, obviously, though without a drink the blokes seem less attractive. I still dance a lot, six hours sometimes but all this is becoming less interesting.

Seeing Mum is getting more difficult too. She's so on my ex's side. Unnaturally so. It takes me about an hour to get her to see how it is for me and by the time I leave she's more supportive, on my side. The side of her daughter. Then next time I see her he, my ex-husband-to-be has been and talked her back round again. He's making it hard to stay in touch with my *own* mother. And so is she. Why does he even keep visiting my mother? Our mother-daughter position is vulnerable enough, what with her hating women.

Grace's the same. It's like he's worked on them, over the years, drip, drip, drip. I just never saw it. Or their part in it. Or *mine*. Why's he trying to take everything I have left?

Going to AA meetings has become an important part of my life. I get talking to some of the sober drunks. One of them, Terry, stood in the corner, knows a lot about recovery. He's just split up from his wife. He's not young – late forties, tattoos and a diamond stud earring, stocky with his belly hidden behind his shirt. You know the way some blokes do that, specially on a Friday night – wear a smart shirt tucked into their trousers but the shirt comes out really big and looking like it's full of air though really it's full of fat and muscle? Or just fat. Shaves his head. Mean fucker.

Yet he seems to talk sense about alcoholism. Quietly, each word calculated. Almost serene in his wisdom. Been drink and drug-free (cocaine) for two years. He tells me where he lives in a council flat next door to a woman I know from meetings.

When she's out next day I think, sod it, I'll pop next door, see if his kettle's working. Sometimes you – I – *need* to speak to someone else in recovery. Like anything it helps to talk with others who've been through something similar: birth, death, miscarriage, difficult knitting pattern, cordon-bleu recipe, shagging a psychopath.

Weird, his flat. But then so is he. Frighteningly grown-up or just frightening? He opens the door like he's Lurch's understudy. Eyes dart everywhere, on surveillance as if he's expecting the unexpected. It's so dark here. Inside the flat. But he is too, don't know – seems to talk sense outwardly but... The flat's poorly furnished but there are many antiques both in and out of display cabinets. It's a bit 'Steptoe and Son'. He has a shop, Junk and Disorderly and he buys and sells second-hand ornaments, furniture, pictures. Clears houses. He makes money from people who don't realise the value of what they have.

He smiles in the wrong places, laughs at the bad things like other's misfortune or when he's hurt someone. Sinister, this, and I shiver but *stay* and drink the too-strong, shit cup of coffee.

I admire his fire surround. Honestly that's all! I don't think of him in that way. He's so old – and dark. There's something about him – like he's buried people in the back garden. He's clearly depressed about his ex-wife but it's not just that. Has he buried himself in the garden? He's guarded; says he thinks he'll die by the sword. Exciting. Shady. Mysterious. Like there's a secret world going on for him which no one else knows about. And guess what? Apart from he's shorter, he looks like my dad!

When he agrees to measure up my fire surround we haggle over the price but he won't move on it. Instead he looks coldly straight at me, through me, threatening.

"I *have* got to make a profit!" He spits it out quietly but I step backwards. Instantly, I feel guilty. And frightened, silly me! So I buckle on the price. When he asks about my love life I tell him I've decided to stay on my own for two years, make some money, sort out my life.

"What if you fall in love?"

"I won't."

"But what if you do?"

"I won't."

Some people at the meetings are hugely helpful. Specially Phil, who's become a close friend, teaches me much about sobriety. He's in his early fifties, a big bloke with a gold chain, gold rings, posh watch and a very young girlfriend, his friend's daughter. Phil's been 'around' for years and helps many, many people. Men, women, teenagers. Gives talks in schools, prisons, you name it. He's almost revered in 'the rooms' – the holy rooms of Alcoholics Anonymous.

We speak on the phone every day. Phil tells me he loves me which is odd because I don't know what to do with it. Is he saying it as a friend, a shag, a boyfriend – what? Mostly when he says it I ask him how his girlfriend is, the young woman he now lives with.

"Can you stop saying that, please? It really pisses me off!"

Not sure if we're just friends but we nearly go too far in his car one night. I've been upset in the meeting. Happens all the time, people crying at meetings, before, during and after. Laughter too. Sometimes it's such a crack it's like having a freebie at a comedy club.

But why's this thing happening in the car when I used to think him so old? Tell you when I stopped thinking he was too old. It was the night, sat next to me he shared for some reason about his very young girlfriend. Pointing out her actual age which makes her younger than me. He knows my age. I do sometimes think his 'shares' are directed at me but don't recognise it as manipulation or grooming. Luckily we pull apart so we can remain friends.

"You're still vulnerable, didn't wanna take advantage of you," he tells me later. We both forget I was the one who pulled away.

Phil takes me flying. He flies. Oh – like my birth father! From the same aerodrome too! He used to own the plane but now rents the same one which he'd sold back to them. It's old, rickety, like an old Ford Anglia. Hope the doors don't fall off. When we fly over Essex he shows me Walton-on-the-Naze, has to shout over the rumblings of the 'Ford Anglia'.

I look and look but can't see or hear the horses on the merry-go-round. In a moment they'll fly up and meet me in the sky. Dad must be about here somewhere too, then we can all be back together, him, me and the horse that's going nowhere just round in circles. Safe but always going back to where we started. I remember that Dad stuck up for me when Mum had a go... and she'd hated me for it.

Where is he, my dad? Will I always look for him in the strangest of places? After he died I kept thinking I saw him; a bloke on telly, a bloke in the fag shop, a bloke at the bus stop. Ha – my dad at a bus stop? It never was him though and I still haven't seen him.

"Easy to believe in a Higher Power, being up here." I mean it too. Thought Phil, middle-aged, big-like-my-dad, Phil, would smile in agreement. He doesn't. Did he even hear me?

There's a huge bouquet of flowers turns up next day. The card simply says 'Why not?' When I phone the flower shop they've been told that WHEN I ring up they're not to tell me who sent them. After a few days Phil confesses, laughing.

"They're beautiful, but why *did* you send them?"

"Why not?" He laughs.

There's a few people I can call on when I fancy going out to dinner and that. Life gets its own little pattern. Quite pleasant in some respects. Except for the kids' dad who demands more and more of their time. It's like their lives are on hold – always at his beck and call.

In November I ask My Lodger if he fancies a shopping trip to New York. He's into America. His sister lives there, Illinois. And he's done New York already and likes it.

"Yeah, when?"

"Next month?"

"Game on!"

He's so sweet, always cracking jokes and having a laugh with the kids and real into being safety conscious. He emanates safety. It drips from him like Rumpelstiltskin's gold. I tell Grace about him.

"… And I wouldn't mind some sex. Ooh, no, I don't mean him, I don't see him that way."

The nearer we get to the trip the more reason there is for me and My Lodger to phone each other, obviously. He phones at least once most days. I notice how happy I get when he phones. I nip up to see him at work, grab a coffee from the canteen. As we walk over from the gatehouse he's really moody.

"It's not a hard job – but they can't fucking *do* it!" Clipped, furious. Blimey! I've never seen him this angry and I'm impressed.

Oh, no, look at that…it is, it's Dot Cotton from EastEnders! Others too – over by the fish and chips is Grant Mitchell and his screen brother Phil is already sat at the table. On the way back to the gatehouse we pass Pauline Fowler taking her dog for a walk. With the executive driving I've been here on jobs but there's not always a herd of them together, celebs. I remember when Pauline was that dolly bird in Are You Being Served. How glamorous was that woman? Bet she'll last forever after a good start like that. Always wished I'd be that gorgeous when I grew up. Oh well.

How supernatural is time? We keep on, one foot in front of the other but meanwhile it's steps and steps ahead of us. Of me. Why've I wasted so much of it? If time was money I'd be skint. Well, I *am* skint but right now at last life seems a bit hopeful, like anything's possible.

It's the Friday before New York and My Lodger asks me to recommend a club for him and his friends. I suggest a couple including one I'll be going to later tonight which I recommend as the better option if it's a shag they're after.

So I'm here now, dancing away with my size ten arse in tight, tight ski pants, trilby on my head when I feel something tickle the back of my legs.

"Ha! It's you!"

"We decided we'd come here when you told us about the clientele."He's such a laugh, My Lodger, cuddly, funny, safe, soothing. We even dance, no mean feat (feet?) as he doesn't usually. He jokes the whole way through with me and his friends. Such fun, I'm so happy. He seems happy too.

He gets a lift home in my car. We're in the lounge later with our coffee. Baby-sitter's left.

"Would you mind if I asked you for a no-strings-attached hug?"

He obliges and we sit holding each other on the settee, his big safe arms around me. All night. ALL night. Only once do I have to shift his hand when it begins a journey up my back and under my top.

So, so safe I feel, next to him. You ever done it? Just sat snuggled up like this the whole night without shagging? It's delicious. Then, bless him, he has to go to work in the morning. Supa-stamina!

It's December '93 and we're flying into New York. The children will spend a few days with their dad. From the moment the cab picks us up me and My Lodger hold hands. We do that the whole journey as in the *whole* journey. In the cab, the airport this end, during the whole flight, the airport that end, the limo and then to the cheap-shit hotel in Manhattan.

"Double or twin?" says the receptionist.

"Twin, please," says My Lodger but over his shoulder I mouth "double" to the receptionist, who clocks it with a grin.

Suppose it's not too bad, the room. Get what you pay for. My Lodger doesn't mention if he's noticed the double bed.

He starts to unpack, folds clothes neatly into the drawers. Me living out of my suitcase, I'm impressed at this precision.

"Used to work with survival equipment."

"So well house-trained!" He grins that grin he has that makes his eyes twinkle, like someone threw a pinch of magic dust over his face. He turns away quick.

"Fuck was that?" I scream and jump onto the bed.

"It went behind the radiator," says my protector lodger, laughing.

It peeps its head out. It's only a flippin' mouse. A grey mouse. In our hotel room. Oh no, please no.

"There's another one. It's black." He points. It follows its friend behind the radiator, the twitching tail poking out.

My Lodger isn't perturbed. I guess he's seen a whole

bunch worse – he saw a man blown up once when he, My Lodger, was eight and on his way to school in Belfast.

"I'm having a shower."

"Don't leave me! If they show their faces I'm coming in that shower!"

I shed my clothes just in case and luckily my threat doesn't bother him. Safety first! He pretends he doesn't notice I'm naked under the towel, doesn't murmur when I step into the shower with him. But he turns round with an enthusiastic greeting.

After me and My Lodger, or rather My Lover, change to a mouse-less room he shops for presents and I shop for an AA meeting. It's in a church hall and there are so many people they're sitting or lying on the floor so I do too. The ceiling is so high it almost reaches the heavens. The acoustics are crap and I can't hear jack but the spirit of the meeting is still here.

My Lover brings me back a new hairdryer – I forgot mine – and two cups of coffee to feed my addiction. The perfect man or what?

The rest of the trip we hold hands except when we walk up the three hundred and fifty-four steps of the Statue of Liberty. Nice word, liberty, blows clean air over you. One day we're sat on the steps at Wall Street. All these steps! But where would we be without them?

"Let's... keep it casual." He says.

"A casual fuck, you mean?"

"No, no, that's not what I mean." It is, though. It's exactly what he means but...

On the last day we drop by to say fare thee well to Tim who still works on Fifth Avenue. It's all done up for Christmas like the rest of Manhattan. As we get in the cab for the airport, still holding hands, it starts snowing. Huge, huge flurries. Gentle, safe, won't-leave-me-flurries which guide us on our journey like white stars guiding us on to a new life.

The snow causes a flight delay so we sleep on the airport floor still holding hands. Wrapped up in coats I snuggle underneath the blanket of hope, bathe in its warmth. I've never had this before.

We can't stop looking at each other, like each of us is a newborn, precious. He's beautiful when his eyes twinkle, calls me his princess, calls *me* beautiful! During the flight back, still holding hands, he starts to speak and it looks important, like I should listen.

"I should tell you something." Oh, no, he's a Jehovah's Witness! A priest! A woman dressed as a man!

"What?" I'm seriously worried now.

"I don't talk very much, never have. Other people have said about it."

He talks enough for me, about any subject I bring up. Been non-stop! No worries there.

What to do when we get home? My Lodger no more, should I ask My Lover to move out so we can date? Otherwise we'll be living together and we've not even been to the pictures.

After the kids go to school he and I sleep off the jet lag. I get into his single bed in the box-room with him. He says later he was chuffed. He hadn't known which way I'd swing it and was glad I chose to still be with him. When we wake we move his things into my room. Giving them the preparation time of a gnat's tea-break I explain the new situation to the kids. They're happy because they really like him.

When the children next see their dad we watch a

video of The Bodyguard and I cry because I think my new man is like that – will protect me the way Kevin Costner protects Whitney Houston in the film. Bliss. Is this what heaven is? I go to sleep thinking I'm a white Whitney Houston. Her bodyguard leaves her in the end but it *is* only a film. Safe at last I look at my bodyguard, his form next to mine, before we fall asleep lip-locked in a kiss.

In two weeks it'll be Christmas. Before then I make him tell his mother about me.

I'm sat next to him on the bed when he phones.

"I've met a girly," he says. She asks mother questions. Things like: is she nice blah blah? I talk to her too. She's friendly and she likes her son – how lovely.

We – he and I – figure we should go out on a date now that we're living together. At the restaurant we're talking, he is, about the state of the country.

"I blame the government," he says. Brrrng Brrrng Brrrng. That's the alarm bells I hear. Normally I'd take the piss out of someone if they talk like this. But instead of listening to the alarm bells, I, we, make a joke out of it, about people who talk like that. Everyone but him, of course. Oh, what a laugh.

Christmas is great. His mum stays a few days the week before, his sister too, over from the States. Hang on – look at that! I just noticed he smiles and does his twinkly eyes to me when his mum or sister are looking but stops when they look away. It's such a split-second thing I barely notice it and if I do clock it I look away. I must've imagined it. Me being oversensitive, picky. Instead I concentrate on the bits that make me feel we're a normal family with his mother who cares.

They're all gone by the time Mum comes over on

Christmas Day.

After her Christmas ritual *the kids have got too many presents, they're spoiled*, then it's, "So long as he puts his foot down with you. I know what you're like." She doesn't often give me relationship advice. She doesn't often talk at all lately. Never rings, always me does the ringing.

As we're about to dish up the Christmas dinner the kids' dad turns up unexpected, takes everyone down the pub, my Mum, the children. Me and My Lover keep the dinner hot and await the return of said children and mother. Though unexpected we make the most of the precious time alone.

When I tell Phil about my new man I feel guilty and worried about offending him. I shouldn't have worried. He reassures me, warmly welcomes my new man into the Phil-Amanda thing. Soon the triangle swizzles around, becomes just the two of us – me and My Prince against the world. Will he keep me safe and protect me from the hate blowing over from my ex-husband-to-be?

Within a month me and My Prince talk about marriage. Okay, it's me that brings it up. He hesitates.

"I'm just not sure." He's gentle when he speaks.

I guess it feels safe enough to even be myself. Even to get irritated, the whole bit.

"But why NOT?" The empty coffee cup I throw across the room assertively speaks volumes.

"OK then, okay," he says. Blimey, that's it?

"Blimey, that's it?"

"Yes… let's just do it." It's true. It really is true. Now we're getting married. Is it this easy to get a husband, just throw your cup across the room? Simply throw china against his better nature? I should throw out those self-help books. What do they know? If people need to know about relationships they should just ask me.

"You're beautiful. I never thought I'd marry someone beautiful."

No one has said anything like this to me before. I'm floating.

Before we have the 'let's get married' talk though, we start trying for a baby.

"How would you feel if I found out I was pregnant?"

"Be quite chuffed, I think."

That's good enough for me. He smiles his twinkly-eyed smile. Woman on a mission, me.

Being with My Prince makes me see things differently. With someone in my life who doesn't hate me I start wondering things like why's Grace so friendly with my ex, who *does* hate me? Mum too. Why's this happening? Is this what best friends do? What mothers do?

I need to sort this out so I'm in Grace's front room which smells of cats. Always has, was just too polite to say so but I can say it now. Fuck it – it *stinks*. She's sneering…

"You always talk about this loyalty thing. Don't know what you're on about. I'm not going to stop being friends with him. Why should I have to choose between you? You can't force me to choose," she says.

"Thought you said I'm your best friend. Is this what best friends do to each other?"

"I said you're my best *woman* friend."

You ever get round to seeing that film Gaslight?

"Not asking you to stop being his friend. I wouldn't. Just don't understand why you'd *want* to be."

I talked about her with Sarah from the hospital.

"She says she likes the 'underdog."

"She wants *you* to be the underdog," Sarah said. I hadn't looked at it that way.

And as I leave her 'smelly cat' flat I see it clearly. The same books, same music albums on her shelves in her comfortable lounge in her comfortable flat – all unchanged for ten years like she's Miss Haversham in training. One child, all neatly under control. Who stays this unchanged for ten years? She puts so much energy into standing still. Strange, she has this thing about her friends' husbands. She always worried she'd never have a husband. It's not true – she's had several.

I wonder if it's jealousy that turns her into a cuckoo. I'm loyal, perhaps too loyal and she's a pathetic creature who doesn't realise loyalty comes before sex in the dictionary. Maybe her dictionary is written in American.

Terry's at the next AA meeting.

"Remember you asked me, what if I fall in love?"

"Yep."

Wish he'd smile more.

"Well, I have." Big smile, me, at his gift of prediction.

He nods. Smile, for fucksake.

We've agreed to marry in June, six months from now. Quickly have a tidy up, apply for the decree absolute. And tell Mum.

"Why June?"

"That's when we want to get married."

"Hmmmph!"

When she sees My Lodger, Prince, New Man she tries to have a laugh about me with him, criticises me over something, anything: my clothes, parenting, cooking, breathing. He doesn't laugh, doesn't join in.

Oops. A first. She's used to having someone to side with against me. Only in jest, obviously. She probably doesn't mean anything by it. Thing is, I know she *does*. It doesn't feel right to be hated by your mother. Wasn't my choice, the adoption. It was hers. *She* chose *me!* I just want her to love me, thought this is how it is between mothers and daughters, assumed she loves me like I love her. But no – she doesn't.

There are certain words that have got family, like everyone else. Take Denial. It's got a younger cousin called Assumption. Assumed. That's what I did. Don't assume, they say – it makes an ass out of you and of me. Me anyway. EEYORE.

The kids are at their dad's when our curly-haired boy tells him I'm getting married to My Prince. He's not happy.

"How DARE you make silly jokes like that to me!"

He flies out the chair and whacks the boy across his back. Hard. The school call me in about it.

"His teacher noticed the hand mark during PE." says the head-teacher. She's recently widowed and got a soft spot for (men) my ex who still visits her often about …something… the children, I guess.

"Well." I guiltily think, everyone loses their temper, as I remember the thrown coffee cup that bagged me a husband. My Prince. My perfect, perfect Prince.

"Everyone loses their temper – has an off day," I quickly defend my ex against this act. His act.

"That's true. Everyone loses it. It's just that I'm obliged to tell you, to have this talk. And I'm supposed to keep a record of it."

The hand print lasts for days on our son's back. The strong arm of the law. His father's law. And I start to feel like shit that I didn't protect him from his father. That means I'm doubly to blame because it's true about the wedding plus my ex is bound to feel bad about that.

Triply to blame, then.

Six months to the wedding. I'm not working so spend time organising it. I book the hall – as in, the BBC say we can have the club-house. I meet them all in the bar after filming of Top of the Pops. He's funny, My Prince. They all like a drink.

Next month we find out I'm pregnant. Thrilled, we keep it to ourselves till we know it's safe – once the first twelve weeks are over. I don't think I'm showing yet but Mum thinks different.

"You in pod?"

"No." I *have* to lie – not even the kids know! She thinks we're marrying quickly because I'm pregnant but that's rubbish and totally separate.

Mum's suspicious when anyone marries quickly. She fell pregnant herself after her first time, can you believe? At seventeen. But she refused, refused and refused again to wed Dad before the baby was born. She'd this feeling he'd throw it back in her face later, that he'd say he 'had' to marry her – that and her HRH father telling her to say no *my Dad always said I should never have married your father*. After the support she got from her mother, *what will the neighbours say?* she went to a mother and baby Home.

Dad wasn't pleased she kept turning him down so he wrote to the Home, said she had venereal disease. After that the matron kept her isolated, the seventeen-year-old-Joan. First while pregnant and then with her new baby. Kept her separate from the other girls, separate bathroom, wasn't allowed to mix, made to wear cotton gloves all the time, made to scrub everything after she'd touched it.

It's funny she kept her baby, Adrian, yet ten years later Bernadette didn't. Mustn't grumble. Mum said she did it so she could be home in time for Christmas otherwise it'd be another month.

When Adrian was a month old they married at a register office with a 'do' back at her mum and dad's house in North London in December 1947. She was wrong about him, Dad, throwing that back at her. It was other things he threw back instead. Forever threatening to leave, he was.

"I'll leave you. Then who'll want *you* with your scabby kids?" He's hinting at the horrific eczema which caused hospital stints, bandaged from head to toe, and still remains. For HIS son Adrian it was five long years and HIS son Tony it was three. It was at the hospital that Mum turned up one day to find Adrian's hair had been shaved off by the nurse.

"The sins of the parents are visited on the children," she said.

That hospital. That's the one.

One sunny summer evening Mum and Tony had a row. As he slammed the front door the glass smashed.

"Fucking sick of it – I'll leave you if this doesn't stop." Oh, hello Dad, thought you were watching Ironside.

Mum didn't know where it came from, she said later, but come it did. I remember watching her, scary, standing up to him like that. She got big(ger?) like a big fat snowman or Michelin Man as Dad always called her. Red-faced she leaned forward in her chair pointing her 'special knife', smeared with steak juice.

"Go on, then. Go! And TAKE YOUR BLOODY KIDS WITH YOU." She says now she wishes she'd said it before, not waited the twenty years.

"D'you know he never said it again after that."

"Oh."

She doesn't need an answer. Not from me.

At eight weeks pregnant I start bleeding. Bed rest doesn't work. Our baby comes away in my hand. I've always loved sea-horses and it's what it looks like, curved with a long spine. I put it in tissue, give it to the hospital. A trainee doctor, Russian or something else spy-like shoves fingers and metal up me. Blood gushes out. My Prince holds my arm, watching this man put things up me.

"Mmm – not zure vots wrong." Stinks of fags.

A proper doctor turns up, looks in the tissue. She knows immediately. She tells us and we cry, both of us. And because I'm in hospital when the kids return from their dad's, My Prince tells them what's happened. Goes over their heads, mostly.

I'm in the kitchen one morning after the school run when the doorbell goes. Funny, not expecting anyone. It's Colin from the DSS fraud squad. Everyone knows Colin. He also visits all the attractive single mums, makes friends with some of them. Jan's known him ages. And as the weeks and visits go by we become good friends and I invite him and his wife to the wedding. He's great, friendly, tells me all the tricks people get up to on social. Terrible! He's good to us too and lets me keep my benefit book an extra week after the wedding so we've got spending money for the honeymoon: a week in a caravan on Mersea Island, Essex.

For the wedding reception My Prince lets the facilities manager choose the DJ, some woman she knows. I go to visit My Prince at work one day, have a chat with the facilities manager. She walks to the exit with me.

"You might have got your clutches into this man but *I'm* the trollop round here. Alright?" Wonder if she's finished her BBC customer service training?

My new Prince comes to an AA meeting. Sits there, seems to take it all in.

"What do you think?" *How was it for you?*

"Lot of brave people in that room." He's so sweet, says all the things I want to hear. It's delicious having someone on my side. I can't remember this happening. Not since Adrian, sometimes Gloria, Dad a bit.

I think he's tired, my man. He works long hours – a seventy-two-hour week at the Beeb, sometimes a hundred when he needs to cover shifts. Top of the Pops day is fifteen hours. He's bound to get moody a lot. Snap at the kids. Snap at me. He apologises at first. Then he tells me he hates it there, hates the people. Odd, because he's always laughing and joking with them.

My ex-husband comes round one day when my husband-to-be is at work. As I go to close the door he juts his foot in the way forcing it open. I'm shitting a brick but calmly watch him come in, don't say anything. He sits down on my settee and spills his toxic shitty guts into my front room. He's going for the self-pity angle. Old habits.

"I just want to see my children. Will you be reasonable? Can't we talk? It'd be nice to discuss the kids' progress." He doesn't mention the four nights a week he sees the kids. He *is* talking inside out and back to front.

I don't tell him I know he's spouting bollocks. Don't

tell him anything. Just nod in all the right places, use my active listening skills – straight from the assertiveness books, plus my bereavement training of course. All I can think about is keeping safe and getting him out of here.

After he spills what he needs to, he leaves. Phew. I make sure the door's shut properly. I look back into the front room. It's as if he's pissed, shit and spunked all over the settee, the floor, the walls, the telly. I can almost smell it, the mix of it, his own special cocktail. His presence – to me it's like he's the devil himself. Or at least an agent. He's like a giant killer cat, assumes a territorial position.

Two weeks before the wedding my ex-husband has the kids for the weekend, as always. He wants me to know something about him and Grace and he wants me to know it now. So he takes the kids over to hers to stay. While he sleeps in her room some of the kids sleep in the front room. Others share the same bedroom as the fifteen-year-old-boy she fosters through Social Services. The one she's paid hundreds of pounds each week for to provide a new, healthier way of living.

I speak to Phil about my ex, his support ever welcome.

"It's purposeful, his behaviour," he says.

We carry on chatting and he tells me of the time he got ill with his stomach, went to a private doctor, but they found nothing so he insisted the surgeon take another look, convinced he had cancer. The man found a tumour the size of a pinhead and removed it. All's well that ends well.

The pain of the Grace thing is huge, as planned. It's like a cancer that won't go away. Next to taking control of my mother it's the most toxic thing he could do.

And the timing – is that why he's doing it? If yes then his plan is working. The fear, always there, is bubbling up to a conscious level. It's frightening to be hated this much. I realise it's always been easier to go back to him as at least then he leaves me alone and things ease up for a while.

My husband-to-be is worried I'll go back with him. Gets moody with me about my ex. Silent anger. Then he loses his temper but says sorry when he calms down.

"Just wish we were married. Be alright once we're married."

But first we need to deal with the kids' sleeping arrangements at Grace's. My Prince phones my ex and asks him to not repeat last time's sleeping arrangements.

"It's alright – the boy's harmless. He's got the mental age of a twelve year old." His charm doesn't wash with my ex-Falklands man.

Why'd I never realise how thick he is when I was with him? Thick but wily which then makes him sort of clever. He certainly seems to live by a different set of rules from everyone else.

How easy is it to nick a bag off an old lady? Lemon-squeezy. But most of us don't because of the rules we live by. But his are different, methinks. Sometimes impulsive yet also patient, he bides his time to get the goodies. He plots, charms, seduces and when that stops working, intimidates.

My Prince first writes then phones Grace asking her the same. She also refuses. So I write to Social Services expressing my concern for my children's safety and the boys' too. They do nothing so I call them.

"We don't have a problem with it. She's apologised for her mistake and assured us it won't happen again."

They put it in writing. A mistake? Over and over? Or an accident? Like accidentally getting pregnant? Argh – how'd that penis get inside me?…Get OUT.

My ex is playing up and it's scary. He sends messages. Spiteful, frightening messages, little notes. Gets punitive – withholds money for any old reason. Turns up early, makes sure he brings the kids back late.

I'm too frightened to say no which is why I've never done it. Who knows what he'll do?

My ex-husband sends a condolence card about the miscarriage. So caring. Almost as though he gives a shit. My Prince is furious with the intrusion, treading on our new life together, talking about our precious baby that is no more.

I get an appointment with this child psychologist at Family and Child guidance because one of the kids is having problems at school. I see an older woman, loads of experience, wise. Just before the appointment I get another note from him requesting he has our daughter an extra night on her own. For some quality time.

"He takes some or all of the children four nights a week and just asked for a fifth night. He always wants more – it's impossible to make him happy. My New Man says he's trying to break up the family. I'm not saying he's not a good father…"

"The children of good fathers don't go to a women's refuge."

I can't believe I did the assertiveness courses. Yes, plural – I did the advanced one too! Ha. I'm a wreck when it comes to this man. *So* afraid of him. It's like he'll stop at nothing to injure, take what he wants. She, the child psychologist, talks to me about saying no.

"Best to start small," she says.

"I'm scared to."

"It's hard to do the right thing." She says. How freeing is this? Permission to be a good mother, to do the right thing by the children.

And I know why it's so hard. It's that I've seen things through his eyes, convinced I'm wrong for even being upset about this toxic shit. Words I utter come through a sieve of his making but maintained by me. I see his face in front of me, hear his voice, making his case, strong, giving excuses, eliciting pity and generally talking bollocks.

When I go home I send him a note through the post saying it's not convenient to send our daughter for that extra night. I'm shitting myself.

How *am* I supposed to have romantic times with My Prince when this is going on? My head's exploding with the fear of it, scared others believe him and never me. I probably am obsessed by it. Who wouldn't be? It's maximum punishment, that someone who's always implied or inferred you're a shit mother – *needs* you to be – then acts as if he's trying to take the kids away.. and ups the ante just before the wedding.

Which is today. The wedding. The sun is shining. It's Midsummer's Day, 24 June 1994. The register office is booked for today, Friday, church for the Saturday – a bigger affair.

We're at the house and Mum's arrived. She's wearing an old black skirt and a short sleeved top. New tights though. Well, I think they're new. As I come down the stairs in a borrowed and beautiful dress she looks me up and down. Expressionless.

"You look nice." Flat. Matter of fact. "I promised your ex-husband I'd get a photo of the children."

"I prefer you not to show him ones of the wedding."

"Hmm." Hope that's a yes but know it isn't.

Friends supply a horse and carriage. Basic make-up. No nail varnish. No engagement ring. A plain wedding band. And no flowers in the bouquet, just all greenery – foliage and herbs. This time it's meant to be about being natural, being real.

Over a hundred guests appear like magic into our lives in time to go on the guest list then disappear soon after the wedding. A lot work at the BBC with my husband. You hear that? Oh, best I say it again. My HUSBAND. My Prince. Protector. Provider of security. We're very lucky, wedding-wise – been given loads of help.

In the church I get the giggles and can't stop. It's nerves really but the whole church ends up laughing. In the photos Mum stands at the end, nowhere near me.

When someone comments on it she says "That's the sort of relationship we have." Fuck does that mean? Does it mean *my ex-son-in-law has homed in on me and tells me things which may or may not be true but the purpose it serves is to keep me and my daughter apart, helps me to hate her more, makes bad worse*. Is that what it means?

I spent ages recording a tape of classical music but the DJ forgot to bring it. The reception was delayed by over an hour because we were waiting for my new beloved's alcoholic father (who never even gave us a card) to finish drinking. Bit like waiting for the moon to turn into cheese.

At the end of the do we're supposed to leave under an arch formed by well-wishers. Fucking DJ only does it early so we have to leave the reception an *hour* before we'd planned to. We haven't got our going away outfits on. My husband goes along with it and I guess, so do I. Jesus. I'm upset because after months of detailed planning the end of the wedding's spoiled. Well, not for anyone else. Just for me. The bride. I'm upset and tell my new beloved, who gets angry. Not with the DJ – with me! So it's doubly fucked.

My eldest boy, twelve, has fallen out with his dad and been refusing to ring him. So my mum, his grandmother, calls my son an ignorant shit. He's also drunk from the welcome sherry left out on the table and spews his guts out in the bushes outside the reception. They film this area, the BBC use it as the hospital entrance on Casualty. Please God my son's vomit isn't in shot.

Most of this goes unnoticed. Everyone else has a great time and sees us off to our promising future. We drive to the caravan. He's quite moody but cheers a little on the drive. Married. We've done it. Phew.

We stand, arms round each other looking up at the beautiful moon and the stars in the clear, clear sky. It's all so full of promise.

On the Tuesday we do a pregnancy test. The line goes blue. Yippeeeeeeeeeeeee!!

Chapter 15: The Borrowers

It's October '94 and we've moved house. Our new home is under three miles away. My ex-husband is furious, threatens the kids he'll take me to court to make sure they don't move schools, change doctors or dentist.

"Mummy will go to prison if she keeps on."

He writes toxic letters via his equally toxic solicitor, furious about the outrageous distance he now has to drive to see the children. Fifteen minutes away, he says.

My husband is furious about my ex-husband and furious with me for keeping talking about he who he's renamed Git-Face. Bit awkward because when my ex plays up I'm being attacked from outside but then my husband gets nasty and I feel attacked from inside too. He's moody with the kids, making it easier for their dad to entice them with treats; days out, McDonald's, Chinese, cinema and ice-skating. Fear, fear and more fear. I'm trying to stay fluffy about the new baby, my new husband, our new home but...

When I'm furious I smash our few cups, plates and bowls – throw them across the kitchen, empty or otherwise. Start off with fuck all – end up with even less. The kids escape upstairs, frightened and sometimes, seeing me sat on the kitchen floor, crying, they help me clear up. It doesn't occur to me to drink. AA told me FEAR = Face Everything and Recover. I'm facing it, I'm facing it. As are the children.

And we do our best, me and my husband, practical-wise. He makes the packed lunches, irons their uniforms. My husband's job doesn't pay much even with all the overtime but I'm grateful-grateful-grateful for this time with the kids, giving them some of what they've missed over past years. The paradox is they're getting better parenting – routine anyway – and me full time – but life's still shit. A different type of shit. With barely enough food we live for long stretches on super-giant sacks of potatoes and baked bean toasties.

With the support of Mrs Woman at Family and Child guidance I reduce the older kids' four-times-a-week de-stabilising visits to their dad. My husband is not happy but what can I do? What's good for the children isn't necessarily good for our relationship. Is it just that? Hark at me being thoughtless. He's bound to get angry, bound to put his fist through the glass in the back door like he does, red-faced, blood everywhere. He kicks the hoover, and mine and the kids' things. *Only* ours, things we care about. *Never* his. How's this happening a few short months after the wedding?

The day after my birthday I decide I've seen Mum for the last time. She comes out to wave me off as I drive away from her house.

"Bye, love."

Habits of a lifetime. I sound the car horn as I leave the Close for the last time. Why is it so easy to do, this? No heart-wrenching struggle, no rushing of motherly love to bring me back. Does she phone to see where I am? Nope. She's not seen Tony for six years either but at least she tried with him. He got a letter *and* a poem!

How is it this easy to end a relationship with my mother? I don't go see her and she doesn't care. So long as she still has my ex-husband and Patrick around to criticize me with, still has all-important men in her life. Though I'll try again with her every few years she will still ooze poison in my direction.

The same month I start seeing Elizabeth the therapist. She's no longer seeing my ex-husband.

"What do you hope to get from coming here?"

"Want to get this shit out of my head."

She nods a therapist's nod. Tells me that yes, she can still have a positive regard for me as well as him.

We go to birthing classes run by an independent midwife. My husband's smiley and friendly while we're there. The midwife agrees to deliver our baby at home. Tee hee. Baby's growing well. We hear its heartbeat at the hospital. It sounds like a race horse and we nickname the baby 'Red Rum'. This baby is some Light in our dark world.

My ex begins a new court case. Unbelievably stressful but useful because when we go to Court more and more truths come out, things I never realised and my perception changes, deepens, all over again. Court Welfare get involved and compile a fantastic report. For the first time in twenty plus years I'm shown some behind-the-scenes work.

I naturally assume the Judge will prefer my ex and dislike me but I tell the truth regardless.

"Would you trust me to make a suggestion… if I felt I knew the solution?" He says.

"No… I don't think you've got the depth of knowledge."

Did I really just say that to a Judge? Fuck did that

come from? I'll tell you where from – from the place where it's crucial that the kids are safe. The place where I don't care what anyone thinks. It's about doing the right thing.

The Judge sums up. He says my ex 'may have been putting on a performance' for his, the Judge's benefit and that 'it's not uncommon'. And that he admires my 'honesty and directness'.

"You were shooting from the hip," says my solicitor.

The Judge makes an order which is better for the children.

It's hard to enjoy the baby growing inside me. I worry it might pick up the stress that's bandied around the house night and day. So much of it, my skin looks like the surface of the moon, my hair's falling out and I keep losing my voice. Ha.

My husband barely talks. He *was* right that time on the plane. He speaks a bit but not in a friendly way unless someone's looking. It's difficult for him, all this shit that's going on. We're back to holes-in-doors land, though no dinner on walls as yet.

When I'm laid up with pleuratic pain, I'm screaming out. Like arrowheads the pains jut into different parts of my torso, each one a surprise. My husband shouts at me.

"I *am* pregnant!" I say.

"*I am pregnant.*" Mimics, high pitched, screws up his face.

I feel shame and guilt then as well as physical pain and when the doctor asks if I'd like something for the pain I'm truly shocked because I'd expected a telling off for being so bad, like I've been making it up, exaggerating. The unexpected sympathy is a welcome balm.

The kids are excited when we live by candlelight for three months because we can't afford to fix the lighting ring-circuit. When the telly goes for three months too, couldn't pay the licence, they're good about it. Look at that – *my* kids reading and playing chess by candlelight! Cosy happy families. Dickens would be proud.

My new black shoes are three years old with holes in the soles where the rain pays surprise visits. My eldest son gets a paper round and at the end of the week it's his first pay day. Bless him, that'll be gone quicker than you can say 'life is shit'. But it's his money, earned through riding his bike on early mornings in all weathers including snow, him wearing a black 'puffa' jacket with frayed cuffs.

He comes home, doesn't speak, won't look at me. Oh, no, *now* what's happened? He strides into the kitchen and places a brand new pair of my size trendy shoes on the table. I cry, realising they've cost him exactly a week's wage.

My husband's good side is his practical, providing one. Handily at the BBC there's *all* sorts. When the kids have a school trip he brings home crisps and cartons of drink from behind the bar at the Queen Vic in EastEnders. He brings the goodies in a sack like Pod does for Homily and Arrietty in The Borrowers. We all gather round to see what treasures he's brought back.

"Been borrowing," he says, grinning. There's always something to get excited about; old sandwiches or cakes from the canteen, school uniform from Grange Hill – just have to take the badges off the blazer pockets, socks, needles, cotton, light bulbs, extension lead, pillows and material from the market stall on the EastEnders Lot so I can sew my daughter a new dress.

It's kitchen curtain material so now my daughter walks around in a dress covered in fruit, like she's jumped from a not-so-still-life at the Tate. There's also; paper, pens, pencils, sharpeners, files for their school projects, drawing pins, dressing gown, slippers, tights, hairbrush, ironing board, shampoo.. biddy-boo – biddy-ba – diddy-do.

When our washing machine breaks down he does the washing in the costume department's laundry room. They give us fruit and veggies from Walford Market – they're throwing it out anyway. There's usually a great big Christmas tree from the Top of the Pops studio as well as coloured filter paper they use for lighting. I use it to make ceiling mobiles that catch the sunshine first thing in the morning.

The baby's nearly three weeks overdue. The midwife recommends the three H's –hot curry, hot bath and hot sex. We take her advice – only time I ever have a Vindaloo curry – and the baby, our beautiful son, my FIFTH (6 Pounds 13 Ounces) is born in the front room during that night. How gorgeous is he, eh?

My husband's mother stays for a week. Mostly my husband doesn't speak to anyone including his mother. I try filling in for him. Though I've asked a hundred times he won't use my name. I've stopped asking now and if someone phones he calls out my name. I always know it's a phone call or someone's at the door if he's speaking to me like I'm a person.

Desperately broke, we're bored with potatoes, potatoes and more potatoes. But at least it means the kids will eat fruit and veggies. I phone Jan, crying, tell her I miss the old days at the airline – for someone's birthday we'd buy cream cakes – hate the old-fashioned décor in the house, the self-designed overrun garden.

She arrives next day with cream cakes, a buggy for the baby and a free haircut. More tears.

When I take a silly, puny, pathetic, desperately-craving-a-kind-word type of overdose, he's angry.

I don't want or really need to go to hospital.

"Go and be sick in the toilet!" He snaps the words and my daughter over-hears. He's okay though with me going to bed, trying to sleep it off. At least I get a couple of hour's kip. Maybe it's worth it just for that.

I've stopped going to AA meetings but me and Phil still speak. We phone each other, meet up occasionally.

"The cancer's come back. My spine this time," he says.

He marries his young girlfriend. Wouldn't anyone clutch at those straws, grip on to any bit of life? A select few visit him once he's home from hospital. I'm privileged to be one of them. He loves to see my young son, remembers his drinking days when he wasn't trusted near a baby. He knows he's dying but won't talk about it.

"I don't let myself think about the future. It depresses me."

Yet he plans his funeral with Exocet precision. When the time comes it's exactly how he wanted it. Hundreds and hundreds fill the chapel. Whole families helped in their recovery by Phil. Alcoholics, partners, parents, teens, children. On the way out we're handed a white laminated card with the serenity prayer on it. This more than anything, Phil told me, is what helped him cope first with living and then with dying.

God grant me the serenity
To accept the things I cannot change

*Courage to change the things I can
And the wisdom to know The Difference*

More shit with the ex. We change the pick-up time one Friday night by two hours. I'm normally too scared to change anything knowing a punishment will follow. So for two hours he's stood outside the house with a huge placard.

THIS WOMAN USES CHILDREN

I assume *eeyore* it's a suggestion from one of his new extremist friends, the minority that give helpful organisations a bad name. There are fruit-loops everywhere, the kindly man assures me when I phone.

Inside, most of the kids cry. My husband pulls the curtains and my eldest son says nothing but puts his arms round his stepdad. First and last time.

My ex, the cheeky fucker, smiles, says hello to the neighbours on both sides and when the kids come out he's got this instant enormous teethy smile for them and a big, bouncy "HIYA" – like he's Coco the Fucking Clown.

When the baby's six days old Mum turns up unexpectedly at the house. Didn't think I'd see her again but she needs me to sign something. She peers over at the new baby.

"Hmmph – tiny little thing, isn't it? What did you call it?"

I tell her and she asks why I didn't use a different name – exactly like she did with the other four.

It's now or never. Here goes. "You never loved me."

"How can you *say* that? Course I loved you!"

"OK… *think assertiveness*… I didn't *feel* loved."

"That's rubbish. Anyway you lied to me."

"What?"

"Said you weren't pregnant but your ex told me you miscarried."

Fucksake.

"We didn't tell *anyone*, even the kids…"

"But you lied to me." She looks at my husband like I'm an asylum in-patient.

"How long she been…like this?"

"Since the pregnancy," he colludes.

Fucksake. Thanks for the support!

I speak to my husband's mother more than he does, tell her how he's doing now he's got ulcerative colitis. He tells me it's my fault he's got this illness but I don't tell her those bits, let her think – and me a bit still – that life's almost normal. People rarely come to the house any more – visitors, the kid's friends.

Occasionally some of the older kids try standing up to my husband. The eldest boy does it once. He flies off on one, shouts the boy down, the *street* down. Everyone else goes silent and still. I feel bad because there's loads of pressure on him; the poverty, the debts, the ex – and I know it annoys him when I talk.

He sometimes doesn't bother being nice even in front of people unless it's his work people. When I pick him up he'll smile and wave goodbye to a workmate then turn his face back into the car, moody. I wondered – well, Elizabeth wondered – if he's got a kind of autism. You can imagine his face when I mention it.

At Christmas the BBC crèche need a Santa. They ask him because at work he's still the jolly visiting uncle, laugh a minute, kind, warm, safety still dropping off him like Rumpelstiltskin's gold. I take a photo of him smiling in his Santa outfit, holding the baby with my daughter and curly-haired boy standing either side. They're all smiley, the two older children smiling up at him, him at me. But when I put the camera down he immediately snaps at my daughter and son. How can life be that good in a photo but this bad in real life?

Everything's got a sarcastic 'as usual' at the end. 'Blah blah a hundred, different, grisly complaints... as *usual*.'

I'm sad for my curly-haired boy. In the early days before the baby came along he was taken under his stepdad's wing. They'd do science experiments, draw, play dinosaurs. In a story he writes at school he's supposed to say who his best friend is and he says it's his stepdad. Not anymore. Friends don't treat you like this – shout, spitting sarcasm calling us all 'fucking cunts' as he stomps upstairs. Am I being unfair – that was only the once?

Somehow he keeps me separate from his people at work. He moans about them, tells me how much he hates them all. So I hate them too, upsetting him like this. But he gets on with Shirley. She tells me later how "We *talk*, me and your husband." Arms folded like we're talking over the garden fence. I assume he tells her about us or worse. By now he rarely speaks to me so her comment hurts like fuck. Much of my time with My Prince, my husband, hurts like fuck, truth be told.

He keeps me separate from his family too. There's very little contact with them. Who knows what they get told? One day a package arrives from Illinois. How exciting. When he opens it photos drop out, pictures of his sister's son, our son's cousin and the letter is addressed just to my husband and our baby son. My name isn't anywhere on it.

I've somehow reduced back into myself. So much of what I say isn't OK with him and I get quieter and quieter.

"Looks interesting."

"What!"

"Kilroy – he's doing a program on 'Is your ex a control freak?'"

"Hmmph."

We do go though. They send a car which takes us to the television studios the other side of London. The free sandwiches are *lovely* and me and him both get speaking parts on the show. He's nice, my husband, friendly, calm, sensible when he speaks. But I'm so ashamed at how loud and outspoken I am that I apologise afterwards to the very orange Kilroy.

"Didn't think you were loud *enough*!" He laughs, lovely white teeth against the beautiful sunset of his skin. When I watch the show on telly I can't believe what a little mouse I was! Like a Sunday school teacher after a year in a Thailand prison – someone with all the life bludgeoned out of her.

There's a trip to Florida planned for all his family next year if we can get the money.

"I'm worried – I feel like I'm excluded from your family. It's hurtful."

"No point you fucking going if you're just gonna spoil it!"

At dinnertimes we all of us eat in silence as the mood of my husband controls the very air we breathe, almost supernaturally. He'll spit out something to one of the bigger kids then turn to our youngest who's sat *next* to his older brother or sister and he'll coo over him. Bizarre.

Can you believe we go to Relate? Yep. Deja-flippin'-vu. I read somewhere only fifty per cent of couples have success at Relate because they wait till it's too late.

It's my fault we're going – I can see he doesn't want to be here. He's forever screaming at me to leave him alone and though he's said he feels we've been robbed of our time together because of the kids, I can't think of one incidence when he's suggested any 'us' time.

He moves out for a while, stays with a married friend at work. I'm gutted. Can't sleep, eat, look like shit. The woman at Relate sets us homework to meet up and discuss what's wrong. We meet in a pub only when I prompt but we don't discuss much. It's sending me insane and I feel trapped. If I don't know what's wrong – and I don't – how can I change, make it better? Ha.

"I'm not coming back until the kids stop messing up the house." Fuck did that come from? He doesn't take responsibility for any of it, the relationship. Not one piece of his behaviour does he agree to change. Since the wedding he's regularly threatened to leave. Cleverly that shuts me up because we all know by now I don't want to be 'abandoned', right?

The Relate counsellor tells him to stop that. When I tell her he's cruel she dismisses the use of 'words like that', like I'm a naughty child.

I don't think to or I'm too scared to say that he'll mumble something from the other room, knows I can't hear him, then refuses to repeat what he said. Looks at me, furious, shakes his head. I tried it once myself, just the once, shook *my* head. He went MAD. I thought his head was going to explode. He does it to the kids too but refuses to say why or what's wrong. Or when he does complain about the kids, after he's spilled his shit and I've accepted all the blame, agreed to try harder, etc., he calms down, says, 'They're good kids, really,' but I don't think he means it. If I continue talking, press a point, he still acts like he hates them and starts moaning again, like it's a circle going round. So nothing's changed. He still sees it the same.

I'm worried my husband would like the older four to move to their dad's so only our son remains. He clearly hates me and the older children but not our son. It's a miracle the older kids don't hate the boy. Instead it's the opposite. Our boy gives and receives much love.

They say we should carry our own sunshine around with us. I think my husband's misheard it. Instead carries his own storm around – no umbrella.

After a fluffy session at Relate where the counsellor cries, we, he agrees he'll come home. But nothing's different. Nothing. He's just in a better mood tonight. Maybe his friend wants his spare-room back.

He likes a drink and I've taken it up again too. I can't be an alcoholic, can I? If I compare myself to him I drink the same or less. Drinking's good – it's the magic that calms him.

Night after night we drink and watch telly. Kids are in bed. No talking. The drink soothes as it always did, prevents the pain hurting so bad. His dad's drinking is what split his parents up. That and the violence. I asked his mum about it once, was he violent? Just had a gut feeling all wasn't well in the toy shop. Yes, she said. A lot. They kept splitting up then reconciling which is why my husband went to thirteen different secondary schools. The reconciling is common in abusive relationships. Ha.

"Did my husband know his dad used to hit you?"

"He must've seen the bruises."

I knew his dad used to hit him with a belt, buckle end. You don't have to be a scientist to see his dad cares about no one, only the drink and of what he can get out of a person, getting his son running round doing errands. He was nearly banned from the sister's wedding, pissed up, causing trouble.

I tell my husband about the fossil of information I've dug up expecting him to be intrigued, glad for some answers but I'm in for a shock. He's furious with me, won't discuss it. Fuck have I done now?

Once he's officially diagnosed with ulcerative colitis it's decided he'll give up work. They have a 'do' for him in the BBC bar. Me and the kids sit on our own and no one talks to us. God only knows what they've been told. I've become invisible again. Not just to him and me but to everyone he knows. They even do the speeches when I'm in the ladies!

For two years I work weekend nights as a hotel night manager. He keeps the house tidy, cooks, still puts my nightdress to warm in the airing cupboard for my return on frosty mornings and I don't *get* it. I don't understand why I can't fix the relationship. I still see Elizabeth who suggests a domestic violence group or anger management. He chooses the domestic violence group as it's free. He gets assessed by John who runs the group and he's shocked when they accept him on the course. Goes only twice.

After spending a week at his dad's he wants to talk. I'd written, asking for a sign of hope.

"It's not working, is it?" He says.

That's because you don't fucking want it to work, why you won't get off your lazy fucking arse and do *anything* to help heal this relationship. Not one jot.

"Did you ever love me?" Tell the truth. Tell me it was just the sex, which should have stayed casual.

"Course I did." About to spring free, he's generous. "If you or the kids ever need anything..." Don't ring us.

He does though, keep his word in the years to come.

Sometimes helping his stepchildren where their father won't and always available to help our son. Sometimes me too.

He moves into the garage. When the council come to check, it's legit, so four weeks later they give him a modern one-bed flat in a nearby leafy village.

I am *so* jealous. I don't mind the thousands of pounds of debt he leaves behind, our debt. I'm just grateful he doesn't want money from the house. I couldn't be homeless again, me and the kids, five of them now. Not again, please God, not ever again. Before he leaves he gives it a shot:

"I don't know if it's safe to leave our son here."

Strength bounds into me from somewhere.

"Don't even fucking *try* it!"

This man who can't do people walks away with nothing. Nothing but his freedom. I really am so very tired.

Chapter 16: Without a Paddle

I know it's about six in the morning because I can hear the lorries thunder past underneath my bedroom window. We live opposite a farm but sometimes you'd never know it with the noisy traffic.

Sleep's been a struggle, again, with here an arm, there a leg thrown across my body. And then the three o'clock, four o'clock wide-awake thing. The no-hope-of-changing-anything thing. The fear thing. The wondering what else I could have done to save the marriage, the second marriage…thing. It feels like it's gone on for ages – years, round and round. Problems. Crises. Problems…

I wonder if we'd had a better start with the marriage, taken it slowly, had less 'attacks' from the ex, or the now ex-ex, had a house big enough, enough money, enough food. If. Don't know if it would've stopped him hating me and the kids. Maybe.

When I think about it the nice bit was all over within a few months, if not weeks, truth be told. Sometimes it feels like the last thirty-plus years have been shit. Probably because they have. Steamingly so.

I make my eyes, which weigh a ton, open onto the grey day. My youngest child, my two-year-old, full-of-love son is in his normal clock-hands position across my bed. Don't have to get up yet. If – I – can – just – move – him – over – ooff – a – little – bit… There. I stroke his cheek and grab another half-hour's kip wishing his innocence could counteract the darkness.

Oh, it's Thursday. I get up when I remember that. Thursdays are good. The local paper comes today and it's free so I get to read it cover to cover while my son watches Teletubbies. While I read it I try not to look down at the carpet, the mustard and brown swirly patterns. Not sure what's worse, the pattern or the fact that it's threadbare.

First, though, I see the 'big four' off to school with their packed lunches. Their 'barely enough to eat' packed lunches. I know my daughter and her younger brother skank food off their friends because my older boys tell me. Ugh. Where *is* that magic wand? I wish to God it'd hurry. At least the kids don't get brought home by the police any more now we've moved.

"Found your son playing in a disused warehouse…"

"Found your daughter in a field feeding the horses…"

"Your son will have to pay for the window…"

I envy my husband in his nice tidy one-bedroom, warm, clean, not very old council flat. And the peace and quiet. And the takeaways.

Looking over at the fruit bowl I see we've still got carrots but the bananas have gone. Course. They're always the first to go. And the kids nick a whole one each if I don't get there in time to divide them up.

Sick of being skint, me. When I get my shopping it's so depressing. If I had a quid for every time I've cried in Sainsbury's! Sometimes I just stop wheeling, put my folded arms on the trolley, lay my head down and cry. Other times I nip off to the toilets. Specially when I see what's in other people's trollies. Specially when it's Christmas. And extra-specially when I realise this week I've got specially bad PMS. Poxy Money Stress.

When I'm rich and famous I'll buy all our food – and I mean *all* of it from Marks and Sparks. Even the bread and milk. There, what do you think of that? I'm sick of buying the economy brands. I mean, the supermarkets are good, keep changing the name to stop people like me feeling shit about it. They have good solid names now too like; 'Everyday', 'No Frills', 'Value' and 'Basics' which ooze with a charitable mask of respect. But when I take it off the shelf my trolley seems to quickly rename it with things like 'Paupers' Pap', 'Trailer-Trash Delight', or 'Pay Shit – Eat Shit'. And we're not supposed to notice it tastes inferior. Did I say inferior or did I say disgusting? For sure, the burgers and sausages taste like something the kids left behind on the toilet bowl.

Sainsbury's, they package in white with orange writing. Then the Tesco's lot covers theirs in blue and white stripes. One day I swear I'll come home and the house and kids will be covered in blue and white stripes!

I mean, you do your best, don't you, me? But there's only so much I can do on my own. The kids are sick of it. They're good but I know they've had enough. Sometimes I mix up economy cornflakes with proper Frosties so they think they've got a treat. I've got away with it so far. You won't say anything, will you?

The embarrassment, the humiliation. My friend Jan hides her few economy items under the rest of her shopping but I'd have to spread my coat across it, which would look a bit iffy. Besides my coat's not great either. Oxfam. When I'm rich and famous I'll have a brand-new coat still with that hangy-up bit on the inside of the collar. And no bobbly bits on the material that make you look like you've just rolled around in a hawthorn bush. A dead hawthorn bush. Ten dead hawthorn bushes.

At first the economy brand seems nice and jaunty but the sight of those colours soon slithers into something more like a punishment for failing. Failing at being a mother mostly, because how could I let it get this bad? Failing at being a wife definitely otherwise I'd still *be* one. And failure at being a daughter even though I was luckier than most, having two mothers. I know, I know, greedy me. Two mothers, two husbands, two lots of siblings and now it's just me and the kids.

The other reason I like Thursdays is it's Top of the Pops night. The older kids baby-sit. First I get ready, make as good a show as I can clothes-wise. Make-up, clean underwear, brush my hair *all* the way through, not just a 'seeing the teacher' surface brush. It's a night out – well, four hours – and the twenty-two pounds seventy-five pence comes in handy.

Oh, sod it. Who's that at the door? It's a man who wants money for the telly licence. House calls, they're making now. Can't they do it through the post?

"Hmm – if you look at this print-out you can see we wrote to you on the..."

"I'm late for work!"

As I write my tears splodge onto the cheque. I dab it on my sleeve, hand it over, quickly do the sums in my head. The kids hover, know something's wrong. Again.

I'm usually late when I get to the BBC studios so it's not a shock tonight. I'm an audience co-ordinator. My husband got me the job when he worked here. The manager slings me a look like he regrets leaving his job as a knife-thrower.

The audience gets herded into a freezing cold room, like a holding room till they go into the studio to be pounced on by the warm-up men. They love it and usually pounce back.

First though, the audience get searched. They have to walk through a metal-detector machine just like the ones they use at the airport. Just like that, except it's broken.

After they've seen their musical heroes, the best dancers win some CDs they'll never play. Doormen are hired in. It's good as then we get to hear who's shagging who, who gave who a blow-job in exchange for a 'TOTP CREW' t-shirt, etc.

Each week we're put in a different position. Like in the cloakroom, which is boring. Or the studio which can be fun. I even get to dance as long as I make sure I'm not on camera. That *did* happen once. Argh! Or by a dressing room. I like that because the bands leave things behind. Things like really good fruit – big juicy fat orange oranges and refreshing apples straight from Eden. It's very tempting. Sometimes even cans of Coke. I reckon some people might take these things home with them hoping they don't bulge too much in their handbag. That's what I reckon.

Once when my husband worked here he got me put opposite Michael Hutchence' dressing room. He knows I'm mad about Paula Yates. Paula stayed behind when Michael's band INXS went into the studio. She was breast-feeding Tiger-Lily.

My heart breaks that she's presented as a bad mother and she *so* isn't. She thinks the world of her kids. Sometimes people just make poor choices in their relationships, don't you think? It's easy to get your buttons pressed if it's what you're used to. Specially if it's been happening for a long time. Then it's double easy to be your own worst enemy. Acting loud, contrary, simply covers up the bad behaviour of the button presser who might stand back, calm, collected, looking saintly while in control.

Wrote to her once, Paula. Never got a reply, though. Anyway I tell her I think she's doing brilliant and I think she is, what with all the bad things in the papers – custody battles and shit. My voice breaks with the honour of meeting this woman.

"Thank you," she says. I watch her looking at Tiger-Lily, feeding at her breast. She grabs her daughter's bare toes, smiles at her child.

Getting someone's autograph is a sackable offence, my husband said, so I collect bits of eye contact. Lots of them. People I love, like Diana Ross. I cried when she sang. Sting too. When I was pregnant I came in to watch Kylie Minogue. She's like a perfect size minus 3 and I felt so old and ugly. I collect eye contact off people I don't like too, like Ant and Dec.

People can look different close up. Have you any idea how *old* Status Quo look in real life? Face it, they're old men with scruffy jeans and scruffy hair. If they weren't famous they wouldn't get away with it – looking like dirty old men from the British Legion.

It's funny how celebs get loads of attention too, sometimes for no reason. It's weird. Like the time when I'm standing in the corridor and Robbie Williams is waiting to be called into the studio. There's a line of about eight people behind him. When he cracks a couple of jokes that aren't funny it's like that domino thing the way the whole line of people start laughing as if he **really is funny**.

The producer and some of the crew are nice and treat you like you're a person. But sometimes it's not so good. I was stood there the other week near to the wall and they pulled a black felt curtain across in front of my face. I think it was a lighting thing but hey, like I'm not already invisible enough!

Tonight I'm in the studio – have to be careful of the cables that snake around – so I whisper a shout at a colleague who's near another fire exit.

"Whose on next?"

"It's… " whisper-shouting back.

"PETER ANDRE!" Hollers a warm-up bloke.

In comes Peter Andre. He's a good little singer but I don't think it's just his voice that interests the girls. Jolly handsome. I have a little dance when no one's looking. His outfit shows off his chest – lovely tan – which is shaven. Ugh. I do so like a hairy chest.

When he finishes, the girls scream. He dashes out of the dark studio to his dressing room and I get me some eye-contact for my collection. As he goes past his hand accidentally brushes mine. He smells of rose petals. How lovely! His mum must be so proud. Then I'm reminded about my own family and the state of my life.

As much as it's good to get out once a week it's also a stark reminder of my own reality. Which is shit, frankly. It's depressing to see how these people live and how I don't live. I'm reminded again I've already lost half my life over to crap and I don't know how I'll make it different for the kids. I really don't. I really, really don't. Whatever I do, things just don't seem to get better.

Sometimes things appear in the newspapers about the celebs here. A mole, that's what they call it. A mole. Can you *believe* someone would do that, just ring up the papers and sell them information? They must be real desperate. Though it's only ever harmless stuff that wouldn't hurt anyone, like where the celebs Christmas party is, who's had a ruck, blah blah. But they love it down at the papers. It's never anything like a well-known EastEnders actress shagging someone in the car park which gets recorded on the security tape. Nothing like that ever goes public.

The kids at least have holidays and treats with their dad which is good for them. But it's difficult to watch when our life together is so crap. Probably hard for them too, coming home to it.

Do you know something? I wouldn't dream of having anyone come round the house – I'm so ashamed. Do you know what's worse than that, though? A whole bunch worse? My kids are ashamed too.

It's Christmas. Time to eat shit and beg. The Churches are good, helping out with parcels for the ashamed and skint at this time of year. The British Legion give us a lovely big parcel of food. The Catholic Church too. Bags full of food shopping, crackers, everything and I'm hugely grateful.

When I phone the Baptist Church I speak to this bloke Michael, the minister. Says he'll help but first wants to meet. The church is big with its own little café on the side. Mostly it's full of very old, nearly dead people, obviously, being a church.

"The reason I agreed is because of the sincerity in your voice."

He puts an envelope on the table then, thank God, he pays for the coffee. This is the most soothing, easy, comfortable talk ever. Peace. There's silence in our talk and it's an alright silence, not an *if you'd been good we would've kept you* silence or an *if only you'd change* silence or even a YOU'D BETTER WATCH OUT type of silence.

He asks me about myself, my life. I tell him how I've kept choosing people who held me back blah blah.

"Aah… the tall poppy syndrome."

"Never heard of it."

"There's a field of poppies and one of them is taller than the rest. The others don't like it and try to knock it down so that it becomes shorter than them."

Oh God.

We shake hands firmly like it's been an important business meeting. As if lives depend on it. Back at the car I rip open the envelope. Thirty quid. Plus the greatest gift I've ever been given. I put my head on the steering wheel and 'whole-body' sobs take over in my private silence.

We pull off another Christmas, as always remembering the less fortunate Cratchits. God Bless us, Every One!

Chapter 17: The Sixth Sense

My kids. My five beautiful children. Young ones who keep a family together when it's not their job, whether it's contributing financially or carrying emotional loads they're not supposed to at their ages.

The eldest three are at the same school. They're real good at communicating with each other, keep a strong bond. Once, they're having this detention together, the three of them one lunchtime. And they do this coughing thing. There were two others plus mine being supervised by a teacher. One of mine coughs then his brother coughs back. Then their sister joins in till all three kids have got this cough-speak thing going like they're birds of a feather, which they are of course.

The school's not the sharpest tool in the box. The students who get expelled from surrounding schools end up here. With my kids. They do their best, the school. Mostly. Except the drama teacher. My daughter loves drama (ha) but her bitch drama teacher shouts at them, intimidates with her bulk, frightens the life out of my daughter who gets put off a subject she loves. I make an appointment, make sure I'm sitting with my back straight, no chewing gum.

"My daughters frightened when you shout at her."

She shrugs her shoulders, just says, "Well."

"*Well?*"

"It's part of the package."

Nice. Without words, slowly I get up and leave, let the door slam back on itself.

But I don't blame the teachers for everything. Some try really hard but still my high-spirited kids get themselves suspended. Me, I thought if I never told them what I got up to at school it would be different for them. But it hasn't worked. Simply keeping secrets doesn't help them succeed.

The strongest prevention to kids not smoking is having parents a) who don't smoke, and b) who are really anti. So they've got that too. They don't know I started smoking at eleven – only that I gave up years ago and hate it. Hate them doing it. Does it mean jack?

My eldest comes in reeking of cigarettes. All his friends smoke.

"You been smoking?"

"Course not. You're paranoid."

My snowy-haired boy, same thing.

"You sure you're not smoking?"

"I can't *believe* you'd even think of accusing me!"

Usually all my kids are polite. And protective. My eldest gets a mobile phone at thirteen. It's in the early days of mobiles – kids generally don't have them. Bit of a leader, he is.

He's always been good at coming home on time and this one night he phones to say he'll be late, his friends noisy in the background, swearing. My boy's always been respectful of his mother.

"Stop swearing. It's me *Mum*, you cunt!"

He has a fight too when someone calls his mother… actually I don't know to this day what the boy calls me. My son doesn't tell me about the fight but the other kids fill me in. No one tells me about all the other fights he has either. He's good at it but it's another secret I won't know for years.

None of this is good. Have they any idea, my kids, how many books I've read on parenting? Trouble with the parenting books is the kids don't read them and the books forget to tell you not to have kids with an arsehole. It'd save so much time if they did.

When it's your kids it's worse than with a bloke, the crap I mean. Problems, crises, issues, challenges – ha. Truly confirmation of being a no-good rotten invisible nothing is when your kids are in trouble. When you've let your kids down what's the point of *anything*?

There's something even more shady going on though. I've got sons disappearing all hours; hurried phone calls. Quick! Slam! Out the door for a meet. Big, brownish grey circles under their eyes like they've been up all night revising for exams. One day I intercept a phone call one son's having.

"Can you get me another hundred?" He asks my boy.

"I'll ask my brother."

No doubt I do all the wrong things. Like confront the kids. Like phone all the help lines. Like lecture, plead, tell them how bad it is, how good their lives could be if only. I make posters for the wall. But it's stupidly bollocks because they're 'enjoying' it so why would they stop?

Eventually the accused will stop of their own accord. They're dealing now but not always very well, not always making a profit. They just get bigger, greyer eye circles and get themselves in deeper shit, owe people they shouldn't owe money to. It affects their health and their schoolwork. And I shout more.

Another time I do 1471 on the phone, find out it's a

bigger fish phoning. I'm not having it. I'm just *not* fucking having it so I call him back.

"It's his brother that's your friend. Why are you phoning *him?*"

"Just a chat."

It's not easy, this. I like this lad. Always polite, always friendly.

"If I find out you've supplied my son *anything* I'm phoning the police."

"I haven't. Never."

"Then you've got nothing to worry about."

Immediately another son phones me. Jungle drums.

"Can't fucking believe you phoned my friend. How dare you phone my friend, threatening to grass!"

"Look! He's my *son*. If he supplies your brother *anything* I'll get the police round."

"You're out of order. He's done nothing wrong!"

"Not a problem then is it?"

But we make up. We always do.

The better the kids surroundings are, the better their lives become. Rocket science. They, we, start to expect more for ourselves, more out of life. I've had work done on the house, even new carpets, new sofas, a new computer. First time in years and years. All the boring badly paid jobs I get don't bring these improvements. It's the constant remortgaging.

My (still) husband doesn't know the half of it. Why would he? He's not too bothered anyway as long as he's left alone – didn't when he was here so why should he now? The truth is he doesn't have a clue and would only makes things worse like he did when he was here. I can't talk to their dad either. Haven't for years though I'd tried over and over but it always ended up with a toxic return: him doing something spiteful, usually within a day or two. So I'm alone. Truly alone. Like I always have been. But now it's official and it's cripplingly lonely.

Sometimes I drink. Then I'll go months and months without. Occasionally I go to AA meetings – almost as an interest. But it gets me out the house and I see adult human beings.

Me and my second husband, we have a bit of a game. It's an apart-together-apart-together game and we try staying friends in between. We even go on holiday, taking our son to Portugal one year. Yeah, I know, abroad! Our son stays as ever in the middle to protect us from communicating with ourselves and each other.

Life shittens when I'm working at the post office. Don't think she, the manager is being racist. I don't think it's because I'm the only white person there. I think it's more that she's a bit thick, makes loads of mistakes, is rude to customers and gives them wrong information to save looking it up. I can *see* her, that's the thing. And she knows I can see her. I point things out. She loves me for it, as I try to help the customers. Shouts at me in front of people.

The manager from the sweet shop we're housed inside says what she thinks. "I wouldn't treat a dog the way she treats you."

Why do I put up with it? Because I don't identify it, her behaviour, for what it is until it's too late. Plus I'm *used* to it. It's my husband that tells me.

"Work-place bullying," he says. Ha.

I read up on it. But I'm only a part-timer so she gets only a verbal warning for something the manual says is on-the-spot-sackable. Nice. And they offer me some hours in another office. It's eating away at my energy pool, this.

My husband's back with us at the moment and I realise something else: I'm being bullied at work, then bullied at home. He leaves the house, again and I leave the job. But what have I learned? Really learned?

I'm still seeing Elizabeth, my ex ex's old therapist. She is old too by now, late seventies. So she *must* be nice, eh? I'm off there in a minute. Doesn't charge me a lot – I sometimes think she keeps me on for the entertainment value. Sometimes think I distract her from her screwball finicky husband in his spick-and-span shed. He who picks her up on every word, every action, tells me on the way out how she's getting forgetful. That's reassuring! She tells me how *he's* getting forgetful. Head-fuck.

We're talking about my first husband. Elizabeth talks about what attracted us to each other in the beginning.

"He said it was the sex, for him," she says. And she laughs in that way she does, in odd places.

I'm gutted, remembering the conversation he'd said he had with Gloria at Relate. What he'd said about the nice, fluffy reasons he gave for liking me in the beginning *sweet and interesting to talk to*. Whereas 'you were an easy shag' isn't so nice, is it?

Elizabeth's told me before he wants people to think he's 'nice'. She's also said he's self-centred. It's like he's wired up wrong compared to other people. I'm so relieved I got out when I did.

The boiler's packed up. You any idea how much they cost? No heat for a few months till the RAF Benevolent Fund do all their paperwork, raise the money from different charities and get us a new one.

My angry first husband stops the maintenance for a

while. I tell him we've not got food so he offers to cook the kids a meal but won't part with actual money.

The house is on the verge of repossession by the building society – not the devil. Ha. Phone's incoming only. So I'm in the phone box opposite the house being fed up to Sandra from school who agrees to phone me back. She's broke too but not *this* broke. She's wiser than me sometimes.

"I can't phone out, can't go anywhere, no petrol, no money for bus fares, can't even write to anyone because I've got no paper and not enough for a stamp."

Mustn't grumble. Stop crying, woman! I'm so tired. Really. Hello, who's that at the door? No, please, no, not again, please God, no. Let it be someone nice. I open the door tentatively like there's SAS officers behind it. I shouldn't have worried. It's Andrea and Lenny. How lovely. Stick the kettle on.

"Thought you'd like this," she says.

Andrea puts bags of shopping on the table. Lenny does the same. This is all so silver lining.

"Oh my!"

They're grinning like Cheshires and I'm… not. For three weeks running they do this, bring us bags of shopping. Chocolate digestives, proper marmalade with bits in, cakes, bananas – enough for one each! And look at this – real Frosties!

PART 3 – THE BEGINNING

Chapter 18: Predator

My husband's gone. This time it's for good. I sink. I haven't had a drink for a few months, have gone back to AA. I go to quite a few meetings, fiddle around with the Steps, read more.

I also go to this women's group. It's the other half of the domestic violence group my husband went to. I continue with it because I like learning. Going to the group gets us to look at our own behaviour, same as at AA. What's my fifty per cent? Why do I keep turning up for a 'kicking'? Yes, he's this and he's that but it's *me* puts the drink to my lips. It's *me* goes back into something that hurts me. Again. I know that now. Is putting down the drink enough? Is ending the relationship enough? I've spent my life bending over backwards to accommodate others then bending over forwards for another shafting and a good kicking up my jacksy. Is that me having a balanced life?

I've joked with friends at how it's been… "Oh, you bought me a Chinese meal. Here, have half my house."

Or, "Don't worry I can easily cook up another five courses – I'm just glad you arrived safely."

Or, "I'll come to you. It's only sixty miles."

Or, "You, Tarzan. Me piece of shit – small 's'."

Rebecca runs the women's group. She's another one like Elizabeth, laughs in the wrong places. Even my daughter spotted it.

Rebecca'll be like, "If you go back to him you're putting your life in danger." Then she'll snigger and snort, her nostrils curling likes she's a horse that's just won the two-thirty at Aintree. She's helpful to women, means well, calls her sister-in-law 'a little madam'. Rebecca tells us about her friendship with a heroin addict. Like soul mates they are, but after twenty years they never quite got it together. How she's the one he needs when he's holed up in a hotel room with his heroin. Brings him his fags. His heroin and his heroine – is she his rescuer? It's good she felt comfortable enough to share it with the group for forty minutes. However, she's found a new man and one day she surprises us all.

"Ta-dah!" She flashes a (mediocre) engagement ring at us. It's good to see some people can do it after all, eh?

"See! There *are* some good ones out there!"

Engaged after three months. It's good to have a role model like her for the group. Us women who tend to make unwise, sometimes impulsive choices. We who'll do anything but face the fear of being alone.

Each week we go round in a circle sharing where we're at. When a new woman turns up, a wreck already and hears about others' experiences of shit, it helps because she identifies and starts to speak out for, sometimes, the first time.

Shit, abuse. Let's call it abuse shall we? Call it what it is. It's over-used, this word, and makes me think of glue, well, Copydex for some reason. Then I'm off on one, thinking of the children's TV programme Blue

Peter, thinking Valerie Singleton with her cereal boxes and Copydex – wondering if she'll make a guest appearance and make us all a model husband, partner, man.

"Here's one I prepared earlier. Look! No hidden agenda, no sadism, no manipulation, no denial, no minimising, no half-baked excuses or crazy-making tactics for avoiding proper talk. He's complete!"

Mind, that's about making things – where *abuse* is about breaking things. Lives. Broken lives. Literally and in spirit.

Despite these tentacles of support in place I'm sinking fast but it's okay because I'm realising the extent of how dark it's all been and I *can* handle it being this bad. I'm almost serene about it, calm. The women's group say it's the denial falling away. Like scales from my eyes? *If thine eyes offend thee*. Could it get any worse? No matter, I've made a decision. Finally. A solution.

Handily, Big Brother is on TV at the moment and it uses up a lot of time. I sit in my green hand-me-down leather chair and that's where I stay day and sometimes nights too. I don't move from the chair, sit there watching telly and I'm up to date on all the adverts, see all the daytime telly I want and don't want. I'm embarrassed to admit I'm addicted to Big Brother. I cry at the end when Kate wins. I'm so glad because she reminds me of my girl, sporty and gorgeous, and I'm bereft I won't see her again now that the show's nearly over.

How lovely for these young women to have their whole lives yet to go with all things possible. All good. All hope. But it's too late for me. I've lost half my life through bad choices so I've made this decision and I'm not displeased with it. It's the most practical one too.

The kids are sorted and don't need me. They're all doing better than they ever have before. Most know what they want to do with their lives and they've got dads who they can go to. Soon I will be sorted too. I know what I've got to do. My answer to life's problems.

I'm getting to AA meetings and the women's group and I see Elizabeth. But outside of that – zilch. I've decided I'll stick to only seeing 'official' people like this because I don't seem to know how to keep myself safe. The few close friends I've got don't keep themselves safe so how can they keep me safe?

How could I end up being bullied at work and at home at the same time? For years and years I've hopped from one abusive situation to another. And the deprivation! How the fuck did that happen? *Why*?

My decision, I believe, is well thought out, rational, sensible, logical. I've looked at it from all angles and plumped for the wisest move. The decision is calming, almost soothing. I've decided to kill myself, do the off. My life's over anyway and I'm so very, very tired. I can't keep doing this. I've had enough. Even if it's not *all* my fault I'm too tired for any more, too tired to go on. Whatever I do it doesn't seem to get better. As far as I can see there are no benefits to staying alive. None.

I share it at meetings, AA and the women's group where I know I won't be talked out of it. But I don't mention it to Elizabeth or anyone else. There *is* no one else. No family. I've cut contact with all but the kids and no one's battering the door down demanding an explanation or a cup of tea. I don't answer the phone or the door.

"I'll get it, shall I?" My snowy-haired boy gets the door, the phone, the post.

I try not to burden the kids but it's hard to stay

cheerful now I've made my decision. One weekend I'm phoning the Samaritans because it's overtaking me a bit. I'm sorry to say I won't speak if it's a woman – keep hanging up till I get a man. Is this my only chance of having a man listen to me?

"It's as if my suicide, my dying has got a life of its own and it's in control."

And I can feel the adrenalin of it, the buzz swirling through my bloodstream, the best white-knuckle ride ever. They're good, the Samaritans. Good-hearted. For all of their six weeks' training they do a lot of people a lot of good. But not me. Unfortunately I've out-researched him so there's nothing he can say that I don't predict. But it's nice to have a bit of company.

The thing is I'm not ready quite yet. If I do it in the school holidays the younger kids can get over it, settle down before the new school term in September.

At an AA meeting I see an old face – Terry, who once sold me a fireplace. He still looks like my dad but he's all smiley now, laugh a minute (specially with women), the cuddly joker. Cuddles – isn't that the name of the killer whale they had at Windsor Safari Park?

He does this weird thing, bizarre. Out of nowhere he grabs me in a too-close, too-firm, too-quick hug which makes me jump. I don't wanna seem impolite so I act like nothing's happened. He laughs, sinister. Sinister or cheeky? Did I just past his first test? His first 'can get away with things because she'll do nothing about it' test? The first boundary-smashing test?

He's really been through the mill though. He's been sober and cocaine-clean over ten years now. That's really something. For me it's been seven months without a drink so I think he's really wise. Plus he tells me that newcomers look up to people who've been sober a few years – the 'old timers'.

He talks a lot about his sponsor in Florida who puts him up for free, loans him a flash car. Says she's an ex-model. Model what, though? When she's over for a visit she comes to the meeting. She's lovely and tallish, slimish, blondish and looks like a bloke. What? No really, she looks like a bloke. In drag. She's even got the deep husky voice of a drag queen roughened by smoky working men's clubs.

The thing about the programme is it teaches us tolerance and not to be judgemental, right? 'Live and let live.' So it's up to her how she wants to look. The main thing is to work the programme, be health-and-spirit oriented, right? She's married and okay, her English lover is violent towards her but… at least Terry gets his freebie holidays in the sun. And she's his sponsor so she helps him, gives him wise advice. She's even a counsellor so knows what she's talking about, obviously.

"We're so relaxed with each other we walk around in our underwear," he says.

Next time I go he's here again. Last time he was scruffy, looked like he'd just finished work and was covered in builders' dust like God mistook him for a mince pie, sprinkled him with sugar. Tonight though, he's smart. Shirt, trousers, the whole bit. That's the shirt that's supposed to disguise the belly behind it, tucked into the smart trousers.

So I share at the meeting about my big grown-up decision. About committing suicide. In the rooms people share whatever they like. A lot of people have seen a lot of chaos. There's often tears and distress but what's important is that people get to share whatever they need to.

Sometimes there are jokes cracking like eggs in a greasy café's frying pan. Much laughter, tears. Whatever feelings are afoot they spill out into the room. It's like being washed, going to a meeting. Sometimes though, a lot of bollocks gets spilled and you know if a person's talking it but not walking it. *Please God, I'm as honest as I know how. I try, anyway. Is that why I don't make too many friends?*

Terry though, homes in on me. He's nice in a repulsive sort of way. Bit fat, bit old, bit crude but in a funny sort of way. One night a crowd from the meeting go for coffee. Me and him are sat together.

"I'm going away on Monday for three months." Good because you've taken to texting me a lot.

"That's nice for you."

"Nottingham. I'm the carpenter on the set of a new TV show."

"Oh, interesting." Like an empty bag is interesting.

"Would you like to go out to dinner at the weekend?"

"Shall we speak in the week?"

See, I'm being brave like this with you yet I'm compelled to keep listening. Partly it's been so long since I've felt heard but partly I'm programmed not to say no and I don't want to be rude. So, while I'm not attracted to him there *is* something there. Surely it's not just that he looks like Dad? Surely not!

He's funny when he shares.

"My wife used to say I'm the devil re-incarnate." Everyone laughs including him. "She took out an injunction, said I tried to kill her!" More laughs. "I *didn't* try to kill her – just put my hands round her throat because I wanted her to shut up, that's all." More laughs, canned, like we're in an episode of M.A.S.H.

He grins too and likes it when people warm to him. I like it too.

"Wanted her to stop being unreasonable, to stop saying things like 'Where've you been?' 'What time you coming home?' and 'Shouldn't you cut down on your drinking?'"

The room's in stitches. He's done it all, he tells me, smiling. In the early days he was on and off the drink. Once he burst into a meeting.

"You're all CUNTS." He'd shouted.

Did the same at his wife's church too: burst through the double doors like Samson without the hair.

"You're all CUNTS."

They prayed for him. She always believed it was her Church that got God to get him to 'the rooms'.

For my birthday the kids have arranged a surprise 'do' at home. They've paid for the food themselves, specially my daughter. A few friends and the kids are here. Terry too.

"I didn't get you a present so I'll treat you to dinner."

Fuck. I smile. "Lovely!"

Bit of a reprieve when he does go away to work so I'm safe during the week from his presence but not his spirit as he keeps texting and phoning. After many, many texts and calls I agree a day for dinner.

He arrives suited up, looks smart. As I get in the car I notice the single rose on the back seat. Shit!

"This is for you."

"How lovely." Bollocks.

At his favourite restaurant it's empty but for us. He has the veal – likes his meat bled dry, I guess.

He tells me a story about his son's wife, who's asked him to baby-sit.

"Said I'll do it but I made her feel guilty first," he

sniggers.

So… this bloke *wants* to make someone he cares about feel guilty. Even thinks it funny. But I stay anyway.

"This is lovely and I'm grateful but I really don't want anything more than friendship."

He looks like a wounded animal but he agrees that's fine. Then he sulks a bit, goes quiet. I feel guilty.

Then, fuck my old boots, during the following week he only keeps on texting and phoning. In the end I have to say something.

"Would you like me to back off a bit, leave you to contact me?" He says, sweetly.

"Yes, please."

Grateful he's making it easy. But does he wait? Like fuck, he does. He's grovellingly polite by text. It's repulsive, makes me feel physically sick and because I don't text straight back he phones. He makes it difficult to say no to him. He makes a point of saying how he can't bear to be rejected. I think I'm being brave and grown up expressing clearly how I don't want a relationship, only friendship.

"I realise it's good to start off being friends first before getting into a relationship," he shares in the meeting, sat next to me. He's good at this. But I can see the manipulation – so what do I do next?

Take the kids camping to Devon, which the kids have paid for. And while they're off doing holiday things like swimming the loneliness pours out a storm over me and I'm unprotected. I start texting *him*. Here a sunset, there a beautiful view of the bay, here a cream tea, there some wild flowers. Maybe I like it. He's polite and attentive – it's easy to want more. It's addictive, intoxicating. Weird because although I haven't changed my mind about wanting to die it's like he's become a temporary respite.

Terry's home weekends and we meet up for dinner, pictures, walk in the park. I still feel repulsed. As soon as he picks me up he shows his concern about me.

"How are you feeling?"

Blimey. It's like he really wants to know all about me. So I tell him. He seems genuinely interested in my history, the marriages, blah blah. Reads to me from the big book of AA. So soothing is he. So wise.

"The truth will set you free," he says. He's always saying it. And "Some are picked but others are chosen." He's so...special..holy, almost. Eh?

Terry's got grandchildren. That's a bad thing, his age.

"I'm fifty-seven."

I've a sinking feeling then because he doesn't look over fifty. But I carry on anyway.

We're at the park today, sat on a bench overlooking a lake. He's wearing shorts.

"They're new," he says.

"Oh." I smile. Interesting.

"Do you like the material? Feel it, look."

He grabs my hand, shoves it on his shorts. I grab it back, startled and repulsed. Again. But I carry on anyway.

"Are you free for coffee tomorrow?"

"Urgh, busy tomorrow…" He puts his head down, serious, quiet, like someone's just died. "But I can the day after," I reassure.

Suppose he's a welcome distraction from the rest of my life. He brags about his wages and I'm suitably impressed, showing the admiration of a skint person, like he wants me to.

Terry talks about his ex.

"It was eighteen months before I stopped driving past her house every day."

Bit obsessed. He must *really* have loved her. He was good to his wife. How lovely – the opposite of my first husband. He tells me he gave her everything when they sold the house! Even the last few bob he was left with he gave back to her for a car. Curious, the timing though. When he gave her everything was around the time he bought his one-bed house and put a huge deposit down – half of the purchase price.

"The council wouldn't give me a place so I stayed in for eighteen months, saved up, did a few shady deals and bought this place. I was renting it till then."

The 'programme' is about being honest. No one's perfect though, eh? Fact that he takes 'parcels' in for people, the big-boy dealers – well, fair enough, eh? Isn't it? He likes doing favours for people. Then they owe him. Some of his people are in prison. He's been to prison too, he tells me.

"What d'you go down for?"

"Attempted murder."

Nice. And while we drive along he tells me about it. I get all the graphics in colour, mostly red, about this bloke he had a ruck with. I switch off a bit but it started in a pub and ended up in hospital where, Terry says, he went back to finish him off.

"I was a pub-fighter."

Are there categories? He's certainly proud of the one he was in and he's full of stories. How he was good with a knife, known for it. They called him Mack the Knife. He tells me too about this other bloke he had a word with. The accused had been giving Terry's mum a good seeing-to. She who liked a drink. Terry says his dad, a mild-mannered man and liked by everyone, sent him after the bloke, as he often did with her other blokes she picked up from the pub. Terry and a mate dragged him to some woods. He said he doesn't know to this day whether he lived or died.

He laughs, sniggers, smiles most of the way through this story. His face lights up like we've just won the war. Excited. Proud.

"Awww – you're scared of me now, aren't you darlin'?" He rubs my knee.

"No, no."

We both know I *am*. Truly. Course I am. It's why he did it, no? I know this…and I carry on seeing him anyway.

I'm in the kitchen talking to my snowy-haired boy. He's twenty, not quite so snowy-haired. In my mind he will always be that same boy who used to scrunch his hand up like a spider and talk for hours to 'Ladybird' – underneath the sensible man he's become. Every time I'm in the Co-op and buy five bars of chocolate for my kids, age range seven to twenty-one, I know them for the children they were as well as the gorgeous people they're growing into.

"I don't want a relationship but Terry's really persistent. He's not listening to me. I don't know if I should go out with him."

"So you're considering going out with someone who doesn't listen to you?"

Who's the child and who's the parent? What am I doing? Life's all twisted sometimes, isn't it? The thing is, I don't even majorly want to live yet here I am thinking about going out with someone.

Why? Because he's there? Certainly I've never had anyone be so persistent. I suppose it's flattering *and* truth be told I like it he's a bit of a hard man. Was.

Makes me feel feminine, girly, a gangster's moll. Is it exciting? Mysterious? An adrenalin buzz? Ridiculously unhealthy? Is it true, even? I think so, mostly – there's too much of it.

Why am I taking on his values? I am, it's true. Like I could give a fuck about cars but because he drives a Mercedes I make this fuss when expected over his car. Actually it's a bit old. It's the car equivalent of gold medallion on a chunky chain. It's more Kojak than it is David Beckham. Yet I coo over it when he demands it. And he *does* demand it. Demands a lot.

He insists a lot too. He virtually begs me to accept money for things – a bill, some shopping, a new pair of shoes, fifty quid I'm short of for something. Being a builder he offers to do work on the house. Like I'm going to say no. It's delicious after having to do everything on my own. Suddenly there's a bit of energy entering the house and I'm truly grateful. I am anyway, plus he makes doubly sure of it. Boy, do I owe him!

There's a day when I'm starting to wish I had a sex life. Isn't that what healthy adults do? He's away this week again but I've made a decision that fits in with his plans. Next time we have dinner I suggest coffee at his.

Chapter 19: Natural Born Killers

It's funny. Although my new man can be respectful he can also be hugely disrespectful. Got a thing about affecttion. As in, like after about a week there are no hugs. And the way he is with other women – I can't explain it – it's almost like a hypnotic thing. I suppose he's just a friendly person. He's been all over the world. Has he shagged his way round it? He tells me about when he worked in Africa for three years. Though he despises black people (he knows people in the BNP – *it's all gonna kick off one day, you know*), he went with prostitutes when he was out there.

"Bit hypocritical, isn't it?"

"I HAD NO FUCKING CHOICE." He shouts.

He's furious at my outrageous suggestion and I back down. I don't know what's happening to me with this bloke. I'm *drowning* in his 'values'. My own, decent, struggled-for-years-to-find-them values are disappearing. As am I. Bit by bit, slowly so at first I don't notice. It starts by me saying no to something, anything, and him keep pushing, pushing, till I give in. Sometimes it's doesn't take much for me to cave in. A look, a comment, a silence.

All gets discussed with Elizabeth.

"He used to go with prostitutes."

She shrugs her shoulders like I've just mentioned how I prefer crocuses to daffodils. "Oh, well, if he's seeing prostitutes it doesn't need to affect you."

"Not now! He *used* to."

She shrugs again. I wonder about her sometimes. How can she think it's OK to date a man who visits prostitutes? Suppose it's good she's open-minded. Is it me being too judgemental? When I've talked about stopping the sessions over the years she's said she thinks I should carry on, that I need the support. It's true I talk about a lot of things in here. She obviously *knows* that I can't manage on my own.

"Therapists can be controlling."

"Can be." She agrees but I keep going anyway.

Terry's insistent about sleeping over at my house. I don't feel good about getting this thing mixed up with the kids, of making that commitment yet when I haven't even met *his* kids. But he keeps on. I feel guilty and cave in.

I've been seeing Terry as more than friends for a few weeks. He keeps giving me things, little things I don't want: very old food from his freezer, freebie soaps from hotels, tins of paint I hate the colour of. Tonight he brings over a carrier-bag. Looks like it should contain something exciting the postman just brought.

"Thanks. It's very kind of you." You have to say that. Always have to be grateful. He goes on and on, makes sure you are.

Mum was the same. You'd buy *her* a present and she'd glance at it in distaste or she was indifferent.

"Thanks, Mand. That's lovely." Words that didn't match her face. She'd whack it on a shelf, never to be spoken of again. But Jesus, when it was the other way round you'd have to be utterly grateful and say so in ten different ways. Then she'd carry on, "You sure you like it, though?"

The game was about giving her compliments on her brilliant choice while denying my efforts, my existence. But, hey, look – I thought this man reminded me of Dad yet here he is acting like Mum!

"Is that any good to you?"

It's hard saying no to him. If you're in a restaurant and don't like the potatoes he pulls a face. Not just a face but *that* face – the face that sends a message up my spine. I smile, gratefully.

"What is it?"

"Co-Proxamol. They come with my diabetes prescription. I don't use them so I thought it'd help you out, darlin'."

He smirks. Weird he's giving me this huge carrier-bag full of tablets when I don't get headache, toothache, arse-ache. Suppose like he says he just wants to help out. He's a good provider which is handily tempting at the moment. Isn't it? And I don't want to offend him when he's been good to me. To us.

"Why d'you do that?"

"What?" Snaps. Angry. Scary.

Defensive, I carry on, perfectly calm.

"Smile like that when it's not funny? It's... sinister."

I hate it when he shouts. "You're always so FUCKING PRECISE, always picking me up on things."

That's the evening lost then. I spend the next three hours trying to get him to cheer up.

"Cup of tea?"

"Nope."

At bedtime he stops halfway during sex, gets off. Just like that. He knows I think I'm shit in bed. My first husband told me I wasn't great and how Suzanne's better than me because she sticks her finger up his arse. He knows I'm self-conscious about my scarred lip, the one the dog bit. And he's taken to sort of squidging his mouth to one side, like to avoid my lips when we kiss hello, goodbye.

"Saw Anthea at the meeting. The one with the big tits."

He always, *always* looks at other women. Specially tits and arses; at meetings, funerals, restaurants, shopping.

"I'm not," he laughs if I pull him up on it, the days it's safe to.

"I'm just thinking what a lovely pair of trousers she's wearing. I like a nice pair of slacks on a woman."

Million guesses at what I start wearing. Yup. Trousers, tight as. I try to entice his approval with my arse. And thongs are about now so I've become the Queen of them. I'm trying to keep him interested and feel myself slipping (back) into slapper-dom.

We have a few holidays, go to AA conventions in the Uk, in Spain, in Greece but mostly we stay separate from his friends. Sometimes even a different hotel to the one designated. It's nice he wants us to spend time on our own. Isn't it?

One time we're away and we go to a restaurant where this young girl welcomes us. He stands right up close to her, smack-bang in her personal space, inches away as if seeing whether she'll move. It's like a tried-and-tested technique. To discover what? Whether she'd eventually give in to a shag if he had the time to pursue it? Yup, she passed his first 'smash the boundary' test.

At the end of the week when he tips a young waitress he puts the money in her hand and folds both his hands over hers, fixing her with his eyes. Another test?

Do my kids like him?

Eldest boy – "Whatever makes you happy, Mum."

Snowy-haired boy – "Well, I think he's a dick but if you're happy…"

Curly-haired boy – "He's a dick."

Youngest boy – "If Mummy likes him, I like him."

Gorgeous daughter? Bit of a problem here. She's not taken to him well. Not at all. She's eighteen, wants to sleep in my bed instead of him.

"Can you at least stop him sleeping in your bed?"

"No! Look, I know it's hard for you. Can't you give him a chance?"

Even the boys get fed up with her.

Terry says he talks to his sponsor about it.

"She's grown up with an alcoholic mother. What d'you expect?" he says she says. She means well, his drag queen childless sponsor who's accepting violence from her lover.

My daughter's taken to sleeping on the landing outside my bedroom and she cries. Blimey, does she. My eldest boy gets so fed up one night he packs her a suitcase.

"You're going to Dads!" he threatens.

"No!" she screams. Snot and tears.

Another time as we pull away from my house for a night out I look up. She's at the landing window, hands sliding down the glass, howling, begging me not to go, not to leave, like he's gonna try and murder me or something. Ha.

I feel sorry for my new man. He doesn't need this from my daughter, who I secretly think he's never liked. Kids, eh? What can you do?

Beth from school invites us to her summer barbecue. Me and my new man go and take my curly-haired son, now seventeen and his girlfriend, who's the same age. It's really embarrassing when a friend gets drunk, slurry, talking bollocks – her husband too. Next thing I turn round and my sober alcoholic partner has fucked off to another table, sat on his own. Guiltily I join him, at a loss to decide what's the best thing: pissed-up friend or rude-fucker boyfriend? It's true I don't find it easy mixing with drunk drinkers any more but my friend was upset, I discover later, so I make amends, don't want to cause bad feeling.

When my man's speaking to my boy's girlfriend he gets animated. It's like he doesn't realise what age she is, like he's oozing something onto her – poison, like those snakes that anaesthetise before going in for the kill. If I didn't know better I'd say he was flirting. Or is it me being over-sensitive?

Over coffee later the subject of prostitution comes up again. He tells me how, in Africa, they tell you to make sure the prostitute's under twelve so she's less likely to have Aids. Why's my skin crawling?

We argue. A lot. He's hard to get on with but says it's me. Maybe I should try harder to explain what I mean. So I do try harder. It goes on for hours, him not understanding no matter how I say things. We usually calm down before we go to bed but not always. Sometimes he storms off.

"I just want us to have a happy, loving relationship," he says.

He's good, buys me clothes, underwear and tells me about his ex.

"She wore trainers and puffa jackets when I met her. When we finished she was wearing Armani suits."

Bit fucking controlling, if you ask me. And I carry on anyway.

But the rows! And I find myself doing insane things. Like when I stay at his I often can't sleep, which makes him angry. So one night last week I started walking home, middle of the night, country lanes. He went mad, looking for me, calling my mobile, which I ignored. Truth be told I'm loving the attention, the adrenalin...but the *price* I'm paying for it!

Sometimes I feel like a prostitute when I'm with him. This morning when I got out of his bed he jumped up and took thirty quid out the drawer.

"Treat yourself when you go to the school fête."

Did he mean it how I took it? The money, like that. Sometimes I feel like he's laughing, saving so much money. If he had to pay out for prostitutes – I'm such a bargain!

He's trying, though. We've agreed that once a week he'll cook for me. Trouble is, I *have* to like it all, eat it all or he gets the arsehole. And I try to make him happy – he's gone to all this trouble. He cooks then we eat but don't talk. We watch his telly. Boring, empty, useless wasted time.

He's not into talking these days, keeps a lot to himself. He knows I like talking, crave it. I ask him questions and he gets angrier. It's almost as if he's deliberately withholding. Surely not?

At Christmas the kids all go to their dad's. Terry sees his family, including his ex-wife, but we're together at New Year. We're off to one of the many AA New Year's Eve dances.

"Hello, gorgeous bloke. You look lovely." Maybe if I love him more? He says nothing.

We argue on the way. He's sullen, makes it awkward and unsafe to speak. Shouts at how wrong I am. Do I have high expectations?

Weird now we're here, hundreds of people all dressed up but not drinking. We dance a little though he's reluctant. Try to hold his hand, he pulls it away.

Suddenly some blonde woman appears, jumps on him, shoves her tits in his face. Quickly he becomes smiley, wise, cuddly old Terry who's been around the 'rooms' a few years – an 'old timer'. He's prepared, knows what to do.

"This is my girlfriend, Amanda."

She runs off a quick half-smile like, whatever, then dances next to us with her friend for five minutes. Terry ran his hand up this friend's leg last week at a meeting: more arguments. I didn't cave in, felt he was wrong this time. He knew it, backed down in the end. Blimey!

"Fucking what NOW?"

Attempt a dance, virtually beg him. He relents though we've barely spoken all night. He won't. When it comes to the 'knock on wood' part of the song he taps his knuckles on my head. Sniggers. Suddenly he's decided to be a jovial cunt. Probably I'm overreacting but I don't like it. He's furious with me and shouts all the way home. As in ALL the way home. An hour and a half.

"You've *ruined* the fucking evening now. All I want is for us to have a happy, loving relationship."

I feel guilty then and wish I hadn't caused him this distress. He tells me he can't handle the stress, not with his diabetes.

I'm supposed to be staying at his. The sex is cold. Icy. I mouth a whisper to him, got a plan. "Goodbye." He doesn't hear me, he's not meant to.

Once again during sex he gets off abruptly midway, says nothing.

"What's wrong?"

"Nothing."

Clearly nothing is wrong as he turns over, asleep within minutes. We've only been together three months. Maybe he'll change with counselling. That's what Elizabeth says. Maybe that will work where the anger management she recommended didn't. He was furious about that – spending out all that money on the course and it didn't work. I felt guilty.

No matter what happens the rejection always outweighs anything else he's done. So I'm relieved he comes round for a cup of tea next day. Thank God we're still on. He's forgiven me.

Later that night I'm sat at the computer wondering, what's the point? What's the fucking point to my life? What? My purpose has only ever been to give service to others. The kids don't need me anymore. *And* it's the school holidays. Terry will replace me within a week. I don't know if he's shagged the blonde woman from last night yet. I thought I had it sussed, which women are his type but no, because it looks like most women are! What's the point of me carrying on, existing for the sake of it?

I play sad music and write sad words at the computer. Logically speaking, why be me anymore? It's never worked. I ring the Samaritans, talk and cry for over an hour. She does mean well, the young woman I speak to. I really warm to her, she's pretty wise.

"It's a shame that *you* should be the one who takes your life because of what other people have done."

I think I'll be sensible about this. I start a fresh 'page' on the computer. Let's call it… 'Honesty is the best policy. 3.30 a.m. 2 January 2003'.

I write down some thoughts. One is I'm not sure Terry is the person I want to be with. Although I'm not the person I want to be with either, and I realise I may simply be too damaged to have a relationship with a man.

My daughter's hovering.

"Mum – what you doing?"

"Go to bed. It's late."

"You coming up?"

"Later."

I write out a pros and cons list: the pros and cons to living or dying. The cons far outweigh the pros, as I knew they would. I fetch the carrier-bag of Co-Proxamol, take out ten boxes. Each box is neatly covered in the chemist's label. Each label with Terry's name and address typed out by the chemist's computer. Counting out seventy tablets I put three boxes in my cardigan pocket. Reserves.

My girl's back.

"What, love. What d'you want?"

"What you doing, Mum?"

"Nothing, nothing, be up soon. By the way…"

"What?"

"I love you."

I call Terry, need to say my goodbyes. I've woken him.

"What is it?"

"Nothing." Click, prrr prrr.

I take the tablets ten at a time. With water. Do it properly. That's ten done, good girl. Twenty. Thirty. Well done. Whoah… starting to feel nice already. Forgiven? So soon? Forty, water. Phone Terry. Slurring a bit. Me, not him.

"What is it?"

"I'm just phoning to… release you."

"What?"

He's funny and I giggle, slurring. Fifty, water.
"What's that noise?"
"Nothing." Giggle, wipe my mouth on my sleeve.
Sixty, keep 'em down, water, water. Seventy. Done.
What's that? Oh, my daughter's laughing. No, she's crying, being a drama queen.

It's all a laugh, really. Like the rest of it's been. My life – all one big laugh. I can see it so, so clearly now. When I was a teenager I had this thought I wouldn't live to be twenty-one. But it came and went – I even failed at that. Soon there'll be no more pain. Thing is, for me now it'll be peaceful, serene, safe and I'll have my freedom.

Chapter 20: Keeping Mum

"Mum, Mum, what've you done, Mum?"

"Nothing, nothing."

She rarely cries, my daughter – my daughter who's had far too much put on her plate. By me. But she's crying now. Why? Why can't she see the funny side of it all?

What's that blue light doing? Oh – a woman in green. I remember that exercise woman who used to be on the telly. The Green Goddess – all in shiny green first thing in the morning, making you stretch, turn, pull, stretch, breathe, breathe, breathe.

"Breathe deeply, that's it, in…out…"

It's a woman with rubber gloves on, a paramedic. There are two of them, and my daughter has stopped crying and switched into her Red Cross mode. Ever sensible.

Terry's arrived. He hovers in the background.

"Want Terry, I want Terry."

My daughter insists he follows in his car.

"It's important she stays awake," says the ambulance driver.

"Mmm, sleepy," I giggle.

My daughter loves this next bit. She shakes me, shakes me, whacks me round the face, then laughs guiltily. Nervously?

Later, at the hospital I'm out of it. I don't know what's going on as I drift in and out of consciousness. It seems to be morning. All five of my children are round my bed. I can't talk properly.

"Her dad's arrived." It's the nurse. My daughter and my snowy-haired boy laugh quietly. Dad?

Terry walks over to the bed. Blimey, the nurse thought...

"Have I had a stroke?"

"No," says Terry.

Oh my hero. Where would I be without him? He doesn't hang about, soon leaves for work.

My two oldest sons have got their suits on. Isn't it suits for funerals? Children gathered round hospital beds – isn't that for the dead or dying?

My eldest son on my left grips my hand tight. My daughter mirrors him on my right. My snowy-haired boy, curly-haired boy and my gorgeous youngest fan out round the bed.

My eldest boy bends down to whisper. He's crying. "Promise me you'll never do it again!"

It's hard to think straight, floating in and out. Struggle, struggle to stay awake. Hang on, if he's saying that does it mean I might live?

I look at the kids, try and work out their ages, can't. Too much, too much. But I do know they're not a fraction through their lives yet, know it's not right for them to lose their mother at this age.

"Am I gonna live?" I ask my boy, now a man.

"Yes." He's still crying.

Truth is he can't know that yet. Test takes twenty-four hours.

I think it's night-time and I'm in intensive care. I

vomit like there's no tomorrow. Ha. A lone oriental male nurse patrols his patch. There's no stomach pumping. They've given me jack. Maybe they don't mind if I live or die.

"YOU'RE NOT HELPING ME MUCH, ARE YOU?"

Nothing.

"Scuse me, scuse me."

He comes over. He's quiet, gentle, clean, innocent, forgiven.

"Am I going to *live?*"

"You want bedpan?" He walks off.

"Am I going to live?"

"Okay, okay, I get you bedpan."

"Am I going to LIVE?"

A woman's voice comes from somewhere behind me, from a bed behind a curtain.

"Answer the poor woman – she wants to know if she's going to *live!*"

He slides over, silent as a geisha. Bends down.

"Not at this moment," he whispers.

I'm frightened now. It's all gone dark, must be the middle of the night. Think positive, think positive, mustn't think negative. Don't think the thought, 'I don't want to die', mustn't jinx it. Think POSITIVE.

"I WANT TO **LIVE**."

If anyone hears me shout out loud, they don't say. I figure if I stay awake, stay awake, stay awake and fight it then I'm in with a chance.

The kids are here again. They're so precious I'd kill for them, die for them and, importantly now, live for them. My daughter looks chirpy.

"The test says you're going to live." She says.

"God's got a plan for you," says Terry later,

mischievous laughter in his eyes. "Your daughter helped me find where you put the rest of the tablets and I've got rid of them."

Awww. He's so wise sometimes. I'm lucky he's in my life. He does care really, always saying he loves me. Even buys me flowers sometimes. Finding and destroying the tablets just proves it. Along with what he says next.

"Whatever you've been doing isn't working, is it? You'll have to find another way."

So… woman on a mission, me. I up the AA meetings, desperate to do things differently. Terry suggests a couple of women who could be my sponsor. One's a lesbian so I ask the other one figuring I'll get more identification.

"They call her Mother Teresa because she's had so many sponsees. She's good, lives in a big house."

Tentatively I ask her and she agrees we'll meet up. I've got blind faith. I've seen a lot of people in the rooms make a good recovery and it's what I want too. I've had enough fucking around being a dry drunk as they say. I've been sober for a year but with *no* recovery.

She gives me loads of her time – on the phone, going over for coffee. I do a lot of meetings, ten or more each week. I *have* to. After a couple of weeks my new sponsor helps me go through the Steps. I do it quickly. Some tell you not to rush it but I've already wasted ten years in and out of AA. Time now for the real thing. But the arguing with Terry makes it difficult to concentrate on my recovery.

"I can't have you *and* get well. We'll need to leave it for a while."

My sponsor suggests that will be easier. No distractions.

"I'll wait for you," Terry says.

He must *really* love me! But instead, the break I need to honour my recovery is broken into by his texts and calls. Then he texts he's in the coffee shop – would I like to join him? Within two weeks the safe haven is broken. Sabotaged. I'm magnetised to him. I've allowed this. I want to be wanted.

However I do go through the Steps and I do everything my sponsor suggests. *Everything* – sharing at meetings, even give a chair once I've completed the Steps. But it's not easy, not at all. That's OK though. It just has to be possible. I phone my sponsor when it gets too much.

"I don't think I can do this."

I don't even care I'm crying, a grown woman, to another grown woman. Again.

"Think of it as a steam engine. Your whole life the engine's been going one way, now you need to turn it in another direction. It's hard, hard work and you'll need all your strength but once the steam engine's facing the right direction it gets easier and easier. You can pray – ask your Higher Power for help and guidance." She suggests I keep a journal and write a daily gratitude list.

She's right and often is, about early recovery. She's great with 'newcomers'. That's what I am – a newcomer. Ha. I'm grateful she gives up so much time. She's lovely, wise, knows a lot, has been sober seven years.

> **Step One** – We admitted we were powerless over alcohol – that our lives had become unmanageable.
> **Step Two** – Came to believe that a Power greater than ourselves could restore us to sanity.

Step Three – Made a decision to turn our will and our lives over to the care of God as we understood him.

Step Four – Made a searching and fearless moral inventory of ourselves.

Step Five – Admitted to God, to ourselves and to another human being the exact nature of our wrongs.

Step Six – Were entirely ready to have God remove all these defects of character.

Step Seven – Humbly asked Him to remove all our shortcomings.

Step Eight – Made a list of all persons we had harmed, and became willing to make amends to them all.

Step Nine – Made direct amends to such people wherever possible, except when to do so would injure them or others.

Step Ten – Continued to take personal inventory and when we were wrong promptly admitted it.

Step Eleven – Sought through prayer and meditation to improve our conscious contact with God as we understood Him – praying only for knowledge of His will for us and the power to carry that out.

Step Twelve – Having had a spiritual awakening as the result of these Steps, we tried to carry this message to alcoholics, and to practise these principles in all our affairs.

As I go through the Steps the most profound things happen. The shit departs from my head and my body and doesn't come back. Then I receive the AA promises:

If we are painstaking about this phase of our development, we will be amazed before we are halfway through. We are going to know a new freedom and a new happiness. We will not regret the past nor wish to shut the door on it. We will comprehend the word serenity and we will know peace. No matter how far down the scale we have gone, we will see how our experience can benefit others. That feeling of uselessness and self-pity will disappear. We will lose interest in selfish things and gain interest in our fellows. Self-seeking will slip away. Our whole attitude and outlook upon life will change. Fear of people and of economic insecurity will leave us. We will intuitively know how to handle situations which used to baffle us. We will suddenly realise that God is doing for us what we could not do for ourselves.

Are these extravagant promises? We think not. They are being fulfilled among us — sometimes quickly, sometimes slowly. They will always materialise if we work for them.

I give Terry more and more chances over the months. We have huge arguments. Are they arguments though? That implies it's two-sided. But it's me sitting there, trying harder to get him to understand; him screaming, shouting, swearing, calling me a FUCKING CUNT. We fall out over the way he is with other women.

It's not the being in a hotel for a nice weekend away, being chased along the corridor, him barefoot, raised fist, screaming out, "You FUCKING WHORE."

It's not his moving to within an inch of my face, screaming at the top of his voice,

"YOU FUCKING CUNT, I NEVER EVER WANT TO SEE YOU AGAIN."

It's not even the calming down afterwards, him confessing, "I didn't wanna lose it with you."

My sponsor tells me that was a threat. I never looked at it that way. I thought he was being thoughtful, kind even. He does throw in kind words sometimes and it's crazy-making.

It's not the fact I know it's heading towards physical violence, like he's prepping himself and me, cranking up towards to it.

It's not the increasingly secret life – two mobiles, both on silent, never answers calls, only returns them. Or the withholding of affection and approval or information, even over silly, stupid things, getting angry when I ask things like, 'Shall I take your coat?'

It's not the guilt inducing… "It costs me FIVE POUNDS, the petrol to your house," in his old 'medallion on a chain' Mercedes.

The wrinkled skin lines under the cheeks, as his arse hangs there, rests on the back of his legs, patient, knowing it's seen its best at now nearly sixty years old. Because what is he to me? Without the fear and adrenalin of his sadism, anger, cruelty and aggression? He's just a bald, fat, uninteresting old man. It's not that.

No, the most painful trick he pulls off is when he takes me to see this Sri Lankan woman he's shagging and wants me to know. He's dropped enough hints about her inviting him to dinner blah blah. He knows he's laughing because it's not safe now for me to accuse him of *anything*.

Terry takes me to price up this job in her house, rubs my nose in it. She ignores me, but looks him straight in the eye. Pleading, angry, still in the early stages.

"You haven't returned my calls, Terry." she says.

"Well," prepared, innocent, looks at me, "we've been

busy today, haven't we?"

As he follows her up the stairs she walks slow, wiggles her arse, seductive, like Marilyn Monroe. They carry on talking, ignoring me.

"I'm going to the car,' I say. 'I don't feel well."

He laughs but stays another thirty minutes. It's only a small job.

We've been arguing all day, the one-sided kind, been begging him can we go to dinner, anything to make up, to make him stop.

"Shall we go to dinner now?" He sniggers, back in the car, after he's had a go at me for walking away, offending her.

"No, too ill."

"What did you come for if you're gonna make yourself ill?"

He's almost pissing himself, he's so tickled.

I still see Elizabeth.

"What are we going to do about your jealousy and insecurity?" I don't know where to go with this one. Is it my fault then, is she telling me that? I'm not sure I feel the guilt I'm supposed to feel.

A friend showed me a doctor's report on her ex who was diagnosed as a sociopath/psychopath. When I research the Internet for symptoms of a sociopath/psychopath, they're screechingly, achingly familiar: self-centred, narcissistic, without conscience and empathy, great liars…

It's a relief when I read what Susan Forward says about them in her book *When Your Lover is a Liar*. They're "the best actors in the world" she says. The sociopath/psychopath "is single-mindedly concerned with the question 'How am I coming across?'" Ha. Spookily I'd skimmed the book at a bookshop but dismissed it as not relevant to me! It was only later I got a copy after a friend recommended it, can you believe? Eghads!

Susan Forward goes on…They have "… hidden agendas. In many cases a sociopath" (psychopath) "will detect a window of vulnerability – a small rip in the woman's emotional fabric." He will have "… registered everything."

He's a "man without a heart'. The sociopath" (psychopath) "has big missing pieces inside of him, he may be the best and most romantic lover you've ever had. But despite his charm and the aura of excitement and drama that often surrounds him, he is incapable of love." Yep. Finally I can start to make sense of my deeply painful journey.

Maybe calling a psychopath a sociopath protects us, makes us feel better because it doesn't sound as bad, as scary. But perhaps they're one and the same. And no one wants to a) be a psychopath (necessarily) or b) call someone else a psychopath. Can of worms? Just a shitting little!

Among a heap of others he can be these things too, so says world-renowned expert Dr Robert D. Hare in his book *Without Conscience*.

1. Glib and superficial
2. Egocentric and grandiose
3. Lack of remorse or guilt
4. Without feelings of guilt or anxiety
5. Lack of empathy
6. Deceitful and manipulative
7. Shallow emotions

8 Impulsive
9 Poor behaviour controls
10 Need for excitement
11 Lack of responsibility
12 Early behaviour problems
13 Adult antisocial behaviour

There's loads more – it's not a 'one size fits all' – a psychopath might not have all traits and could well have extras. A biggy is they're profoundly detached. No matter what they say about how they're heartbroken – nope! It's narcissistic injury – they're pissed off, *furious* with you, me. They don't do genuine sadness or many other feelings, no matter how convincing they appear. Any 'feelings' are more likely to hover around the rage department though they do know the glee of getting one over on someone. It's *always* about having power over others, power and control – words that Terry uses often. I realise a psychopath will reconcile a relationship they hadn't ended, just so *they* can then end it. Revenge. Punishment. Fucksake!

As I read more and more, it's so very dark and I crash into another depression as I realise and accept it's been THIS BAD. But…having the clarity, finally, is fantastic – Heaven sent, as I realise I wasn't mad *or* bad after all and gradually the Truth lifts my spirits. I'm beginning to *know* I'm right.

The point is, I tell Elizabeth, this basically describes Terry.

"Come on, you know you sometimes add two and two and get five." She does it again, that smile when she's saying something that's not funny.

Fucksake. *So did you, then, did you get round to seeing that film Gaslight?* Sometimes even people in powerful positions, people like therapists, *Gaslight* other people. Thank God I've chosen Elizabeth, though. She *must* be nice – she's been married nearly fifty years. Stable as a slide-rule, her, and she must know best – she's a therapist!

So despite Terry clearly showing multiple characteristics of a psychopath, as in the label fits him like an oven glove still hot from the pie, I file away this conversation. For now.

But I start to ask myself… What if I *like* being controlled? What if being controlled *feels* like love because it's what I'm used to? What if… when he gives orders it makes me think he cares about me, loves me? It does actually. Or it used to.

Within a couple of weeks I end it. It's when one night he insults me in front of my children in our own home. After he leaves, my daughter and curly-haired boy tell me how they see it. She says I was trying to make it up to him while he was speaking badly to me, mimicking, in front of them. By the time he reaches his house, five minutes away, five quid's worth of petrol lighter, I've phoned his mobile and told him it's over. When he calls back my curly-haired boy speaks urgently.

"Stand your ground, Mum!" So I do. It's finished. Over.

After a few days the withdrawal sets in again like all the other times. The pain of being without him is physical even though I don't want to be with him! This time I sit with it, see it out. And it's horrible, seeing, *really* seeing, how bad it's always been.

I realise and accept that I've never been loved. Not by parents or partners anyway. But I *am* loved by God and my children.

Then I get thinking about the overdose. The carrier-bag of Co-Proxamol. Within a month or so of me sharing my decision to end my life Terry gives me the carrier-bag of tablets, pills that I don't need, and later on, when I was in hospital, he made sure he took the rest from my house and destroyed them. That'll be the tablets that had his name and address written all over them.

He used to say he likes living on the edge, likes crime because of the buzz. At the very least there would be lots of action where he's the hero of the piece, rallying round. Or he could have completed it with my murder. The ultimate power and control. The paradox is there are people in AA whose lives he's saved. No doubt Dr Harold Shipman saved lives too – probably even brought life into the world!

Evil human beings are so effective because most people refuse to believe anyone can be that callous. We judge others as ourselves. Maybe we shouldn't always.

Someone in AA puts me in touch with Poppy. She's good with relationships. It's ten days since I finished it with Terry. She tells me about sex and love addiction which I now clock about myself. There's a 12 Step programme for this too. And co-dependency. How did I not notice my own adrenalin or intensity addiction, creeping around underneath all the shit?

Poppy also tells me that she had to have abstinence from relationships for a while. It's a relief to hear and I do the same.

AA is about a bridge to normal living. I never wanted it to be a bridge to another bridge though I've heard so much about other people's cross-addictions. I know there's a bit more work on my recovery needed.

The bottom line is that ALL THIS SHIT is about

being addicted to abuse, to all things toxic. If I didn't abuse myself, I'd find someone else to do it for me. And it usually starts in childhood – it certainly did for me. I was set up for it.

Of *course* I had to put the drink down before I could even think of dealing with anything else. But it's *so* much more than the drink. It's big, this. **Huge**. And I couldn't get out of it alone. I needed people support but I had to start putting my Higher Power – fuck it, let's call him God – putting God before Terry, who was my God, the one I worshipped, just like I did the others before him. He made sure of it. We *both* did. And I've always done it. Always been attracted to … to what? What type of men? Attracted or addicted to?

The next time I'm at Elizabeth's we talk about Terry. I tell her I've stopped seeing him. I'm crying. It's painful even though I hate the fucker.

"Why do you keep letting these men do this to you?" She shakes her head.

"How could it happen so many times?" I ask.

Normally she tells me what I've done wrong and I bounce out the happier for it, knowing that if it's my fault I can change, do something about the problem, keep the relationship.

But what happens if you disclose to someone you've been abused and they say,

"No, you haven't, it's you being…" Fill in the gaps.

What happens if someone discounts you, me? Exactly! You, I, steam straight back in there, stay in the problem, invite more of the same because you, I, think it's all my fault, I've been exaggerating, etc.

"He's probably a sociopath," she says.

She does that stupid laugh as she says it. That's

sociopath as in psychopath. That's sociopath/psychopath – same as I suggested to her before. *So did you get to see it yet, that film Gaslight?*

Ten years I've been seeing Elizabeth. How much of my life could she have saved me, could I have saved me? How many years have I lost unnecessarily? But that would have meant I stopped seeing her. By now I know that she, above all, wants, *needs* me to keep coming. Does seeing me make her feel powerful enough to face her puny but controlling to the nth degree husband? She adopted four children so she *must* be nice – right? Am I the unofficial fifth? There was a time I wished I was.

My new friend Poppy, a Christian but still nice, talks about being dependent on others, still looking for Mummy and Daddy. Who *me?*

That's it, isn't it? Being dependent on others' approval – but big time. I'm not just talking 'Does my bum look big in this?' approval. The thing is, there can't be control without dependency. In this sick system each needs the other or it can't happen. Keeping dependent on Elizabeth kept me primed to be dependent on others too. It's not what I needed from her. She knows not what she does – or does she?

I've always read but get reading more. *Much* more. We've never talked religion, me and Elizabeth, so I bring it up.

"No, no," she shakes her head, "Jesus did exist but he was just a man, a good person, nothing special."

She knows I've been going to church. I find information about therapists who abuse. Ha. They're not supposed to give these sorts of opinions about a person's faith. She's told me before that she goes to supervision. I wonder now what kind.

Within a few weeks of finishing with Terry I realise I need to end some other relationships too. I go to Elizabeth for one last visit. It's not safe to continue. She's tight-lipped, not happy I'm leaving her. As I'm walking out the door she looks at me, beady.

"Women can be abusers too, you know."

"Yes… I know."

A shiver creeps its way up my spine as I leave her influence. Finally.

Also I let several friends go as well as my sponsor. Sometimes we outgrow people quicker than at others. This is a speedy outgrowing of those I've been dependent on, specially those who wanted me kept as the underdog while they had the upper hand.

That's been me, eh? Limpet. Dependent on fags, drink, 'difficult and or avoidant people,' abusers, psychopaths, almost any shit that will destroy me. And abuse *will* destroy. Cunning, baffling, it feeds off death and destruction. Unless I choose life, which I do. I could feel guilty because there's people worse off. Mustn't grumble. But you know what? There's also people better off.

I realise that Jesus was scape-goated too. Maybe he was the tallest poppy. Maybe Terry was right: God has a plan for me. What do you reckon?

Mum's in hospital.

"Does she need anything?"

"She's got nothing," says the nurse.

Despite being 'cared for' by my ex-ex-husband, still after a month she has nothing she needs: basics like a nightdress, soap, comb, a towel. Next time I visit, the magician has been and – abracadabra – the magazines etc. I brought have disappeared and ta-dah! Look –

there's a photo of her much-loved boxer dog! My ex-husband tells anyone who'll listen how he takes her shopping. It's not a shock to discover he's sole beneficiary of her will. What was it he used to say? *It's all in the preparation.*

On one of the visits I bring two of the kids. She's got six gorgeous grandchildren she never sees. But, despite her dementia, today we have a lovely, lovely time talking about her mum and dad, the forget-me-nots in their garden, her dancing six nights a week at Tottenham Royal. I try getting her to say her favourite word. Antidisestablishmentarianism. She has a go, misses. I comb her hair. She likes that. We even sing, gathering every good moment to treasure later, making the most of a bad job.

She's now just over eight stone but looks the same, to me, her daughter. Her beady eyes piercing, she grabs my hand with a grip like a hod-carrier. I've brought photos.

"Who's this, Joan?"

"Don't know."

"It's Adrian. Look – isn't he gorgeous?"

"Adrian David Trent," she says, then, "I'm frightened." She grips still tighter. How can I help her when she's never helped herself?

"I know. I know you are."

Next day the hospital phone. When I arrive less than an hour later she's already dead. It wasn't great but she was still my mum. I just wanted her to love me.

Chapter 21: As Good As It Gets

Last night I dreamed I returned to being Mandy again. I saw her in the distance, and it seemed to me as I stood by an iron gate on a road leading me towards her she looked sad, lonely. There were trees and bushes, the way seemed barred to me. But like all dreamers I was possessed of sudden, supernatural powers and passed like a spirit through any barriers to reach the goal before me.

Whereas I always thought her the evil one, and so had to become Amanda, I became aware that a change had come upon her. She's been narrow in her choices, and unkempt in her ways, but the drive I had to reach her, the true her, became fruitful.

Puzzled, I noticed the pot of poison always at her centre was still there, the black hole of shame that, little by little, insidiously, the darkness had built upon in strength and stature. She too had added to the pot.

I had to avoid a branch swinging in front of my face so I could see clearly. The more I looked the more I could see the illusion she held for herself. The poison came about not as evidence of her badness but as a result of the attacks, sometimes by self but mostly and originally from others. In the beginning. Toxic others. It was pain she felt, yet when another attack brought about more pain, she, through being long-term discounted, attributed 'that feeling' as evidence of her 'badness'. How can anyone have a decent middle and end after a toxic beginning?

The darkness, always a menace, specially in the past, had NOT triumphed. There were other things I noticed in Mandy – not just all the wrong things, the ONLY things I used to see – but the good. With my heart thumping in my breast, a strange prick of tears behind my eyes, I took her hand, and brought her speedily back out from the dark shadows, the darkness, the bastards now just a thread of their former selves. Gripping her firmly as she clung to me, ever fearful, we walked together in my enchanted dream. Along the path she, no longer an empty shell of a young girl, moved into my body and I walked for both of us out into the sunshine, innocent.

When I woke up I remembered how good life is, genuinely good. No longer an illusion but round pegs in round holes, square in square. Now some memories are reclaimed as good ones, kept in a warm place. I'm no longer thinking that everything in the past has to go. Good things, like times at Walton-on-the-Naze. Things like Adrian's jokes:

Man walks into a doctor's.

Doctor says:

"I'm sorry, Mr Jones, I've got some bad news."

"What is it, Doctor?"

"I'm afraid you've only got three minutes to live."

"Isn't there anything you can do for me, Doctor?"

"Well…I can boil you an egg."

And I have loads of good memories of the children growing up. Hugely rewarding memories. I watch them blossom as I blossom. They help and motivate each other to reach the great heights they'll all reach and are reaching.

Thing is, for me now, it's peaceful, serene, safe and I've got my freedom – so long as I have abstinence from the things that hurt me… and don't replace my Higher Power with something or some*one* else. Now I've got a life – that's The Difference.

P.S.

Reading these books helped teach me how to keep safe.

The Verbally Abusive Relationship - Patricia Evans (Adams Media, 2010)
The Gift of Fear - Gavin de Becker (Bloomsbury Publishing Plc, 2000)
The Betrayal Bond - Breaking Free of Exploitative Relationships - Patrick J. Carnes (Health Communications, 1998)
Out of the Shadows (understanding sexual addiction) - Patrick J. Carnes (Hazelden Info. & Ed Services, 2001)
People of the Lie - M. Scott Peck (Arrow, 1990)
Facing Co-Dependence - Pia Melody (Harper Collins, 2002)
Facing Love Addiction - Pia Melody (Harper San Francisco, 1992)
Alcoholics Anonymous Big Book - AA Services (Hazelden Info. & Ed. Services, 2002)
The Psychopathy of Everyday Life - Martin Kantor (Praeger Publishers Inc, 2006)
Bad Boys, Bad Men - Donald W. Black, (Contributor) C. Lindon Larson (OUP USA, 2000)
Without Conscience - Robert D. Hare (Guilford Press, 1999)
Stalking the Soul - Marie-France Hirigoyd, (Afterword) Thomas More (Translator) Helen Marx (Helen Marx Books, 2004)

When Your Lover Is a Liar - Susan Forward, Donna Frazier (Harper Perennial, 2000)
Violent Attachments -J. Reid Meloy (Jason Aronson, 1997)
Snakes in Suits - Paul Babiak, Robert D. Hare (Harper Collins US, 2007)
Bully In Sight - Tim Field (Success Unlimited, 1996)

And recommended
Survivors Workshops
at
The Meadows, Arizona
www.themeadows.com

An occasional detail has been changed to protect the involved

Printed in Great Britain
by Amazon